Socioeconomic Background and Achievement

Socioeconomic Background and Achievement

OTIS DUDLEY DUNCAN

DEPARTMENT OF SOCIOLOGY
UNIVERSITY OF MICHIGAN
ANN ARBOR, MICHIGAN

DAVID L. FEATHERMAN

DEPARTMENT OF RURAL SOCIOLOGY
UNIVERSITY OF WISCONSIN
MADISON, WISCONSIN

BEVERLY DUNCAN

DEPARTMENT OF SOCIOLOGY
UNIVERSITY OF MICHIGAN
ANN ARBOR, MICHIGAN

∫P SEMINAR PRESS   New York and London   1972

SEMINAR PRESS, INC.
111 Fifth Avenue, New York, New York 10003

United Kingdom Edition published by
SEMINAR PRESS LIMITED
24/28 Oval Road, London NW1

LIBRARY OF CONGRESS CATALOG CARD NUMBER: 72-88537

PRINTED IN THE UNITED STATES OF AMERICA

To

WILLIAM H. SEWELL

pioneer student of social stratification

Contents

Chapter 1. FRAMEWORK AND STRATEGY

Chapter 2. MODELS, METHODS, AND DATA

Chapter 3. THE BASIC MODEL

List of Tables

xi

List of Figures

Preface

This monograph investigates the process of social stratification in the United States. It picks up where *The American Occupational Structure* left off, providing elaborations of the models of status transmission between generations which appeared in the work of Blau and Duncan (1967). We describe the rationale and strategy of our research in Chapter 1. Suffice it to note here that the 1962 benchmark survey of social mobility in the United States ("Occupational Changes in a Generation," the survey whose data *The American Occupational Structure* summarized) provided the point of departure for our project. The "OCG" data file embodied information which had not been exploited fully by Blau and Duncan. At the same time, problems for analysis were posed by *The American Occupational Structure* and a related inquiry, *Family Factors and School Dropout: 1920–1960* (B. Duncan, 1965b), which exceeded the capacity of a single body of data to address. Consequently, we assembled a number of data sets to supplement the OCG data. These were used to extend, enlarge, and improve the treatment of factors relating the characteristics of a man's family of origin to those socioeconomic statuses attained at later stages in his life cycle.

Our work concerns the achievement of three major statuses: education, occupation, and income. We take as problematic the (imperfect) correlations among these status dimensions for American men during roughly the first half of the twentieth century. The analysis concentrates on processes which might account for these correlations, implicating such factors as the social and economic characteristics of the family of origin; capacities and dispositions regarded as aspects of the individual's personality; decisional influences stemming from one's social involvements with parents, siblings, peers, and schools; and events or contingencies in the life cycle (e.g. family formation, divorce, migration). As a result, the monograph may be of interest to a variety of social scientists, aside from students of stratification. For example, economists will find data on the economic returns to schooling and ability; for social psychologists, there is information on the role of attitudes, values, and motives in social mobility; for sociologists, we discuss issues relating to "the culture of poverty." More generally, we regard our work as speaking to a public concerned with the extent of opportunity in American society.

Whatever its potential appeal to various audiences, our monograph represents a self-conscious effort at systematic model construction for the process of social mobility. We have detailed our assumptions and sought to expose the logical implications of our models. Some readers may find the strategy of model-building of interest in its own right, as a methodological paradigm. Where our efforts are defective, we heartily invite correction, reconstruction, and further extension.

The research reported herein was carried out pursuant to Contract No. OE–5–85–072 with the U.S. Office of Education, and this monograph is based upon the Final Report, Project No. 5–0074 (EO–191), "Socioeconomic Background and Occupational Achievement: Extensions of a Basic Model," submitted to the Bureau of Research, Office of Education, U.S. Department of Health, Education, and Welfare, May 1968.

We wish to acknowledge the helpfulness and efficiency of the U.S. Bureau of the Census in preparing special tabulations from the OCG survey. Our project relied not only upon the OCG data but also on several other sets of data collected by other investigators who generously allowed us to have access to their materials and to make use of them in our own way. We greatly appreciate the professional and personal courtesy of C. Norman Alexander, Jr., Ernest Q. Campbell, Harry J. Crockett, Jr., LaMar T. Empey, Archibald O. Haller, Albert D. Klassen, Jr., Edward O. Laumann, Alejandro Portes, Howard Schuman, William H. Sewell, and Charles F. Westoff. None of them is responsible for our conclusions, but we wish to pay tribute to their careful work which made possible our own efforts.

We were fortunate to have the support of a capable research staff. Bruce L. Warren, Elliot M. Long, and James N. Porter served as research assistants at various times; Warren wrote a memorandum upon which a portion of Section 5.1 is based. Ruthe C. Sweet and Susan Bittner, working under the supervision of J. Michael Coble, were responsible for computer programming and data processing. James C. Cramer, Griffith Feeney, Neil Paterson, Steven Peters, Ellen Shantz, and Alexandra Stavrou were statistical clerks. Joanne Raymond, William Allen, and Linda Warren carried out occupational coding. Mary

Scott and Alice Y. Sano typed the Final Report manuscript, and Marjorie Snyder typed the monograph copy. In the final stages of preparing the manuscript for publication, the editorial assistance of Mary Balistreri was invaluable, and the clerical aid of Sue Ward is gratefully acknowledged. The continuity of the project under often trying circumstances was assured by the resourceful administrative actions taken by Helen Dempster.

The research was carried out at the Population Studies Center of the University of Michigan. The facilities it offered, as well as the atmosphere of dedication to research that it provided, made it possible to complete our work.

Monograph revisions were facilitated by support from the College of Agriculture and Life Sciences, and the Center for Demography and Ecology, both of the University of Wisconsin, Madison.

Finally we recognize the cooperation of Jossey-Bass, Inc., in permitting us to reproduce a portion of an article by the senior author which appeared in E. F. Borgatta (ed.), *Sociological Methodology*, 1969.

Otis Dudley Duncan
David L. Featherman
Beverly Duncan

Chapter 1

Framework and Strategy

Two complementary processes interact to produce a growth of knowledge in an area of continuous scientific inquiry. The first is the process of discovery, description, and verification: the establishing of facts and relationships by observation, analysis, and the replication thereof. The second is the process of systematization and synthesis. It eventuates in interpretation and generalization. Factual information is assimilated to conceptual and explanatory schemes, resulting in their enlargement and specification. In the present undertaking, the preponderant emphasis has been on the second process. Some new findings are reported and some familiar ones are reconfirmed, but the primary objective has been to achieve an improved synthesis of an existing body of knowledge. The project was specifically planned as a sequel to two previous inquiries: *The American Occupational Structure* (Blau & Duncan, 1967) and *Family Factors and School Dropout: 1920–1960* (Duncan, 1965b). These were both primarily concerned with the analysis of a single body of data, those derived from "OCG," the March 1962 supplement to the Current Population Survey of the Bureau of the Census, "Occupational Changes in a Generation." This survey was supplemented by various pieces of Census information, but there was no opportunity to consider a range of variables not normally available in censuses. At the same time, the research reports did not fully exploit the analytical potentialities of the OCG data themselves. We have, therefore, taken the opportunity to increase the store of reliably ascertained facts, but our main purpose was to extend, enlarge, and improve upon the previously reported models of the process of achievement.

1

To interpret consistently or to systematize cogently a collection of findings requires the adoption of a point of view. When the logical requisites of the point of view are made explicit in the form of a framework within which synthesis is to be attempted, it is seen that the framework supplies criteria for the *selection* of data. The outcome is then something rather different from a compendium of facts or a comprehensive enumeration of findings. The typical product is what we term here a model. This usage has the merit of continually reemphasizing the purposeful selectivity of the analyst's arrangement and manipulations of data. The purpose is not to construct a faithful portrait of reality but rather to exhibit and rationalize some of the suspected connections between aspects of reality. If the metaphor will be allowed, one can describe the spirit of the investigation by stating that its intention is to develop a special-purpose map of the terrain rather than to provide an aerial photograph of it. More than one such map, evidently, could represent the same terrain, depending upon the purpose.

Sociologists with an amazing variety of perspectives have concurred on the proposition that a focus on occupational roles and statuses is strategic in the examination of achievement in American society. Theory and research conducted with a view toward understanding the processes producing and sustaining a division of labor have enlarged our understanding of occupational differentiation. Studies concerned with occupational status have provided a wealth of information about the allocation of honor or prestige to occupational roles and have confirmed the rather surprising approximation to invariance in the status rankings of occupations over time and place (Hodge, Siegel, & Rossi, 1964; Hodge, Treiman, & Rossi, 1966). A third tradition, that of research in occupational mobility and social stratification, is the more immediate source of the basic ideas with which we are working here. The generic idea is that all known complex societies are characterized by one or more forms of institutionalized social inequality. However, there are variations between societies and, presumably, within a society over time in the degree of opportunity, that is, the extent to which persons are recruited or assigned to roles bearing unequal rewards on the basis of the circumstances of birth or rearing in a particular family, locality, cultural or ethnic group, or social milieu. To the extent that achievement depends upon such circumstances over which the individual has little or no control, we say that a society is stratified. Thus the crucial facts upon which our estimate of the degree of stratification in a society depend are those that relate achieved status to the circumstances of origin. If we aspire to something more than an ability to estimate the degree of stratification, however, we are obliged to consider what processes give rise to stratification of the form and degree that we observe. It is useful, therefore, to discuss the process of achievement in general terms, the more specific and more nearly operational idea of the socioeconomic life cycle, and the ways in which one might begin to think productively about the problem of developing more adequate models of what transpires in that cycle. The remainder of this chapter is devoted to these matters.

1.1 The Process of Achievement

Students of social stratification are interested in jobs and occupations primarily as labels or indicators of social status. The acceptable performance of an occupational role confers upon the incumbent of that role a status which, to a rough approximation, is somewhat uniformly evaluated by most members of the society (Reiss and others, 1961; Siegel, 1970). In addition to the more or less direct status reward associated with an occupation, other rewards and status evaluations are linked to occupation in a variety of ways. Most obvious is the fact that pursuit of an occupation leads to remuneration in the form of earnings, which in turn may be used for consumption and investment in forms that represent utilities to the earner himself and indications of status to his associates.

In the United States, as in other contemporary industrial societies, occupation is typically an *achieved* status (as contrasted with such an *ascribed* status as membership in a recognized ethnic group). That is, the conferment of status is based in some considerable measure on the role incumbent's own performance of the role rather than upon any one of a number of extrinsic considerations, such as his family's reputation or his personal attractiveness. To be sure, there is an interaction among criteria of status, and it can frequently happen that role performance is facilitated or impaired by various "extrinsic" factors or that status evaluations are "contaminated." Thus, one often observes instances of incompetent performance of occupational duties where the incumbent is insulated from the normal consequences of incompetence by his tenure of certain nonoccupational statuses. Hence, the statement that occupation is an achieved status is not equivalent to the statement that occupational roles are allocated to persons solely on the criterion of "merit." Indeed, the main empirical question in the study of status achievement (of which occupational achievement is an important example) is whether or not and to what degree such achievement depends on factors other than the individual's competence and inclination to perform the role on the basis of which status is conferred. The corollary question then becomes that of the extent to which "competence and inclination" themselves depend on factors other than the role incumbent's own capacity or prior achievement.

The problem suggested by the title *Socioeconomic Background and Achievement* can, therefore, be stated as follows: Given that occupation is an achieved status, what factors can be identified as influencing this achievement and thus as accounting for variation in occupational status? In particular, what if anything about socioeconomic background represents favorable or unfavorable conditions for achievement, and how do these conditions exercise their influence?

It is often observed, for example, that an appreciable number of men are found in the same occupations their fathers pursued. Even "occupational inheritance," when it is observed, is not an exception to the principle that occupation is an achieved status. It may well be easier for a farmer's son to become a farmer than it is for the son of a nonfarm worker; but to hold the status of farmer he is required actually to perform that occupational role in at least some minimum degree. By the same token, a doctor's son becomes a physician not by some immediate mechanism of "inheritance" but by going to medical school and carrying on a medical practice, however much his father's prior achievements may facilitate his own. Just as it is easier for a doctor's son to become a doctor than it is for a plumber's son, it is easier for a doctor's son to become a lawyer than it is for the son of a truck driver. The operation of "occupational inheritance" is merely a special instance of the general phenomenon that the socioeconomic background of a high status family of orientation is favorable to the achievement of high occupational status.

The connection between socioeconomic background and occupational achievement, however, is neither perfect nor unproblematic. Indeed, in one sense, the most important parameter of the process of stratification in a society is the *degree* of association between background, or social origins, and achievement (Svalastoga, 1965, p. 70). Moreover, the existence of such an association, of whatever degree, is not self-explanatory. Presumably, it comes about through the operation of one or more mechanisms that produce the observed result. If it is the case, for example, that occupational roles are allocated to a substantial degree on the basis of educational attainment, and if it is true, in turn, that amount of schooling depends in some measure on the status level of the family of orientation, then one would have a good basis for the argument that differential educational attainment is one of the "mechanisms" via which background influences occupational achievement. Of course, this particular mechanism might operate in combination with other mechanisms. Moreover, one might take the very relationship between educational attainment and background as problematic and inquire what mechanism accounts for this relationship. Do children from families differing in status also differ in scholastic aptitude, which in turn affects the amount of schooling received? Or is it the case that the amount of resources a family may invest in the schooling of offspring is sharply limited by its status level, so that an economic mechanism is of prime importance?

As these cursory examples should suggest, there is no clearly specified terminus to the search for "mechanisms" which account for observed relationships and thereby explain the parameters of a process. As the search is pressed, if it is successful, the account of the process becomes more and more detailed and models of it become more complicated. All the work done to date would appear to be at a comparatively early stage in such a search, and we are really only at the very beginning of what may turn out to be a long sequence of substituting new and more elaborate models for old and less informative ones. Whether the sequence has a limit at which curiosity might come to rest is hardly an issue that must be resolved at this time.

1.2 The Socioeconomic Life Cycle

Implicit in the foregoing introductory remarks is a commitment to the strategy of looking at what happens to an individual over a substantial part of his lifetime—or, since our concern is really with populations of individuals, what happens to a cohort of men as they move through an appreciable part of their life cycles. The previous discussion has not only served to introduce the life cycle approach but it has indicated the rudiments of a framework that suggests how to identify some strategic observations on the course of the life cycle. As has been implied, we might think of at least three "stages" of the socioeconomic life cycle, conveniently labeled family, schooling, and job. Concerning family, we clearly want to ascertain the statuses of the families of orientation represented in a cohort of men. Concerning schooling, we must ascertain how the men in the cohort vary with respect to the amount of education they ultimately secure. Concerning job, we must find out how they are placed in the structure of occupational statuses. With only this amount of information, a beginning can be made in contriving some significant measurements of the process of achievement and in interpreting the relationships established via such measurements. Despite the apparent simplicity of this conceptual framework, it is worth nothing that it has become clearly articulated only within recent years (Duncan & Hodge, 1963) and that something approximating adequate measurements on a representative national sample became available only within the last 5 years (Blau & Duncan, 1967). These accomplishments of previous research represent the starting point of the investigations reported here.

Some significant decisions entailed in the formulation of a research strategy can be elucidated illustratively even if, for the moment, we confine our attention to the very rudimentary model: family → schooling → job. Estimation of parameters and assessment of relationships within this model presuppose the capability of measuring the variables taken to represent the relevant condition or status at each of these stages.

Let us consider first the matter of the status of the job held at some

convenient point in the life cycle. Assuming that job titles or occupational desig-
nations are available for a cross section of the men in a given cohort or set of
adjacent cohorts, we have a large number of options as to the ways in which the
jobs may be classified or characterized. Most relevant for the problem considered in this research, as stated previously, are indexes of occupational
prestige and occupational socioeconomic status. We may take advantage of the
rather considerable amount of prior work which has resulted in the construction and validation of standardized measures of these two aspects of occupational differentiation (Reiss & others, 1961; Hodge & others, 1964; Siegel,
1970). Among other things, this work has demonstrated a close correlation
between occupational prestige and occupational socioeconomic status although the two variables are not quite interchangeable. (The present project
sheds some additional light on this matter.) Using either type of index, occupational achievement may be indexed by a quantitative score that has convenient
properties for statistical analysis and model construction.

The measurement of schooling can be carried out even more expeditiously.
In most of the work described in this report, educational attainment is simply
indexed by the number of years (grades) of school completed in the formal
educational system. While refinements of this measure have been suggested,
none can be considered fully operational at this time. Moreover, it is by no
means certain that the gain in precision from such refinement would be worth
the effort entailed in effecting it.

As for the initial stage of the model, "family," the obvious first step is to
measure the socioeconomic level of the family of orientation in the same way
that the individual's own achieved status is measured. Thus, primary emphasis
has been placed on the educational attainment and occupational status of the
head of the family in which an individual is reared, the measures of these two
variables being the same as those already mentioned. Obviously, these two
measures comprise only a minimal selection from the set of conceivable
indexes of "socioeconomic background," although there is reason to believe
that they tap much of the variance associated with such alternative or additional
measures as family income and mother's education.* Even a comprehensive

---

* Recent critics of this view (for example, Schiller, 1970) have argued that current studies
of social stratification underestimate the degree of intergenerational status transmission
because they fail to measure family income (or head's income in the family of origin) and
because of errors in measuring family background statuses like paternal and maternal education and father's occupation. Such errors, if present, will attenuate relationships to measures
of status achievement. While our data address this critique only indirectly (see Section 3.1),
we find no incontrovertible evidence which supports the contention that our indicators of
socioeconomic background underestimate the effects of social origins on achieved statuses.
A better purchase on this issue will be achieved in analysis in progress of a Wisconsin cohort
(Hauser, Lutterman, & Sewell, 1971; Sewell, Hauser, & Shah, forthcoming); preliminary
results do not suggest underestimation.

roster of such socioeconomic indexes, however, would not exhaust the connotations of family as an initial stage in the socioeconomic life cycle. No doubt we still have much to learn about the traits and conditions of families that have an influence on the achievement of their children, although it is already possible to demonstrate the significance of family size and the racial or ethnic classification of the family, even though these are not statistically independent of its socioeconomic level.

Apart from bringing up the issue of the choice of variables, the rudimentary version of the model forces one to give explicit attention to the manner in which the process of achievement is to be represented. As already stated, the model posits a statistical dependence of schooling on family background, and a subsequent dependence of occupational achievement on schooling. Thus, schooling is regarded as an intervening or intermediate variable which may operate to transmit the influence of family background on occupational achievement. But two other logical possibilities must also be reckoned with. First, schooling may operate not only as a mechanism transmitting the influence of the prior stage, but it may contribute variance to the outcome that is independent of that stage. Second, even though most of the effect of family background on occupational achievement is transmitted via schooling, some of it may be transmitted in some other way. As long as we stay within the confines of the model under discussion, we must acknowledge the possibility of *direct* effects of background on achievement as well as the *indirect* effects via schooling.

Despite the rudimentary nature of the system of relationships discussed thus far, it clearly is one of sufficient complexity that strictly verbal description of it threatens to become excessively cumbersome. Therefore, at this point, it is advisable to introduce the two other modes of representing such a system that will be employed throughout this report, the diagrammatic and the algebraic.

Figure 1.1 exhibits a diagrammatic arrangement of the variables discussed thus far as being implicated in a rudimentary model of the process of achievement. At the far right, as the ultimate outcome of the whole process, is the respondent's occupation. The letter Y stands for the variable, occupational socioeconomic status, as measured on the scale developed by Duncan (1961a). Four arrows lead to Y, representing the assumption that occupational status depends (directly) on educational attainment (measured by years of schooling, U), on family head's occupation (measured on the socioeconomic scale, X), on family head's education (years of schooling, V), and on unspecified residual factors summed up in variable B, which is taken to be uncorrelated with the other three determinants of Y. The second relation depicted by the diagram is the dependence of educational attainment (U) on family head's occupation (X) and family head's education (V) as well as unspecified residual factors, summed up in variable A, taken to be uncorrelated with X and V.

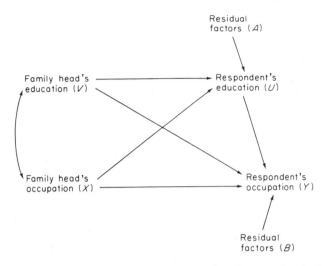

Fig. 1.1. Schematic representation of the basic model of occupational achievement.

The system we are discussing thus has two dependent variables or outcomes, respondent's education and his occupational status. Each of these is taken to be *completely determined* by factors recognized in the model. The assumption of complete determination is rendered tenable by the introduction of the variables A and B, which are the "residual factors" influencing U and Y, respectively. The implications of this assumption will become clearer in Chapter 2, where the conventions appropriate to this mode of diagrammatic representation are spelled out more fully. At this point, only one further word of explanation is needed. The arrows leading from one variable to another (except in the case of the curved line with arrowheads at both ends) symbolize the notion of *direct* dependence. If we assume that dependence is transitive, then the pattern of arrows also conveys information about the way in which indirect dependence is assumed to operate in the model. Thus, if Y depends on U and U in turn depends on A, then Y depends indirectly (though not directly, on the assumptions of this model) on A. Moreover, since Y depends on U and U depends on X, then Y depends indirectly on X as well as directly; and the same may be said in regard to the dependence of Y on V: Both direct and indirect dependence are involved. Indirect dependence is ascertained from the diagram, therefore, by reading back along a compound path of connecting arrows.

We shall use interchangeably such terms as "depends on," "is caused by," and "is influenced by." At all times, statements about the "causes" of a variable will refer to the particular model under discussion and are not intended to have any special ontological validity with respect to the real world.

That is, if we say that Y is caused by (influenced by, depends on) U, X, V, and B, we mean that we are considering a model that represents a process assumed to work in this fashion. Such statements about the *properties* of the model are to be sharply, clearly, and consistently distinguished from statements about the *validity* or suitability of the model as a representation of what is actually "true" about external reality.

An alternative, but completely equivalent, presentation of the model depicted in Fig. 1.1 can be stated as a set of two equations (in which the symbols have the same meaning as in the figure):

$$Y = p_{YU} U + p_{YX} X + p_{YV} V + p_{YB} B$$

$$U = p_{UX} X + p_{UV} V + p_{UA} A$$

To these equations must be added the specification that residual A is uncorrelated with variables X and V and that residual B is uncorrelated with variables U, X, and V with residual A. The coefficients symbolized by p's correspond to the straight lines bearing arrowheads in the diagram. The algebraic presentation makes it explicit that the model is a system of *linear* equations. Thus the algebraic translation of "U depends on X, V, and A" is "U is equated to a linear combination of the values of X, V, and A."

1.3 Incremental Strategy of Model Building

Thus far it has been indicated (a) that the study of the process of achievement will be effected by taking the socioeconomic life cycle as a conceptual framework; and (b) that it is possible to translate assumptions about how the process operates into an explicit model which can either be represented by a diagram in which causal relationships are symbolized by arrows linking variables or expressed algebraically as a system of linear equations. The example given of such a model is the somewhat rudimentary one that we shall term, for convenience, the "basic" model of this research. The model is basic only in the sense that it represented the point of departure for the project, the intention of which was to develop "extensions" of it. The nature of the extensions that were attempted is the subject of the present section.

A good model serves not only to rationalize and interpret a pattern of empirical relationships but also to raise questions whose answers require further empirical inquiry and/or modifications of the model. Thus the long-run course of research in an area of inquiry may be guided, more or less explicitly, by an incremental strategy of model building. The history of previous work in in the area of socioeconomic achievement becomes more intelligible on the assumption that this strategy was implicit in the collective efforts of research workers.

For a long time, investigators were preoccupied with the problem of "occupational mobility"; their basic concern, in effect, was to establish the nature and degree of relationship between respondent's and father's occupations (Y and X, in the notation introduced previously). Once reasonably reliable estimates of this relationship were in hand, it was natural to inquire into its mechanisms. At that point, it was suggested that schooling is an important intervening variable. Studies of occupational mobility, such as those of Glass (1954), Carlsson (1958), and Svalastoga (1959), began to include attention to this variable, and it became pertinent to suggest a simple three-variable model treating schooling as dependent upon father's occupation, and son's occupation as dependent upon both schooling and father's occupation (Duncan & Hodge, 1963). Once this model was available and its properties had been explored, one logical next step was to incorporate into it an additional measure of social origin, to wit, father's education, on the supposition that schooling might depend on more than one aspect of family background. Such was the genesis of the basic model outlined in the previous section, which was treated in some detail in the research of Blau & Duncan (1967).

As the strategy of model building became more explicit, it was evident that further progress need not be limited to the consideration of one additional variable at a time. Moreover, the tradition of studies emanating from the original interest in occupational mobility was seen to be converging with that of investigators concerned with such variables as educational plans and occupational aspirations (for example, Turner, 1964; Sewell & Orenstein, 1965) and those considering the role of psychological variables in the process of achievement (for example, Centers, 1948; Kahl, 1965; Stacey, 1965; Crockett, 1966). The hunch that it would be fruitful to attempt a merging of these lines of investigation underlay the proposal to attempt a whole series of "extensions" of the "basic" model. A review of the literature provided suggestions for the kinds of variables to be considered in such an endeavor and leads for locating pertinent bodies of data.

After even a cursory examination of the basic model, the student of social stratification and occupational achievement will have no difficulty in suggesting ways in which it might be extended. Our intention was not to generate an exhaustive list of such hypothetical extensions but to attempt seriously to effect some significant number of them.

To begin with, it seemed desirable to consider enlarging the number of *background* variables. It was mentioned in Section 1.2 that the two measures of the family's socioeconomic level (head's education and occupation) hardly exhaust the list of possibly relevant variables of this kind. Yet there was reason to believe that substantial marginal improvement of the model would not be achieved merely by including more of this particular kind of variable; hence this task was not given high priority. Instead, attention was focused on other kinds of measures pertaining to the family or deriving from the use of "family" as an initial stage of the socioeconomic life cycle. One obvious candidate, in view of its demonstrated association with educational attainment (B. Duncan, 1967), is family size, or number of siblings.

Another kind of background variable is suggested by the fact that belonging to a given family of orientation confers ascriptively the status of member of the ethnic category into which that family is socially classified. Hence, race and ethnic classifications are taken to be potentially significant "background" variables. Much the same could be said of religious (denominational) group membership, which tends to be an ascribed status, although by no means an entirely fixed one. Little or no attention was given this factor in the present project, however, primarily for lack of readily available data.*

Two other important initial conditions of achievement are linked up with membership in a family of orientation. These are the individual's locations in time and space. His location in time is irrevocably fixed by his date of birth; and, from some standpoints, of all the advantages or handicaps conferred on the offspring by the parents, few are more important than those depending on the historical period within which life is to be lived. It will not be expeditious to treat location in time as a "background factor" in quite the same sense as family size or socioeconomic status; but the importance of this factor dictates a continuous attention to the historical dating of information and the age classification of respondents. As for location in space, certain regional differences in achievement are well known. A more extensive treatment of the implications of such differences would have been entirely appropriate, but it turned out to be impossible to improve much on the results of earlier work (Blau & Duncan, 1967, Chapter 6).

A most interesting category of variables comprises those we shall term *intervening* variables. The import of this term can be explicated by referring back to the basic model. That model, if it be accepted as a rough first approximation, discloses a substantial connection between occupational achievement and socioeconomic background and also a similarly substantial one between educational attainment and background. As already suggested, we may regard the amount of schooling secured as a factor that intervenes between background and occupational achievement, operating both to transmit part of the influence of background and also to induce variance in achievement not associated with background. Educational attainment, therefore, is our first example of an intervening variable. It qualifies as such by virtue of two properties: First, schooling itself depends on antecedent variables in a causal sequence, and, second, it influences a variable (occupational achievement) taken to be an

---

* The reader is directed to the work of Warren (1970a, b) for a thorough analysis of the religious factor within a framework closely related to the one used here. See also Duncan and Featherman (1970) and Featherman (1971c).

outcome of such a sequence. Both conditions are necessary for us to accept the interpretation that it is a significant intervening variable. From one point of view, much of the scientific quest is concerned with the search for intervening variables that will serve to interpret or explain gross associations presumed to reflect a causal relationship.

Granted that education is one important intervening variable, the demonstration that this is so merely heightens one's curiosity about others. For one thing, the connection of education with background factors is itself not unproblematic. What variables are involved in the mechanism producing this causal relationship? Moreover, as we shall see, while education is indeed of great importance in transmitting the effect of background, there is in the basic model a nontrivial direct influence of background on occupational achievement. How does this come about? Can we introduce into the model intervening variables other than education such that the estimate of the direct influence of background shrinks to zero? In this event, the extended model could make a fair claim to have explained fully the association between background and occupational achievement.

In view of the central role of education in the basic model, an obvious candidate for another intervening variable is intelligence, for some differential psychologists now take the position that intelligence as measured by standard mental ability tests is essentially "scholastic aptitude."* It will be of interest to learn whether, or to what extent, the influence of family on schooling operates via intelligence—or rather, it will be of interest to see what issues are raised by this manner of posing the question. Moreover, if intelligence influences achievement, it will be relevant to estimate how much of this influence operates via educational attainment and how much is independent of the factor of amount of schooling.

Along with ability, some social psychologists would name motivation as a prime candidate for an intervening variable. Indeed, it was at the end of a chapter entitled "Intelligence and Motivation" that Lipset & Bendix (1959, p. 259) suggested "that by merging the sociological and psychological approaches to the study of social mobility we may be able to advance the study of the mechanisms by which individuals and groups reach their positions in the stratification structure." No doubt these authors did not mean to imply that "ability" and "motivation" exhaust the list of psychological factors that represent significant intervening variables, even though from a commonsense point of view these may seem to comprise an adequate classification of such factors. In any event, the spirit of the present investigation is nicely characterized by the remark just quoted.

---

* See Jensen (1969) and Herrnstein (1971) for a review of this issue and a commentary on the development of intelligence tests and what they measure.

It is not within the scope of the present enterprise to achieve a taxonomy of "psychological factors" that will rigorously satisfy the theoretical criteria of a science of behavior. Thus the elaboration of distinctions between and relationships among motives, goals, values, aspirations, dispositions, and the like is a task left to the social psychologist. Insofar as this kind of work in social psychology has influenced research on the process of achievement, it suggests the advisability of some attention to one axis of classification of such variables. On the one hand, as suggested by the term "motive," there may be postulated dispositions that are deep-seated, enduring, and diffuse and pervasive in their influence on behavior. On the other hand, as suggested by such terms as "plans" and "intentions," are dispositions that are comparatively specific and temporally localized in their influence. A generalized "need for achievement," illustrating the former, may, therefore, be conceived as underlying the more or less definite "occupational aspirations" of a youth or the even more specific set of intentions tapped by a question on "college plans." Both sorts of variable will be considered as candidates for incorporation into an extended model, within the rather severe limits placed on the inquiry by present techniques of measurement and available data.

Another group of intervening variables may conveniently be labeled "social influences." Here we have in mind the patterns of social interaction between an individual and relevant "others" in his social milieu that may influence his dispositions or direct his attention to opportunities. The family of orientation, already considered in terms of its relevance to background, is here thought of as providing specific role models and as molding characteristic dispositions, both directly and indirectly. Further, we wish to subsume under this category the suspected impact of peer groups on the formation of occupational goals or tendencies relevant thereto, whether this impact is disclosed in dyadic relations with friends or in the patterns common to an entire category of peers (as in alleged influences of "school climate"). To temper expectations in regard to this whole category of variables, it had best be stated at the outset that treating them in the format of the present inquiry poses some severe methodological problems, and the success of the venture is quite limited. Fortunately, one aspect of the investigation will be supplemented by an ambitious study of "school effects" by Hauser (1969; 1971).

The next major class of variables to be discussed might well be regarded as a subclass of "intervening variables"; but it poses some issues sufficiently special that it is convenient to have a distinct label, to wit, *career contingencies*. Here we have in mind decisions taken or circumstances encountered in the course of the life cycle that may have significant bearing upon occupational outcomes. Such contingencies may be related both to background factors and to other intervening variables, and thus serve to mediate the influence of either of these on occupational achievement. From another point of view, the recognition of certain career contingencies may be tantamount to a proposal of a more detailed sequence of stages in the life cycle. The difficulty with this viewpoint is that the contingencies in question—those associated with entry into the labor market, selection of place of residence, initiation of a family of procreation, and liability to military service—do not arise in a fixed temporal order, and different individuals may not encounter all of them in the same way.

In purely conceptual terms, there is no apparent limit on the number of career contingencies that might be fruitfully examined. Here, as in the study of intervening variables, the operative limits on the inquiry are imposed by the availability of data. The project did, however, seek to consider (albeit in varying degrees of detail) the following contingencies: (1) age at first job; (2) the occupational level of the first job; (3) residential migration; (4) marital status; and (5) fertility, that is, size and timing of increments to the family of procreation. Each of these has been implicated in the process of achievement by results of previous research. A further contingency, probably a good deal more important than its scanty treatment in previous research would suggest, is military service. This topic has been opened up by an important survey (Klassen, 1966); unfortunately, however, in the present inquiry we have not been in a position to follow up the leads developed there.*

In addition to the general caveat that applies to all the work reported here— to the effect that all results are to be regarded as tentative—it must be stipulated that the work on career contingencies falls considerably short of what would be regarded as an adequate investigation. Our work on these topics is not only placed at the end of the report but was in fact undertaken toward the end of the project, under considerable pressure of time. If the data reported suggest something of the complexities of the issues at stake, the effort will not have been wasted.

The final class of variables to be incorporated in our models comprises the *outcome* variables. The principal one of these has already been identified as occupational status, whether measured by a socioeconomic index or on an occupational prestige scale. Although concentration on this particular outcome is dictated by the primary goals of the study, it is not irrelevant to consider other outcomes that may equally well represent outputs of a process of achievement —most notably, income or earnings, to which we shall give passing attention. A whole series of further outcomes could also justifiably claim attention—for example, job satisfaction, feelings of economic or status security–insecurity, social class identification, and other measures of "subjective achievement." Our study of such variables has been quite restricted, again primarily for lack

---

* Fortunately, the survey data reported by Klassen (1966) have now been analyzed by Mason (1970) to render estimates of the effects of military service and training on later socioeconomic attainments.

of clearly relevant data suited to manipulation within the framework of our models.

To be sure, we are considering outcomes other than those mentioned. Indeed, each intervening variable or career contingency in a model is to be conceived as an outcome of a process traced up to a given juncture in the life cycle. Educational attainment is perhaps the clearest example in our work of an achieved status which is both an outcome of the earlier phases of the life cycle and an intervening variable with respect to later phases. The very nature of the kind of model we shall be developing is that "outcomes" at one stage become "antecedents" with respect to a subsequent stage.

The reader may have noted the omission of a kind of variable that is often discussed in reports of research involving moderately complicated designs, that is, so-called control variables. The omission was not inadvertent, for we should wish to argue that there is no clearly describable role for control variables as such in the strategy of model building to be illustrated here. Upon inspection, variables proposed as "controls"—if, indeed, any clear role is predicated for them whatever—will be found to fall into one or another of the categories already proposed: background variables, intervening variables, career contingencies, or outcome variables. When a causal model has been made explicit, "control variables" will have been properly allocated to one of these functional slots.

It might seem that an exception would have to be made for the sort of "control variable" that specifies the population within which the process is assumed to operate. In the present research, for example, all the data examined pertain to males so that one might wish to assert that sex has been "controlled" by disposing of one of the categories of the sex classification. Our strategy does indeed rest on the assumption that patterns of achievement for men and women are quite distinct: Different variables may be relevant, or the same variables may have different weights. But we should want to claim that, in principle, models of the process of achievement could just as well be constructed for females as for males. Construction of such models in parallel would be tantamount to the recognition of sex as a background factor, albeit one with especially pronounced interactions with the remaining variables in the models. Confining our work to relationships observable in the male population was merely a tactic to make the investigation manageable and does not represent an acknowledgment that this classification (or any other such classification that might be proposed in addition to those considered here) enjoys some special status as a control variable. It would undoubtedly be all to the good if investigators would relinquish that term entirely in favor of making more explicit and defensible the rationale on which controls are introduced in statistical analyses.

1.4 Prospectus

This introductory chapter is intended to acquaint the reader with the questions raised for investigation and the general strategy for seeking answers. Specific problems relating to definition of variables, securing and manipulating data, and techniques of model construction will be discussed more fully in subsequent chapters. In Chapter 2 we shall present at some length the essentials of the technique of path analysis, which is to be employed throughout the remainder of the study in explicating models and securing estimates of their parameters; sources of data are also described. Properties of the basic model and estimates made on it are treated in Chapter 3, in preparation for the series of extensions to be considered in the remaining chapters, which review the work done on the project in regard to the several background variables, intervening variables, and career contingencies identified previously.

This monograph does not cover all work done in the course of the original project nor does it treat evenhandedly all the topics discussed in the Final Report on which this monograph is based. A number of topics, suited to separate treatment, have been summarized herein from their published sources, and the reader is encouraged to consult the latter for a more thorough analysis and comment. Finally, several of the analyses in the Final Report have been revised or updated in this version of our work, although these changes do not alter any of the provisional conclusions drawn from the original research regarding the process of status attainment.

If it were necessary to assume that the reader will approach the material in this report uncritically, a number of caveats would be in order. Without stating these in detail, may we simply assure him that all the work reported here, insofar as it involves interpretations of findings or postulates embodied in models, is regarded as tentative. In no case is it assumed that the last word has been said, and many of the models obviously do no more than suggest leads for more thorough investigations. Such investigations, when and if they are carried out, will assuredly render many of our interpretations doubtful. A high rate of obsolescence of models is devoutly to be desired, provided that the old ones are replaced by superior versions.

Chapter 2

Models, Methods, and Data

The preceding chapter was intended to indicate both the breadth and the narrowness of the problem accepted as the task of this research. It is a broad problem in the sense that a rather diverse set of variables has been designated as appropriate for study, and the general framework is one that is purportedly susceptible to more or less indefinite expansion to accommodate such a list of variables. The problem is greatly narrowed, however, by the resolution to exploit a single self-conscious strategy of model building. Thus the project places rather stringent requirements on sets of observations or measurements in determining whether they shall be considered relevant to the task at hand. We have no way to make use of impressionistic evidence or scraps of data that cannot, even conjecturally, be tied in with our basic model in some formal, quantitative way. We accept the opportunity cost of being deprived of the benefits (if any) of attending to the immense lore surrounding our subject in order to realize the more tangible benefits that accrue from being able rigorously to manipulate bodies of systematic, quantitative information. (The justification of this strategy in terms of a general philosophy of science is beyond the scope of this report; the reader who is completely skeptical of the possibility of such justification may be well advised to read no further.)

The first task of the present chapter is to provide the mathematical and statistical rationale of our procedures of model construction and estimation. We have drawn heavily from the germinal work of Wright (1960a, b, and literature cited therein) on the technique of path analysis. No detailed elaboration of this technique is included here, and the reader is encouraged to consult

17

recent expositions written for social science audiences (Duncan, 1966; 1970b; Land, 1969; Heise, 1969). The text assumes that the reader is fluent in the terminology of path analysis, and although the present chapter recapitulates some of the fundamentals of this technique, it constitutes a review and not a primer of path analysis. A second task of this chapter is to enumerate and describe the principal sources of data, on which was based the incremental strategy of model building, as detailed in Chapter 1.

2.1 A Recursive Model

Included in Duncan's (1966) exposition on path analysis models is an illustration drawn from the work of Ralph Turner (1964). Coincidentally, Turner's data, as represented in Fig. 2.1, comprise a five-variable recursive model of the process of stratification or of status attainment. While we shall not interpret the substance of our representation of Turner's data, we have included Fig. 2.1 as an occasion for a review of recursive path models and their interpretation. A particularly instructive feature of this example is that Turner himself had not presented the entirety of the model in a single connected account, and he had made no use of the technique of path analysis or of the type of diagrammatic representation illustrated here. Nevertheless, it is possible to show that the model is implicit in his verbal statement of hypotheses and relationships, even though the statistical manipulations that Turner reported are not the ones that are seen to be appropriate once the model is made explicit. He does, however, provide in scattered contexts (Turner, 1964, pp. 49 and 52, Tables 11, 17, and 20) the essential data for estimating all the path coefficients of the model, in the form of intercorrelations of the five variables identified in Fig. 2.1.

The statements made by the author that appear to imply this particular model may be summarized quickly. At one point, Turner (1964, p. 17) states, "background affects ambition and ambition affects both IQ and class values; in addition . . . there is a lesser influence directly from background to class values, directly from background to IQ, and directly between IQ and class values." Elsewhere (pp. 54–61) he suggests that school socioeconomic rating operates in much the same fashion as (family) background. In discussing the relationship between the two—family background and school rating—Turner notes that "families may choose their place of residence," but he also concedes that "by introducing neighborhood, we may only be measuring family background more precisely" (p. 61). In short, the author does not unequivocally postulate a causal ordering of these two variables with respect to each other; accordingly, the diagram inferred from his statements makes no commitment on this point either.

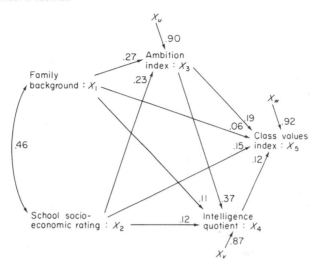

Fig. 2.1. Path diagram representing causal model implicit in Turner's (1964) study of the determinants of aspirations, with path coefficients estimated from correlations reported by him.

The model as formulated verbally and represented diagrammatically can also be rendered algebraically as a set of linear equations:

$$X_3 = p_{32} X_2 + p_{31} X_1 + p_{3u} X_u;$$

$$X_4 = p_{43} X_3 + p_{42} X_2 + p_{41} X_1 + p_{4v} X_v; \text{ and} \qquad \text{(Model 2.1)}$$

$$X_5 = p_{54} X_4 + p_{53} X_3 + p_{52} X_2 + p_{51} X_1 + p_{5w} X_w.$$

The symbols are those denoting the variables appearing in Fig. 2.1. The three variables with literal subscripts (u, v, and w) are the residuals for X_3, X_4, and X_5, respectively, which must be included in the model to satisfy the condition of complete determination. In a recursive model of this type the usual assumption with respect to these residuals is that each is uncorrelated with the other variables directly influencing the dependent variable in question, and that they are uncorrelated with each other (Blalock, 1964). It is this set of assumptions that provides the leverage needed to make numerical estimates from the empirical data. In the case at hand, therefore, the equations of the model are supplemented with the specification, $r_{1u} = r_{2u} = r_{1v} = r_{2v} = r_{3v} = r_{1w} = r_{2w} = r_{3w} = r_{4w} = r_{uv} = r_{uw} = r_{vw} = 0$. One further stipulation completes our statement of the assumptions underlying further algebraic and numerical work: All variables are taken to be in standard form; that is, each of the measured variables, $X_1, ..., X_5$ and each of the residuals X_u, X_v, and X_w has a mean of zero and a standard deviation of unity. All that is involved here is a simple transformation. If, for example, variable 3 as originally measured had a mean of $\overline{V}_3$ and a standard deviation of σ_3 in the sample under study, then we define $X_3 = (V_3 - \overline{V}_3)/\sigma_3$ with similar definitions for the other variables.

On the understanding that the variables are in standard form, the coefficients (the p's) in the equations are termed "path coefficients," and their interpretation goes as follows: In the first equation (for example), for a unit (standard deviation) change in X_2 there is (on the average) a change of p_{32} in X_3, where p_{32} is the fraction of a standard deviation by which X_3 changes, given unit change in X_2. (It need not be a proper fraction inasmuch as path coefficients may have numerical values outside the range ± 1.0.)

The reader is likely to have encountered path coefficients under the name of "*beta*-coefficients" or "*beta*-weights." The two concepts are interchangeable for a model like the one under examination; but path analysis also applies to cases in which the coefficients cannot be estimated by the straightforward procedure used in calculating *beta*'s. One notational convention may be explained at this point. As is conventional for *beta*-coefficients and regression coefficients in raw-score form, the first subscript of the path coefficient denotes the dependent variable and the second subscript the causal or explanatory variable. Secondary subscripts, used with partial regression and *beta*-coefficients to identify the variables "held constant," as in $\beta_{32.1}$, are not employed in the notation for path coefficients, however. It will always be evident from the statement of the model, either in symbols or as a diagram, what other independent variables are involved. Note that while the order of the two subscripts must be carefully observed for the path coefficients, it is irrelevant for correlations since $r_{ij} = r_{ji}$.

Although the distinction between path coefficients and conventional standardized regression coefficients may seem unnecessary at the moment, the reader may bear it in mind for future reference. For the present, the reader may wish to think of Model 2 as comprising a set of three regressions: X_3 on X_2 and X_1; X_4 on X_3, X_2, and X_1; and X_5 on X_4, X_3, X_2, and X_1. However, we shall later exhibit models in which conventional regression estimates are not applicable. Hence, it is advisable to state the general method by which estimates are secured, noting that it is equivalent to the calculation of a set of regressions under special circumstances, such as those applying in the present instance.

Let us suppose (as is in fact the case in this example) that we know all the correlations among the measured variables, $X_1, \ldots, X_5$, in the sample of respondents for which the analysis is being made. Inasmuch as we are working with variables in standard form, the correlation coefficient takes on a very simple form: The correlation between any two of these variables, say X_i and X_j, is simply $r_{ij} = \Sigma X_i X_j / N$, where N is the number of cases in the sample. If $i = j$, we have

$$r_{ii} = \sum X_i X_i / N = \sum X_i^2 / N = 1.0$$

in view of the property that a variable in standard form has unit variance or that the correlation of a variable with itself is unity. It is now easy to show how any of the known correlations can be written in terms of an expression involving path coefficients and some other known correlations. Consider the first equation of Model 2.1.

$$X_3 = p_{32} X_2 + p_{31} X_1 + p_{3u} X_u.$$

Suppose we multiply both sides of the equation by X_2 to obtain

$$X_2 X_3 = p_{32} X_2^2 + p_{31} X_1 X_2 + p_{3u} X_u X_2.$$

Now, sum both sides of this equation over sample observations:

$$\sum X_2 X_3 = p_{32} \sum X_2^2 + p_{31} \sum X_1 X_2 + p_{3u} \sum X_u X_2.$$

(The p's may be written to the left of the summation signs because they are constants.) Finally, divide both sides by N:

$$\frac{\sum X_2 X_3}{N} = p_{32} \frac{\sum X_2^2}{N} + p_{31} \frac{\sum X_1 X_2}{N} + p_{3u} \frac{\sum X_u X_2}{N}.$$

But $\sum X_2 X_3 / N = r_{23}$ and $\sum X_2^2 / N = 1.0$, and so on, as we have just seen. Hence we may write:

$$r_{23} = p_{32} + p_{31} r_{12} + p_{3u} r_{2u}.$$

However, $r_{2u} = 0$ on the specification concerning correlations of residuals stated at the outset. Hence our final result is

$$r_{23} = p_{32} + p_{31} r_{12}.$$

To refer to the sequence of steps through which we have just gone, we may say that we "multiply the first equation through by X_2 and simplify."

Let us now "multiply through" the first equation by X_1. We obtain in an exactly parallel fashion

$$r_{13} = p_{32} r_{12} + p_{31}.$$

Collecting our results thus far, we have

$$r_{23} = p_{32} + p_{31} r_{12}, \text{ and}$$

$$r_{13} = p_{32} r_{12} + p_{31}.$$

The three correlations appearing here are known, having been calculated from the data. The two path coefficients, p_{32} and p_{31}, are not known at the outset. But we now have two linear equations in two unknowns. Straightforward computational procedures for obtaining the solution for the two path coefficients are readily available.

Next, let us multiply through the second equation of the model by X_3, X_2, and X_1 in turn. The steps already described will lead us to a set of three equations in which appear three unknown path coefficients, p_{43}, p_{42}, and p_{41}:

$$r_{43} = p_{43} + p_{42} r_{23} + p_{41} r_{13}$$

$$r_{42} = p_{43} r_{23} + p_{42} + p_{41} r_{12}$$

$$r_{41} = p_{43} r_{13} + p_{42} r_{12} + p_{41}.$$

The same procedure applied to the third equation of the model, multiplying it through by X_4, X_3, X_2, and X_1 in turn, yields four equations containing the four unknown path coefficients, p_{54}, p_{53}, p_{52}, and p_{51}:

$$r_{54} = p_{54} + p_{53} r_{34} + p_{52} r_{24} + p_{51} r_{14}$$

$$r_{53} = p_{54} r_{34} + p_{53} + p_{52} r_{23} + p_{51} r_{13}$$

$$r_{52} = p_{54} r_{24} + p_{53} r_{23} + p_{52} + p_{51} r_{12}$$

$$r_{51} = p_{54} r_{14} + p_{53} r_{13} + p_{52} r_{12} + p_{51}.$$

We have, therefore, generated the "normal equations" from which we may solve for all the unknown path coefficients, except for the residual paths.

To find p_{3u}, multiply the first equation through by X_3 and simplify so as to obtain

$$r_{33} = 1 = p_{32} r_{23} + p_{31} r_{13} + p_{3u} r_{3u}.$$

The two path coefficients, p_{32} and p_{31}, have already been computed and may now be taken as known. But the foregoing equation appears to contain two unknowns, p_{3u} and r_{3u}. To resolve this difficulty, multiply through the first equation of the model by X_u to obtain

$$r_{3u} = p_{32} r_{2u} + p_{31} r_{1u} + p_{3u} r_{uu};$$

whence $r_{3u} = p_{3u}$ inasmuch as $r_{2u} = r_{1u} = 0$ (by the specifications of the model) and $r_{uu} = 1$. Returning to the first equation in this paragraph, therefore, we have

$$p_{3u}^2 = 1 - p_{32} r_{23} - p_{31} r_{13},$$

which yields the solution for p_{3u}. The same type of formula is readily derived for p_{4v} and p_{5w}. The calculation of these completes the set of numerical estimates for this model.

It will be noted that we gave an expression for each of the 10 correlations in Turner's data, except one, r_{12}. In this particular model, both X_1 and X_2 are "predetermined" variables. Correlations among predetermined variables are simply taken as given. On the path diagram, such ultimate or unanalyzed correlations are represented by a *curved* line linking the pair of variables, with arrowheads at *both* ends. Such a link does *not* represent any assumption or hypothesis as to causal relationship or dependence. Indeed, the model is entirely silent on the question of how correlation between predetermined variables may arise. In this case, someone might wish to argue that X_1 causes X_2, that X_2 causes X_1, that the two variables reciprocally influence each other, or that the two share some common cause which gives rise to the correlation between them. As long as we treat X_1 and X_2 as predetermined with respect to this model, it does not matter what the actual causal relationship between them is, for the only information we need is the degree of correlation between them.

2.2 Reduced Forms and Semireduced Forms

As indicated by the introductory remarks in Section 1.2, one of the attractive features of the type of model investigated here is that it makes explicit both the direct and the indirect effects of causal variables on dependent variables and allows for the possibility that one variable may be "dependent" with respect to its antecedents in a causal scheme but "causal" with respect to subsequent variables. All this is clearly suggested by the path diagram, but to see how these properties of the model work out quantitatively, we must carry out some more algebra.

Let us for the moment ignore the equation for X_5 in Model 2.1. Moreover, let us assume that Turner had proposed that IQ (X_4) depends on family background (X_1) and school rating (X_2) without regard to ambition (X_3). The diagram for this simple model is shown on the left in Fig. 2.2. The model has only one equation,

$$X_4 = q_{42} X_2 + q_{41} X_1 + q_{4a} X_a. \qquad \text{(Eq. 2.1)}$$

We use, temporarily, the symbol q for path coefficients since the coefficients here are not the same as those in Model 2.1. Again we specify that the residual is uncorrelated with the predetermined, causal variables: $r_{2a} = r_{1a} = 0$.

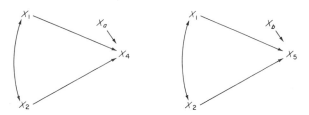

Fig. 2.2. Reduced forms of Model 2.1 with X_4 as the dependent variable and with X_5 as the dependent variable.

Now, if we substitute the first equation of Model 2.1 into the second, we obtain

$$X_4 = p_{43}(p_{32} X_2 + p_{31} X_1 + p_{3u} X_u)$$
$$+ p_{42} X_2 + p_{41} X_1 + p_{4v} X_v$$

or, rearranging terms,

$$X_4 = (p_{42} + p_{43} p_{32}) X_2 + (p_{41} + p_{43} p_{31}) X_1$$
$$+ p_{4v} X_v + p_{43} p_{3u} X_u.$$

This is seen to be of the same form as Eq. (2.1), upon making the following substitutions:

$$q_{42} = p_{42} + p_{43} p_{32};$$
$$q_{41} = p_{41} + p_{43} p_{31}; \text{ and}$$
$$q_{4a} X_a = p_{4v} X_v + p_{43} p_{3u} X_u.$$

From the point of view of Model 2.1, q_{41} is a composite path which sums up the direct effect of X_1 on X_4 as p_{41} and the indirect effect via X_3 as $p_{43} p_{31}$. The relative magnitudes of the two quantities will frequently be of interest.

A more complicated composite path is disclosed when we work out the equation in the reduced form of Model 2.1 in which X_5 is the dependent variable. The same kind of algebra already illusrated permits the deductions:

$$q_{52} = p_{52} + p_{53} p_{32} + p_{54}(p_{42} + p_{43} p_{32})$$
$$q_{51} = p_{51} + p_{53} p_{31} + p_{54}(p_{41} + p_{43} p_{31}).$$

Such expressions, in effect, exhibit the "mechanisms" by which the predetermined variables bring about their effects on the dependent variables of a complex model.

One important comment follows from this demonstration of relationships between reduced form and extended form models. Almost any model, however complex, may be considered as a reduced form with respect to a model which gives a still more elaborate account of intervening variables. But the omission of such intervening variables from the reduced form does not necessarily mean that the latter is invalid. (Matters are not so simple for a "semireduced" form, as is brought out subsequently.) Thus, if Model 2.1 is an acceptable representation of the process under study, then so are the reduced forms in Fig. 2.2. If the investigator had begun with the three-variable equation depicted on the right side of Fig. 2.2, the estimates of the paths q_{51} and q_{52} would have been correct, even though he could not, at that point, specify their composite nature. Two things are accomplished by the more elaborate Model

2.1: (a) The "mechanisms" through which X_1 and X_2 influence X_5 are made explicit and quantitative estimates of their relative importance are secured; (b) variance in X_5 due to intervening variables but independent of the predetermined variables is accounted for. Thus Model 2.1 gives a more nearly complete explanation of X_5 than does the reduced form, as well as a more explicit or detailed interpretation of the dependence of X_5 on X_1 and X_2.

To see how this comes about, let us recall that the residual, X_a, for the reduced form on the left side of Fig. 2.2 was shown to be composed of two terms:

$$X_a = \frac{p_{4v}}{q_{4a}} X_v + \frac{p_{43} p_{3u}}{q_{4a}} X_u.$$

Multiplying through this equation by X_u, X_v, and X_a in turn (remembering the specification $r_{uv} = 0$), we find that $r_{ua} = p_{43} p_{3u}/q_{4a}$, $r_{va} = p_{4v}/q_{4a}$, and $r_{aa} = 1 = (p_{43}^2 p_{3u}^2 + p_{4v}^2)/q_{4a}^2$, and hence that $q_{4a}^2 = p_{43}^2 p_{3u}^2 + p_{4v}^2$.

This result may be rearranged as $1 - p_{4v}^2 = 1 - q_{4a}^2 + p_{43}^2 p_{3u}^2$; or $R_{4(123)}^2 = R_{4(12)}^2 + p_{43}^2 p_{3u}^2$, where $R_{4(123)}^2 = 1 - p_{4v}^2$ is the coefficient of multiple determination (squared multiple correlation) obtained when X_4 is regressed on X_1, X_2, and X_3 and $R_{4(12)}^2$ is the coefficient of determination for the regression of X_4 on X_1 and X_2 only. The former exceeds the latter by the amount $p_{43}^2 p_{3u}^2$, which is easily computed given the estimates of path coefficients for the extended form of the model. Hence, the introduction into the model of X_3 as an intervening variable (between X_1 and X_2, on the one hand, and X_4, on the other) not only serves to elucidate the mechanisms by which the predetermined variables influence the dependent variable but also to account for a greater part of the variation in the latter.

The previous discussion and results do not carry over, however, to "semireduced" form models, and the source of the difficulty hinges on the assumption of uncorrelated errors in a recursive model. Our comments about Fig. 2.2 (the reduced forms of Model 2.1) are valid inasmuch as we can legitimately assume that $r_{a1} = r_{a2} = r_{b1} = r_{b2} = 0$, that is, that residuals to endogenous variables are uncorrelated with predetermined variables. However, residuals among the endogenous variables may not always be uncorrelated (as is usually assumed in the Simon-Blalock solutions of recursive systems). This exception applies, for example, when one of several endogenous variables is deleted in a semireduced form model such as that illustrated subsequently. In such cases, the investigator would be arguing from estimates in the semireduced form model which are biased estimates of the "true" state of affairs in the extended form.

Consider as a paradigm Turner's Model 2.1. To recapitulate, the assumptions of the model are: (i) Residuals are uncorrelated with predetermined variables, that is, $r_{u1} = r_{u2} = r_{w1} = r_{w2} = r_{v1} = r_{v2} = 0$; (ii) the residual in each equation is uncorrelated with the explanatory variables for that equation, so that $r_{3v} = r_{3w} = r_{4w} = 0$; (iii) the residuals of the several equations are uncorrelated inter se, that is, $r_{uv} = r_{uw} = r_{vw} = 0$.

Let us suppose that the "true" state of affairs in the social world is as represented by Model 2.1 and Fig. 2.1, which are, of course, equivalent. Suppose, further, that in undertaking Turner's research we had failed to develop the Ambition Index (endogenous variable X_3) and had represented the determinants of aspiration by Model 2.2:

$$X_5 = q_{54} X_4 + q_{52} X_2 + q_{51} X_1 + q_{5t} X_t;$$
$$X_4 = q_{42} X_2 + q_{41} X_1 + q_{4s} X_s. \qquad \text{(Model 2.2)}$$

We can ascertain the actual, albeit unknown, state of affairs confronting Model 2.2 by elminating X_3 from the last two equations of Model 2.1 by directly substituting the first equation into them. We find:

$$X_5 = p_{54} X_4 + (p_{53}p_{32} + p_{52}) X_2 + (p_{53}p_{31} + p_{51}) X_1$$
$$+ p_{53}p_{3u} X_u + p_{5w} X_w$$

and $\qquad\qquad\qquad\qquad\qquad\qquad\qquad\qquad\qquad\qquad\qquad\qquad$ [1]

$$X_4 = (p_{43}p_{32} + p_{42}) X_2 + (p_{43}p_{31} + p_{41}) X_1$$
$$+ p_{43}p_{3u} X_u + p_{3v} X_v.$$

We can reconcile Model 2.2 and [1] by proposing the definitions,

$$q_{54} = p_{54}$$
$$q_{52} = p_{53}p_{32} + p_{52}$$
$$q_{51} = p_{53}p_{31} + p_{51}$$
$$q_{5t} X_t = p_{53}p_{3u} X_u + p_{5w} X_w \qquad [2]$$
$$q_{42} = p_{43}p_{32} + p_{42}$$
$$q_{41} = p_{43}p_{31} + p_{41}$$
$$q_{4s} X_s = p_{43}p_{3u} X_u + p_{4v} X_v.$$

The fourth and seventh equations in [2] imply that

$$X_t = (p_{53}p_{3u}/q_{5t}) X_u + (p_{5w}/q_{5t}) X_w$$

and $\qquad\qquad\qquad\qquad\qquad\qquad\qquad\qquad\qquad\qquad\qquad\qquad$ [3]

$$X_s = (p_{43}p_{3u}/q_{4s}) X_u + (p_{4v}/q_{4s}) X_v.$$

The "true" model for our semireduced form (omitting X_3) is, therefore, represented by the combination of Model 2.2 and [3]. The "correct" path diagram

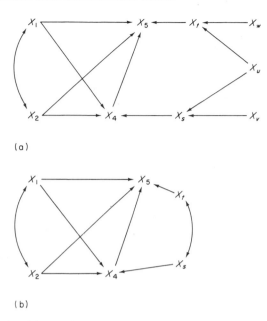

(a)

(b)

Fig. 2.3. Semireduced forms of Model 2.2, in which variable X_3 has been omitted from the causal model represented in Figure 2.1.

under the circumstances is given in Fig. 2.3a. It is obvious from Fig. 2.3a that X_s and X_t, the residuals in Model 2.1, cannot be uncorrelated since they are completedly determined, respectively by X_u and X_v and by X_u and X_w; X_u is thus a "common cause" of X_s and X_t. We can use the equations in [3] together with assumption (iii) to ascertain not only the correlation r_{st} but also all the correlations among the residuals in the two models, Models 2.1 and 2.2. There are five such residuals, and we can multiply each of them through each equation in [3], sum over sample observations, divide by N, and simplify the result. We obtain,

$$r_{us} = p_{43} p_{3u}/q_{4s} \qquad \text{(since } r_{uv} = 0)$$
$$r_{vs} = p_{4v}/q_{4s} \qquad \text{(since } r_{uv} = 0)$$
$$r_{ws} = 0 \qquad \text{(since } r_{uw} = r_{vw} = 0)$$
$$r_{ut} = p_{53} p_{3u}/q_{5t} \qquad \text{(since } r_{uw} = 0) \qquad [4]$$
$$r_{vt} = 0 \qquad \text{(since } r_{uv} = r_{vw} = 0)$$
$$r_{wt} = p_{5w}/q_{5t} \qquad \text{(since } r_{uw} = 0)$$

and

$$r_{st} = (p_{53} p_{3u}/q_{5t}) r_{us} \qquad \text{(since } r_{ws} = 0),$$

or

$$r_{st} = (p_{43}p_{3u}/q_{4s})r_{ut} \qquad (\text{since } r_{vt} = 0).$$

Either of these expression simplifies to

$$r_{st} = p_{53}p_{43}p_{3u}^2/q_{5t}q_{4s}, \qquad [5]$$

but

$$r_{tt} = 1 = (p_{53}p_{3u}/q_{5t})r_{ut} + (p_{5w}/q_{5t})r_{wt}$$

$$= p_{53}^2 p_{3u}^2/q_{5t}^2 + p_{5w}^2/q_{5t}^2,$$

whence

$$q_{5t}^2 = p_{53}^2 p_{3u}^2 + p_{5w}^2. \qquad [6]$$

Simiarly,

$$r_{ss} = 1 = p_{43}^2 p_{3u}^2/q_{4s}^2 + p_{4v}^2/q_{4s}^2,$$

whence

$$q_{4s}^2 = p_{43}^2 p_{3u}^2 + p_{4v}^2. \qquad [7]$$

Substituting [6] and [7] into [5], we obtain

$$r_{st} = \frac{p_{53}p_{43}p_{3u}^2}{(p_{53}^2 p_{3u}^2 + p_{5w}^2)^{1/2}(p_{43}^2 p_{3u}^2 + p_{4v}^2)^{1/2}}, \qquad [8]$$

and Fig. 2.3a can be redrawn as Fig. 2.3b.

If we had computed the path coefficients (the p's) for Model 2.1, having data on all the predetermined and dependent variables, it would be an easy matter to compute all the "correct" coefficients (the q's) for Model 2.2, as well as the correlation (r_{st}) between its residuals, making use of formulas [2], [6], [7], and [8]. In the case of our hypothetical investigation with Model 2.2, however, this information is not available. Hence, we might be tempted to adopt the incorrect (as we now know) assumptions for Model 2.2: $r_{4t} = r_{st} = 0$. We would also be assuming that $r_{1s} = r_{2s} = r_{1t} = r_{2t} = 0$, but these assumptions would not be incorrect, as can easily be verified by multiplying the equations in [3] through X_1 and X_2, recalling assumption (i). Let us see what would happen in making use of the erroneous assumptions to obtain values of the path coefficients in Model 2.2. Multiply the second equation in [1] through by X_1 and X_2 to obtain

$$r_{42} = (p_{43}p_{32} + p_{42}) + (p_{43}p_{31} + p_{41})r_{12}$$

$$r_{41} = (p_{43}p_{32} + p_{42})r_{12} + (p_{43}p_{31} + p_{41}). \qquad [9]$$

This is a set of perfectly good estimating equations, which takes on its pleasing symmetrical appearance in virtue of assumption (i), in particular, $r_{2u} = r_{2v} = r_{1u} = r_{1v} = 0$. Hence, we obtain immediately the solutions for $(p_{43}p_{32} + p_{42})$ and $(p_{43}p_{31} + p_{41})$, that is to say, for q_{42} and q_{41} (cf. [2]). The result is the same as we would have obtained by computing these two q's from the values of the p's in terms of which they are defined. In fact, the second equation of Model 2.2 is nothing other than the "reduced form" of the second equation of Model 2.1.

Difficulties emerge, however, as we try to solve for the q's in the first equation of Model 2.2. Multiplying that equation through by X_4, X_2, and X_1 in turn, we obtain:

$$r_{45} = q_{54} + q_{52}r_{42} + q_{51}r_{41} + q_{5t}r_{4t}$$

$$r_{52} = q_{54}r_{42} + q_{52} + q_{51}r_{12} \qquad [10]$$

$$r_{51} = q_{54}r_{41} + q_{52}r_{12} + q_{51}.$$

We are able to put to good use the results, $r_{2t} = r_{1t} = 0$, which follow from [3] and assumption (i). However, we cannot get rid of the term $q_{5t}r_{4t}$ since $r_{4t} \neq 0$. Indeed, from [3] we have

$$r_{4t} = (p_{53}p_{3u}/q_{5t})r_{4u} \qquad (\text{since } r_{4w} = 0). \qquad [11]$$

But from Model 2.1 we can ascertain that $r_{4u} = p_{43}r_{3u} = p_{43}p_{3u}$. We may now rewrite [11] as

$$q_{5t}r_{4t} = p_{53}p_{43}p_{3u}^2. \qquad [12]$$

Let us transpose this term in the first equation of [10] and rewrite that set of equations in matrix form:

$$\begin{pmatrix} 1 & r_{42} & r_{41} \\ r_{42} & 1 & r_{12} \\ r_{41} & r_{12} & 1 \end{pmatrix} \begin{pmatrix} q_{54} \\ q_{52} \\ q_{51} \end{pmatrix} = \begin{pmatrix} r_{45} - p_{53}p_{43}p_{3u}^2 \\ r_{52} \\ r_{51} \end{pmatrix}, \qquad [13]$$

the solution for which is

$$\begin{pmatrix} q_{54} \\ q_{52} \\ q_{51} \end{pmatrix} = A^{-1} \begin{pmatrix} r_{45} - p_{53}p_{43}p_{3u}^2 \\ r_{52} \\ r_{51} \end{pmatrix} \qquad [14]$$

where A is the square matrix on the left-hand side of [13] and A^{-1} is its inverse. Contrast this correct solution with the one that would be obtained if we were to make an erroneous assumption because of our omission or ignorance of X_3.

We would use a set of estimating equations like [10], except that the term $q_{5t}r_{4t}$ would not appear. Thus we would, in fact, solve for a different (and biased) set of coefficients—call them q^*:

$$\begin{pmatrix} q^*_{54} \\ q^*_{52} \\ q^*_{51} \end{pmatrix} = A^{-1} \begin{pmatrix} r_{45} \\ r_{52} \\ r_{51} \end{pmatrix} \qquad [15]$$

Note that, in general, q^* will differ from the corresponding q and by a magnitude and sign that cannot be known without having data on X_3. The bias is easy to express symbolically. Let

$$A^{-1} = \begin{pmatrix} c_{11}\ c_{12}\ c_{13} \\ c_{21}\ c_{22}\ c_{23} \\ c_{31}\ c_{32}\ c_{33} \end{pmatrix} \qquad [16]$$

be the matrix inverse in [14] and [15]. Then it can be seen that

$$q^*_{54} - q_{54} = c_{11}p_{53}p_{43}p^2_{3u}$$

$$q^*_{52} - q_{52} = c_{21}p_{53}p_{43}p^2_{3u} \qquad [17]$$

$$q^*_{51} - q_{51} = c_{31}p_{53}p_{43}p^2_{3u}$$

are the biases in the respective q^* coefficients. It is worth noting that if either p_{53} or p_{43} is zero, then these biases are also zero. Conceivably, one might have reasons for supposing this to be the happy state of affairs in the absence of direct evidence to this effect. But one would do well to be clear in one's own mind that such an assumption is required for the acceptance of q^* as an estimate of q.

The moral of the tale, of course, is that *any* investigator is likely, on occasion, to be in the situation of attempting to estimate a semireduced form model such as Model 2.2. The case of the phantom intervening variable (X_3) is but one instance of the generic problem of unmeasured "third variables" that induce "spurious correlation." Thus our illustration serves to emphasize the importance of evaluating a recursive causal scheme with respect to its coverage of intervening variables as well as its inclusion of the proper predetermined variables. Additionally, the illustration points up the caution one must exercise in interpreting coefficients estimated for a model which is, in effect, a semireduced form of a more extended model, even if the latter is not explicit in the investigator's thinking.

2.3 Sources and Descriptions of Data Sets

It is customary to complain that in sociology the results of discrete research projects are not additive in the sense that each new contribution builds on those preceding it while the accumulation of research results reveals a discernible pattern or structure. Sociology is, rather, a discipline of bits and pieces. If this judgment is just, it only raises the question of why it is so. Perhaps the usual answer is that discrete investigations do not share a common body of theory or conceptual framework. That answer is not accepted here. While there is merit in the major premise—that investigations manifest diversity in their theoretical orientations—the conclusion does not follow. The simple reason is that research operations—selection and measurement of variables, delimitation and sampling of populations, and so on—are seldom dictated by or even narrowly constrained by strictly theoretical considerations. They are more likely to be contrived by exercising a combination of emulation, expediency, and inspiration.

The more basic impediment to cumulative research is the simple lack of adequate attention to standardization and replication of research procedures. With sufficient attention to these matters and sufficient skill in execution, the results of research would begin to resemble the "interchangeable parts" that came to be used in machinery during the nineteenth century. That is, one investigator's findings could be juxtaposed with those of another working on the same topic, and valid inferences could be drawn from the conjunction of the two, assuming that the form of the inference could be justified in logic. This kind of juxtaposition is often attempted informally in the "commentary and discussion" section of research reports. But in this context, where the rules of scientific inference are relaxed in the hope of encouraging productive speculation, the quasi-inferences reached have only heuristic value. They do not represent an increment to firm knowledge (although, to be sure, they may stimulate some further effort to secure such an increment—but more likely some further "commentary and discussion" on a subsequent occasion).

These generalities preface a statement of the attitude taken toward data in this project. This attitude was rather eclectic, within a pair of constraints suggested by the initial formulation of the problem. The first constraint concerned the specification of the population to be studied. This population was defined as the adult male population of the contemporary United States in the central ages of working force participation. On occasion, well-defined subpopulations within this population are considered for separate study. It will be noted that the vagueness of the terms "contemporary" and "central ages" allows some considerable latitude in making specific decisions. Even more to the point, all sorts of approximations to the target population were accepted when there seemed to be reasonable grounds for doing so.

The second constraint related to the measurement of variables. The general classes of variables of interest to the project have been enumerated in Section 1.3. A prospective data source was considered relevant to the project if it included measurements on some combination of variables in this enumeration.

With these constraints as guidelines, the project undertook a review of literature and a round of communication with investigators believed to be working on pertinent material. The first criterion for accepting a body of data was, of course, its availability, either in published reports or in unpublished files and computations. The second criterion, which served to put the constraints into effect, was that the data should be compatible with, or at least in some sense comparable to, the OCG data sets that were available to the project as a legacy from previous projects or that were tabulated especially for this one. The abbreviation OCG stands for "Occupational Changes in a Generation," a survey that will be described later. Thus, if a prospective data set included some of the same variables as the OCG set and some additional variables of potential interest, and if the population covered was at least roughly (but presumably sufficiently) comparable to that covered in OCG (or some interesting sub-population in the latter), it was considered as having a high potential utility to the project. As it turned out, our hopes for accumulating numerous data sets meeting the project specifications were somewhat too optimistic; yet a number of complete data sets and other fragments of information were uncovered whose availability had not been anticipated.

OCG Data. By far the most important data set, both in terms of logistics of data processing and analysis and in terms of contribution to the overall structure of the project was the OCG set. The existence of this body of information was due to a prior project with which the principal investigator was associated (Blau & Duncan, 1967). It had also served as a major resource in a related study (B. Duncan, 1965b). The data were collected in conjunction with the March 1962 Current Population Survey (CPS) of the United States Bureau of the Census, via the regular CPS interview and a supplementary question-naire, "Occupational Changes in a Generation." In addition to the regular CPS items, including, among others, age, race, marital status, 1961 income, employ-ment status, occupation, industry, and educational attainment, the supplement provided such items as ethnic background, educational attainment and occu-pation of the head of the respondent's family of orientation, number of his siblings, educational attainment of his oldest brother, occupation and industry of first job, and age upon entering the first job. Some 20,700 respondents in this survey represented the approximately 45-million men in the United States civilian noninstitutional population between the ages of 20 and 64 in March 1962. All reports on occupation (that of the head of the respondent's family, that of his own first job, and his current or most recent occupation as of March 1962) were coded to the Census detailed classification and subsequently recoded to scores on the scale of occupational socioeconomic status devised by Duncan (1961a).

Although the previously mentioned projects using these data had acquired rather voluminous tabulations, which were available to the present project, there remained for further analysis a number of interesting relationships not hitherto adequately studied. Hence, we secured from the Bureau of the Census additional extensive tabulations differing in form rather substantially from any that were already available. These permitted somewhat closer specifications of the several subpopulations to be studied and facilitated computations of the kind required by the particular type of model used in the project.

NORC-CPS Data. The only other major set of nationally representative data was another CPS supplement, conducted as an adjunct to the October 1964 survey. The data were collected by the Bureau of the Census for use in a study of military manpower carried out at the National Opinion Research Center (NORC) on behalf of the Department of Defense (Klassen, 1966). Although this CPS supplement covered all civilian noninstitutional men 16–34 years old, this project made use of just the subset of data for white men 25–34 years old. Several variables in the CPS-NORC set were designed to be closely comparable with OCG items. The first major use of the former, therefore, was to secure a replication of OCG results. The outcome of this replication was highly satisfactory. The second major use of the CPS-NORC data was in constructing models involving mental ability (Duncan, 1968a). The respondents in the 1964 supplement who were veterans of military service were matched to their service records, from which there were extracted the scores on the Armed Forces Qualification Test. In addition to mental ability scores (for veterans only) the CPS-NORC set includes such variables of interest to this project as educational attainment, current occupation, total earnings in 1964, occupation and earnings of first job, and father's occupation and education.

DAS Data. Although no original data were collected expressly for this project, the project did take advantage of the opportunity to cooperate with a survey that began at about the same time. This was the 1966 Detroit Area Study (DAS), an annual study conducted at the University of Michigan. The directors of the 1966 DAS, Professors Howard Schuman and Edward O. Laumann, kindly incorporated into their survey instrument a number of questions of interest to this project, so that many of the OCG items are fairly closely replicated in the DAS set. In addition, the latter includes a measure of mental ability, the "Similarities" subtest of the Wechsler test of adult mental ability. Also of interest to this project were efforts made in the DAS to secure indicators of strength of achievement motivation. While the results of these efforts were equivocal, the data did permit an examination of the degree to which such motivations might account for religious-ethnic differentials in achievement (Duncan & Featherman, 1970). The target population for the 1966

DAS comprised native white men 21–64 years of age residing in the Detroit metropolitan area. Thus these data permit a replication in a local setting of the national results secured from the OCG and CPS-NORC sets. In addition to the interest in this replication, the DAS set permitted study of a particular measurement problem: the effect of using alternative measures of occupational status. All the occupation entries on the DAS schedule were coded by the staff of this project, adhering closely to the Census detailed occupation code and associated procedures. It was then possible to recode occupations in any fashion desired. Of particular interest was the comparison between scores on Duncan's (1961a) socioeconomic index of occupational status and scores on the occupational prestige scale resulting from the work of Robert W. Hodge, Paul M. Siegel, and Peter H. Rossi at the National Opinion Research Center, 1964–1967 (Siegel, 1970).

FGMA Data. The FGMA data set afforded material for one of the most intensive analyses of the project (Duncan, 1969). The identification FGMA stands for Family Growth in Metropolitan America, the title of the monograph by Westoff and associates (1961) for which these data were originally collected. These data were of strategic importance, not because of the population covered—it was a rather curiously defined one—but because of the considerable effort that had gone into the attempt to measure motivational variables. The FGMA population consisted of couples who at the time of the survey, in 1957, had recently had a second child. The sample was drawn from birth records of several major metropolitan areas. Psychological measures were available for 941 husbands. Collateral information on these included several items closely similar to OCG variables: father's occupation, number of siblings, educational attainment, occupation and income at marriage, and current occupation and income. The occupation items in FGMA were coded to the North-Hatt prestige scale (Reiss and others, 1961). This precludes a strict replication of OCG results, but provides data roughly comparable to the DAS set, making use of the occupational prestige recodes included in the latter.

Subsequent to the completion of the Final Report, data from the second and third panels of FGMA were made available to us. These follow-up data cover the period 1957–1967 and provided an opportunity to explore the longer-term effect of selected motivational dispositions on subsequent status attainments and to examine the relationship of marital fertility to mobility (Featherman, 1969; 1970; 1971a, b, c).

WISC Data. All of the data sets thus far described, like the bulk of the data available to this project, derive from cross-sectional studies. The time dimension enters in via retrospective questions used to ascertain such information as father's occupation or respondent's first job. In contrast with this type of study, a major research effort under the direction of William H. Sewell at the University of Wisconsin involves a longitudinal design. The baseline measurement derives from a questionnaire survey of all Wisconsin high school seniors in

1957. A probability sample comprising approximately one-third of the initial respondents was followed up in 1964–1965, and a response rate of 87 percent was obtained. Among the more important variables obtained in 1957 are intelligence, high school grades, occupational aspirations, educational plans, and parental socioeconomic status. The follow-up survey provided data on educational attainment, as of the seventh year beyond high school, and occupational status at that time. One other special feature of the WISC data set is that aggregate measures on the high schools attended by the respondents are available, making possible analyses designed to test for hypothesized "school effects."

The present project has not attempted a comprehensive analysis of the WISC data. That task is in progress at the University of Wisconsin (Sewell, Haller, & Portes, 1969; Sewell, Haller, & Ohlendorf, 1970; Sewell, Hauser, & Shah, forthcoming). Instead, we have used preliminary tabulations provided by the Wisconsin research for certain special purposes at particular points in the course of the project as well as a particularly significant replication, given the longitudinal design of the WISC study, as contrasted to the cross-sectional design of the other data sets. The reader should note that our statistics from the WISC data do not always correspond with those subsequently published by Sewell and his colleagues, owing to slightly different definitions of variables.

All of the data sets described thus far were used, in one way or another, to make possible substantive analyses not contemplated by the original investigators. In contrast, sets described in the paragraphs to follow were exploited for more strictly methodological purposes. That is, the problem as formulated by the original investigator was much the same as the one defined for this project, but in the latter case there was a commitment to a particular type of model, differing considerably from the analysis format of the original study.

SRC Data. One of these "secondary analyses" was done on data originally collected by Survey Research Center in 1957 for a national study of mental health. A subsample of respondents, including 715 men, were administered TAT tests for the purpose of indexing strength of achievement, affiliation, and power motives. These data were used by Crockett (1962) in an investigation of the role of achievement motivation in intergenerational occupational mobility. Additional specifications on the population to be covered as well as deletions dictated by missing information reduced Crockett's sample to 368 cases. Further losses were sustained in our reanalysis since not quite all the original schedules could be located in SRC files. In any event, the small size of the available sample means that this material is not well suited to the estimation of parameters. Our interest in the SRC data set was primarily in ascertaining whether Crockett's conclusion on the role of achievement motivation would be sustained in the framework of the kind of model used in this study.

MICH Data. Similarly, in working with data provided by Professor

Archibald O. Haller of the University of Wisconsin, we were particularly interested in reexamining (Duncan, Haller, & Portes, 1968; Duncan, 1970a) a relationship detected in his previous work (Haller & Butterworth, 1960) using methods rather different from those suggested by the basic model employed in this project. These data were generated in a survey of all 17-year-old boys in school in Lenawee County, Michigan, during the spring of 1957. Interviews and test data were secured for 442 persons, but for the analyses of interest here, the sample was restricted to the 329 boys for whom information was available on their best friends. Clearly, this sample does not afford a secure basis for estimates of parameters for the whole United States population. The MICH data set does, however, provide unique or virtually unique information on an interesting set of variables: levels of educational and occupational aspiration of the boys, the socioeconomic status of their parents, the measured intelligence scores of the boys, and their estimate of their parents' encouragement of high achievement levels. The same data are available for the "best friends" of the boys.

In addition to the seven major sources of data that have been described, a number of other items of information were reviewed and sometimes incorporated into analyses. These are bits of data of a more fragmentary nature rather than the somewhat substantial data matrices afforded by the previously cited sources. It should be noted, moreover, that in regard to the latter it was not the intention of the project to perform exhaustive analyses or data summaries. Instead, each data source, whether it was rather compendious or comparatively restricted in the amount of information it provided, was examined selectively in the light of the specific objectives of the project, as outlined in Chapter 1. Given the somewhat unusual character of these objectives, the use of source materials involved the project in rather little duplication of the work of original investigators.

Chapter 3

The Basic Model

The main outlines of the process of occupational achievement, as it is observed to operate in the male population of the contemporary United States, have been established by previous research (Blau & Duncan, 1967). That is, we now have firmly based estimates of the degree to which achieved occupational status depends on the socioeconomic level of the family of orientation, the extent to which education serves as an intervening variable in the transmission of status, the extent to which it introduces variability into occupational achievement that is independent of origins, and the contributions of certain other background factors to level of status attained in adulthood. This chapter will recapitulate some of the results of this prior research but will cast them into a somewhat different form for purposes of better comparison with the results of the present project. It will also summarize a replication of the earlier results and consider a salient methodological problem—that of the variation in findings due to variation in the technique of measuring occupational status. All the data in this chapter pertain to the subpopulation of adult white men. Explicit comparisons between white and Negro men appear in the next chapter.

3.1 Occupational Achievement in Four Cohorts

The OCG data were retabulated for this project so as to secure correlations among the major variables for native non-Negro men in four age groups, as of March 1962: 25–34, 35–44, 45–54, and 55–64 years of age. Table 3.1 presents the correlations needed for calculations on the version of the basic model to be

TABLE 3.1

Simple Correlations between Variables Entering Into the Basic Model, for Non-Negro Men with Nonfarm Background, in Experienced Civilian Labor Force, by Age: March 1962[a]

Age group and variable[b]	Correlation with					Mean	Standard deviation
	X	T	U	Y	H		
25–34							
V	.4885	−.2691	.4017	.3420	.1534	9.17	3.53
X	–	−.2290	.4133	.3534	.2019	34.59	22.35
T	–	–	−.3262	−.2475	−.1523	3.49	2.86
U	–	–	–	.6510	.2726	12.38	3.04
Y	–	–	–	–	.3369	43.34	25.01
H	–	–	–	–	–	6.14	4.29
35–44							
V	.5300	−.2871	.4048	.3194	.2332	8.55	3.72
X	–	−.2476	.4341	.3899	.2587	34.41	23.14
T	–	–	−.3311	−.2751	−.1752	3.77	2.88
U	–	–	–	.6426	.3759	11.95	3.20
Y	–	–	–	–	.4418	44.78	24.71
H	–	–	–	–	–	7.50	5.36
45–54							
V	.4863	−.2395	.3685	.2517	.1902	8.15	3.69
X	–	−.2301	.4454	.3777	.3032	32.99	22.35
T	–	–	−.2997	−.2341	−.1329	4.09	2.96
U	–	–	–	.5949	.3635	11.25	3.28
Y	–	–	–	–	.4376	42.41	23.76
H	–	–	–	–	–	7.74	6.81
55–64							
V	.5313	−.2749	.3534	.3022	.1595	8.38	3.66
X	–	−.2398	.3879	.3543	.1871	34.06	23.16
T	–	–	−.2817	−.2565	−.1122	4.46	3.09
U	–	–	–	.5576	.3071	10.47	3.61
Y	–	–	–	–	.3799	42.73	24.62
H	–	–	–	–	–	6.99	6.37

[a] Source: OCG data set.

[b] V, Father's education; X, father's occupation; T, number of siblings; U, education; Y, occupation; H, income, 1961 ($1000).

presented here. These correlations are for men with nonfarm origins; that is, the head of the family in which the respondent grew up was not pursuing the occupations farmer, farm laborer, and the like as of the respondent's age 16. Although most results differ fairly little when farmer's sons are included, it seems conceptually simpler to deal with the nonfarm sector separately since the perplexing question of status comparisons between farm and nonfarm jobs can be avoided. (There is so little movement from nonfarm origins to farm occupations that it is not necessary to remove such cases from the data.)

There is no immediate need to comment on particular correlations in Table 3.1. They are, in effect, the raw material for the calculations next to be reported. These calculations take the form of three regressions in a recursive set, which are suggested by a causal argument advancing the following propositions: (1) Educational attainment depends on three characteristics of the family of orientation, the respondent's number of siblings and the occupational level and educational attainment of his father (actually, the head of the family, in the event of the father's absence). (2) Occupational status in 1962 depends on educational attainment and the foregoing three family background items. (3) Income depends on occupational status, educational attainment, and the three characteristics of the family of orientation.

Inasmuch as achieved occupational status was ascertained as of March 1962 while income was measured for the year 1961, there is an apparent inversion of the temporal order of the variables relative to the foregoing assumptions about causal order. In view of the compelling considerations that lead one to think of income as depending on occupation, rather than vice versa, we shall have to regard 1961 income as a proxy for 1962 income, that is, as a somewhat fallible measure thereof. This is a customary procedure in analyzing data on income collected by the Bureau of the Census, but little evidence exists on the seriousness of the error it incurs.

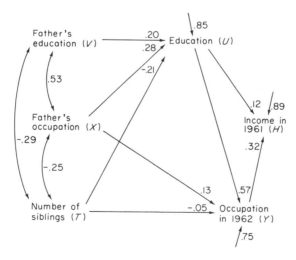

Fig. 3.1. Basic model of the process of achievement, with path coefficients estimated for non-Negro men with nonfarm background, 35–44 years old, in experienced civilian labor force, March 1962. (Source: OCG data set. Path not shown where coefficient is less than .05 in absolute value.)

TABLE 3.2

Partial Regression Coefficients in Standard Form for Recursive Model Relating Achieved Statuses to Family Background Factors, by Age, for Non-Negro Men with Nonfarm Background, in Exprienced Civilian Labor Force: March 1962 (Parentheses enclose each coefficient less than its standard error in absolute value)[a]

Age and dependent variable[b]	Independent variables[b]					Coefficient of determination
	Y	U	T	X	V	
25–34						
U (Education)	–	–	−.2080	.2585	.2194	.263
Y (Occupation)	–	.5875	−.0216	.0744	.0638	.436
H (Income)	.2635	.0556	−.0542	.0794	(−.0124)	.126
35–44						
U	–	–	−.2053	.2780	.1985	.269
Y	–	.5668	−.0540	.1266	(.0073)	.431
H	.3247	.1193	−.0201	.0492	.0494	.216
45–54						
U	–	–	−.1856	.3210	.1680	.260
Y	–	.5245	−.0494	.1442	−.0235	.372
H	.3204	.1153	(.0079)	.1298	(.0059)	.222
55–64						
U	–	–	−.1736	.2562	.1695	.208
Y	–	.4687	−.0810	.1285	.0460	.342
H	.2970	.1293	(.0104)	(.0277)	(.0122)	.159

[a] Source: Table 3.1.

[b] V, Father's (or family head's) educational attainment; X, father's (or family head's) occupational status; T, respondent's number of siblings; U, respondent's educational attainment; Y, respondent's occupational status, March 1962; H, respondent's income in 1961.

Our procedure then, is to regress U on T, X, and V; then Y on U, T, X, and V; and finally, H on Y, U, T, X, and V. (See Table 3.2 or Fig. 3.1 for identification of these letter symbols.) The regressions were computed within each cohort, and the results are displayed in Table 3.2. In Fig. 3.1 the regression coefficients have been taken as estimates of the path coefficients of the causal diagram. Just as a way of simplifying the diagram so that the main results are clearer, coefficients less than .05 in absolute magnitude are not shown and the corresponding paths are deleted (even though some of these small coefficients might be statistically significant on a conventional test). For illustration, the results are displayed in the graphic form for only one cohort, men 35–44 years old in 1962. Most of the important features of the results are, however, shared by all the cohorts.

Each of the three family background factors directly influences education in an appreciable degree. Results for all four cohorts suggest that father's occupation is a slightly more weighty factor in educational attainment than either father's education or number of siblings when all three variables are considered simultaneously. The effect of number of siblings is negative, implying that an increase in family size lowers the number of grades of school completed. For greater detail on this portion of the model, see B. Duncan (1967).

In the regression of occupation on education and the three family factors, the former emerges as by far the most important direct influence. There is an interesting age gradient in the magnitude of the coefficient for education, which runs from .47 for the oldest cohort to .59 for the youngest. These data alone do not, however, permit an inference as to time trend in the closeness of association between educational level and occupational achievement since the cohorts differ in duration of experience in the labor force.

A consistent finding over cohorts is that number of siblings has a negative influence on occupational achievement. The path coefficients p_{YT} measures the direct influence; in addition, number of siblings operates negatively on occupational achievement by way of education, as may be seen in multiplying the paths $p_{YU} p_{UT}$. In the oldest cohort the direct and indirect influences are about equal in size; in the younger cohorts the indirect influence assumes a greater relative importance.

Comparing the coefficients measuring the direct dependence of occupation on father's occupation and education, respectively, points up a prevalent kind of ambiguity encountered in regression models. These two variables are inter-correlated to the extent of about .5 in each cohort. With this much collinearity between independent variables it becomes very difficult to estimate the separate effects of each. Thus we notice considerable instability in the relative magnitudes of the coefficients over the four cohorts. In all cases, father's occupation does have the higher coefficient, as one would expect a priori. In one cohort, however, the two are about equal, while in the immediately older cohort father's education has a coefficient of essentially zero. In another cohort, the estimate of the coefficient for father's education comes out slightly negative, a result which would be difficult to interpret substantively. It appears, therefore, that slight fluctuations in the zero-order correlations of these variables with the dependent variable, given the intercorrelation of the former, suffice to alter considerably the estimate of the nature of their respective direct influences. In this situation, many investigators consider that the attempt to separate the influences of the two variables is hopeless, and they resort to some such procedure as combining scores on the two variables into one composite score with more or less arbitrary weights. In several of the data sets used in this project, such a procedure had been followed so that in later chapters we shall often encounter measures of so-called family socioeconomic status rather than specific variables like father's occupation or education.*

It may be seen that the problem alluded to here appears also in regard to income as the dependent variable. In both cases, we feel that a prima facie case for father's occupation as the more central influence can be made; and such a case is not wholly inconsistent with the results. Hence, if it were necessary to present a single estimate of the effects of family socioeconomic level, we should be tempted to repeat the regression calculations, simply omitting father's education as an independent variable for respondent's occupation and income. Father's occupation would then be in some measure a proxy for the various measures on family socioeconomic status that could be suggested as well as a "cause" in its own right. It appears that the attempt to distinguish between these two roles would founder on the obstacle presented by high collinearity.

To summarize the interpretive conclusion on the point at issue, Fig. 3.1 shows father's occupation as a direct influence on respondent's occupation but father's education as only an indirect influence. As measured by $p_{YU}p_{UV} = .11$, this indirect influence is not negligible.

We turn, finally, to the portion of the model which regards income as the dependent variable with all the five prior variables considered as possible direct influences on it. Reviewing the results for all four cohorts, the main common pattern is that the coefficient for occupation is substantial while that for the direct influence of education is appreciable. In all four cohorts, the indirect influence of education via occupation is greater than the direct influence, that is, $p_{HY}p_{YU} > p_{HU}$. This supports the conclusion reached by less precise methods that "an educational advantage is translated into an income advantage primarily, though not exclusively, by pursuing an occupation in which the prevailing income level is comparatively high" (Duncan, 1961b, p. 788).

The results are less consistent for the three family background factors. In any case, their direct impact on income seems to be slight. We must bear in mind, of course, that two very important intervening variables are included in the model so that it would, in fact, be rather anomalous if family background appeared to have a substantial *direct* influence on income. To report that such a direct influence is slight is not to say that the background factors are unimportant but merely that their influence is largely indirect. To clarify the point, Table 3.3 presents regression coefficients for the three reduced form equations of the

---

* Stratification researchers would be ill-advised to construct these composite socioeconomic variables without first determining the pattern of relationship between each component and the other variables of interest. Hodge (1970, p. 188), for example, finds that socioeconomic status is not a unidimensional construct with respect to various measures of psychological well-being and social integration. However, Hauser (1970) reports that the family socioeconomic status variable in the WISC data is a unidimensional construct with regard to adolescent achievement aspirations and educational attainments.

TABLE 3.3

Partial Regression Coefficients in Standard Form for Reduced Form of Recursive Model Relating Achieved Statuses to Family Background Factors, by Age, for Non-Negro Men with Nonfarm Background, in Experienced Civilian Labor Force: March 1962[a]

Age and dependent variable	Independent variables[b]			Coefficient of determination
	T	X	V	
25–34				
U (Education)	−.2080	.2585	.2194	.263
Y (Occupation)	−.1438	.2263	.1928	.181
H (Income)	−.1036	.1534	.0506	.055
35–44				
U	−.2053	.2780	.1985	.269
Y	−.1703	.2842	.1198	.196
H	−.0998	.1746	.1120	.089
45–54				
U	−.1856	.3210	.1680	.260
Y	−.1467	.3126	.0646	.169
H	−.0605	.2669	.0459	.098
55–64				
U	−.1736	.2562	.1695	.208
Y	−.1624	.2486	.1255	.168
H	−.0603	.1347	.0714	.043

[a] Source: Table 3.1.

[b] V, Father's (or family head's) educational attainment; X, father's (or family head's) occupational status; T, respondent's number of siblings; U, respondent's educational attainment; Y, respondent's occupational status, March 1962; H, respondent's income in 1961.

model, wherein each of the dependent variables is regressed on only the three family background factors. In this pattern of analysis, intervening variables are not explicitly recognized so that one may compare directly the three dependent variables with respect to the magnitude of total impact of background variables on them.

The outcome of this analysis is quite clear: Each of the background variables as well as the combination of all three has its greatest impact on education and its least on income, with the impact on occupational status being intermediate. With one minor inversion (p_{UX} for age group 35–44) this ordering is recapitulated in each of the four cohorts. Substantively, we are led to the conclusion that family background matters most for attainments that are close in time to the period of residence in the family of orientation and has a progressively attenuated influence on achievements coming later and later in the life cycle.

This conclusion must, of course, remain tentative. It is vulnerable to the possibility that we have failed to measure some factor or factors in family background that have a different pattern of impact on achievement. In particular, it will not have escaped the reader that we have no measure of the income or wealth of the family of orientation, although father's education and occupation are in a moderate degree presumably correlated therewith.*

Speculations on this matter may be aided by a hypothetical calculation. Let us imagine a hypothetical variable, Z, which may stand for "father's wealth" or "father's income." Let us say that for respondents in the 35- to 44-year-old age group the correlations of the background variables with Z are as follows: $r_{XZ} = .44$, $r_{VZ} = .38$, and $r_{TZ} = -.14$. Let us take as a further hypothesis that the combination of Z and the other three background variables yields a coefficient of determination,

$$R^2_{H(ZTXV)} = .269;$$

this has been chosen for illustration to be the same as

$$R^2_{U(TXV)} = .269$$

since we want to consider the possibility that income in the hypothetical case is as closely dependent on family background as is education in the observed case. Finally, let us assume that the path coefficients p_{HT}, p_{HX}, and p_{HV} that we have already estimated remain the same after Z is included in the array of independent variables. These three postulates, all quite artificial, suffice to allow us to deduce the path coefficient $p_{HZ} = .36$ and the corresponding correlation $r_{HZ} = .50$. This would appear to be a conservative estimate of the intergenerational correlation of incomes that would have to be postulated to raise the coefficient of determination to the specified level. That is, other reasonable postulates that might achieve the same thing would probably require a still higher value of r_{HZ}. Now, so far as we know, there is no estimate for a broadly defined population on the actual magnitude of such a correlation as r_{HZ}. But we can note that it is appreciably higher than the other intergenerational correlations we do observe, $r_{UV} = .40$ and $r_{YX} = .39$ in this particular age group. The reader may well find it plausible to believe that the intergenerational correlation with respect to income is higher than with respect to occupation

---

* Hauser, Lutterman, & Sewell (1971) find a significant, positive coefficient (about 14¢ on the dollar) for the effect of paternal income on total earnings of sons in the WISC data set. This relationship is net of the effects of paternal occupation and paternal and maternal education, and it holds only for the earnings variable (not for educational or occupational attainment).

and education. If that should prove to be true, it would be slightly surprising, but the possibility certainly cannot be foreclosed.*

Even so, it is difficult to imagine that the coefficient of determination for income could be raised without also raising that for, say, education. If family income is a neglected factor in income achievement, we have also neglected it in regard to educational attainment. How much the inclusion of Z in the model might raise the coefficient of determination for U is indeterminate without stipulating even more assumptions than we have already used. Hence there really is no way to make a useful hypothetical calculation here. However, supposing Z made only a very moderate increment in the predictability of U, we would be back to the pattern we have noted in the actual data—to wit, that educational attainment depends somewhat more on family background than does income. As was stated, this conclusion can be only tentative. Nevertheless, it is difficult to discredit it on the basis of a priori reasoning alone.

3.2 Replication and Scales of Measurement

The work reported in this section takes advantage of the close approximation to a replication of part of the OCG study that was achieved in the Detroit Area Study (DAS) of 1966. The first question raised is that of the transferability of conclusions reached on the basis of a national sample to the situation represented by the population in a particular metropolitan locality. Table 3.4 provides the relevant correlations, means, and standard deviations for the two samples. The OCG data used here are for native non-Negro men with nonfarm background in the experienced civilian labor force of the United States in March 1962. The DAS data pertain to native white men 21–64 years of age in the summer of 1966. The full DAS sample consisted of 1013 men; for some combinations of variables the effective sample size is as low as 900 owing to nonresponse on particular items. The comparison of the first two panels in Table 3.4, therefore, reveals differences that are due primarily to (a) sampling variation in each of the studies; (b) the difference in time between 1962 and 1966; and (c) the difference in population coverage, national v. local. The coding of occupations, which was accomplished as a special task of the present project, was intended to yield results as nearly comparable as possible with those yielded by procedures of the United States Bureau of the Census.

* In unpublished tabulations from the WISC data set, Hauser and Sewell calculate a product-moment correlation of .181 between father's average income between 1957 and 1961 and son's 1965 income; the correlation between father's average income and son's total earnings in 1967 is .147. Both figures are calculated for nonfarm Wisconsin residents in the civilian labor force and therefore are based on restricted distributions. Still, these estimates are substantially lower than the other intergenerational correlations reported elsewhere and in the WISC data.

TABLE 3.4

Simple Correlations in OCG and DAS Data Sets, with Alternative DAS Results for Different Measures of Occupational Status.

Data set	Variable		Father's occupation (X or X')	Respondent's education (U)	Respondent's current occupation (Y or Y')	Mean	SD
OCG,	Father's						
non-Negro	education	(V)	.506	.393	.306	8.63	3.67
nonfarm	Father's						
background,	occupation	(X)	–	.419	.371	34.07	22.72
age 25–64	Respondent's						
	education	(U)	–	–	.610	11.70	3.30
	Respondent's						
	occupation	(Y)	–	–	–	43.47	24.58
DAS-1							
occupations	V		.481	.322	.271	8.80	3.20
scored on	X		–	.338	.306	33.90	23.76
socioeconomic	U		–	–	.599	12.00	3.20
index	Y		–	–	–	45.84	24.03
DAS-2,							
occupations	V		.424	.322	.256	8.80	3.20
scored on	X'		–	.240	.211	39.22	12.78
prestige	U		–	–	.567	12.00	3.20
scale	Y'		–	–	–	42.74	13.44

The major result of the comparison is that the intergenerational correlations (V with U, V with Y, X with U, and X with Y) are somewhat lower in Detroit than in the nation, although the intragenerational correlations (V with X and U with Y) are closely similar. This is precisely what we would expect if part of the national intergenerational correlation is due to between-place covariation superimposed upon the within-place covariation found in each of the nation's localities.

Figure 3.2 shows diagrams that present the comparison in terms of the path coefficients that can be estimated for the truncated version of the basic model that is, of necessity, used here. (The relevant comparison is between OCG and DAS-1.) For many purposes an analyst might well regard the two sets of results as essentially identical, although it follows from the observation on magnitudes of simple correlations already made that the measured effect of family background on educational attainment and occupational achievement is slightly less in the DAS than in the OCG data. Inasmuch as the OCG sample is far larger in size, coefficients of the same magnitude may be clearly significant in OCG results but not so in DAS results. Thus, on a conventional test, $p_{YV} = .03$

is clearly signficant (greater than two standard errors) in the OCG data, but $p_{YV} = .05$ is not as large as two standard errors in the DAS data. In both sets of data, of course, this coefficient is at most of marginal substantive interest (the reader may wish to recall the remarks on collinearity in the preceding section).

In summary, it appears that the OCG results, at least in their general configuration, are readily replicated. Although the "news" value of such a result is not great, its scientific importance should not be underrated. A minimum requisite for the orderly accumulation of scientific knowledge is that findings of one investigation must recur in other investigations, supposing that sufficient precautions to assure comparability have been taken, as they obviously should be if such accumulation is to occur.

The second set of comparisons afforded by the DAS data has to do with a somewhat different problem. This is the question of how to achieve an operational counterpart to the notion of occupational "status." In all of the work with the OCG data, the measure of occupational status is the socioeconomic index (Duncan, 1961a). In the FGMA data set—to take an example from the material used in this project—the measure was a somewhat different one: the

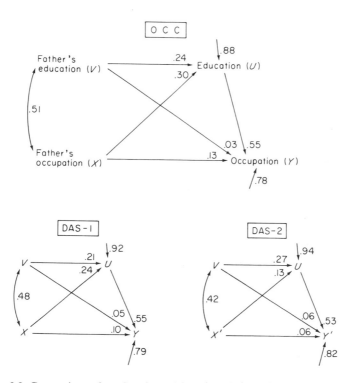

Fig. 3.2. Comparison of results with OCG and DAS data. (Source: Table 3.2.)

1947 set of occupational prestige scores, or so-called North-Hatt scale (Reiss, 1961). In the construction of the socioeconomic index, it was found that for the group of criterion occupations the correlation between the two measures was as high as .91 (Duncan, 1961a). However, this calculation probably exaggerates the correlation of the two types of score for two reasons: First, it is not weighted for the numbers of employed men in each of the occupations; second, the correlation applies only to occupations for which a close match between Census and NORC titles was possible. The consequence of these facts is that comparisons across such data sets as OCG and FGMA are impaired to an unknown degree: Similarity of results could be due, in a measure, to mere coincidence, while divergence of results could be due to properties of the measuring instruments rather than to differences between the respective populations.

An opportunity to study the effect of changing the scale of measurement, in abstraction from other factors affecting comparability, was afforded by access to the DAS data. Here we recoded the detailed occupations, which had been initially coded to the Census detailed list, in two ways: first, according to the scores on the socioeconomic index, and second, according to a new set of NORC occupational prestige scores generated by recent work at NORC by Hodge, Siegel, and Rossi (Siegel, 1970). Results based on the socioeconomic scores are referred to as DAS-1 and those utilizing prestige scores as DAS-2. Thus, in DAS-1, X and Y are measured on the socioeconomic scale, while in DAS-2, X' and Y' are measured on the prestige scale. The correlations between the two scales in the DAS sample are $r_{XX'} = .814$ and $r_{YY'} = .860$. The latter figure probably provides the fairest comparison with the previously mentioned estimate (Duncan, 1961a) of the correlation between the socioeconomic index and prestige, .91. As was indicated, that estimate is somewhat too high.

The comparison of correlations in DAS-1 and DAS-2 (two bottom panels of Table 3.4) yields a clear-cut result: All the correlations in the latter are smaller than in the former (with the exception, of course, of r_{UV}, where the occupational measure is not involved). This result has a curious implication. Suppose we wished to think of one of the measures as a "true" occupational status score and the other as a 'fallible" index thereof. Then $r_{XX'}$ and $r_{YY'}$ would each be correlations of a true score with a fallible score. Suppose further that we have a certain correlation computed on the basis of fallible scores and wish to estimate what that correlation would be if true scores were known. Straightforward methods for this problem, assuming uncorrelated errors, are available. If, for example, we take it that $r_{XY} = .306$ is the fallible result, we should then estimate the true correlation as $r^*_{X'Y'} = (.306)/(.860)(.814) = .437$. Actually, as Table 3.4 shows, $r_{X'Y'} = .211$. Hence the assumption of this calculation is poorly supported. However, if we take $r_{X'Y'} = .211$ as the fallible result, we should estimate the true correlation r^*_{XY} as $(.211)/(.860)(.814) = .301$, an estimate that compares closely with the actual $r_{XY} = .306$. Hence the empirical results in the two versions of the DAS correlations are easier to rationalize on the assumption that occupational socioeconomic status is the "true" measure of occupational status and prestigue is a fallible indicator thereof than on the opposite assumption. Of course, we have no warrant for the premise that either of these assumptions must be true, nor can we wholly trust the assumption of uncorrelated errors. But in the light of these results and in view of the desirability of making comparisons with OCG and comparable data, our further use of the DAS data in Chapter 5 will rely solely on the socioeconomic index as the measure of occupational status.

In Fig. 3.2 the two versions of the DAS data are compared with respect to path coefficients. Two main consequences of substituting X' and Y' for X and Y, respectively, are noted. First, the overall explanatory power of the model is somewhat less in DAS-2 than in DAS-1, as expected from the simple correlations. Second, use of the occupational prestige measure tends to magnify the importance of father's education, relative to that of father's occupation, in regard to both respondent's educational attainment and his occupational achievement.

It may also be observed that there is a small difference between the two versions in regard to the net influence of respondent's education: $p_{YU} = .55$ as compared to $p_{Y'U} = .53$. The supposition that the socioeconomic index might exaggerate the influence of education on occupational achievement is not, therefore, borne out by this result. A similar conclusion on the point at issue was reached by Blau & Duncan (1967, pp. 124–128) in a somewhat different way. In particular, it will be seen that the magnitude of p_{YU} relative to p_{YX} is certainly no greater than that of $p_{Y'U}$ relative to $p_{Y'X'}$. It is to be hoped that this result will effectively satisfy the curiosity of those who have wondered if there is some kind of "education bias" in the socioeconomic index of occupational status.

Chapter 4

Background Variables

In the presentation of the basic model in the previous chapter it has been made clear that family size and socioeconomic level are to be regarded as more or less standard background factors in the analyses described throughout this report. In the present chapter we examine briefly some additional factors that impinge upon life chances by virtue of membership in a given family of orientation. These include what sociologists call the "ascribed statuses" of racial and ethnic group membership. We also look briefly at the question of whether family size is best represented by the simple number of siblings or by numbers of siblings of specified sex. Finally, the possible bearing of the stability of the family of orientation on later fortunes is considered.

With the exception of the matter of the sex of siblings—one which can be disposed of quickly—the material in this chapter has been dealt with more thoroughly in separate publications (Duncan, 1968b, Duncan & Duncan, 1968; 1969; Featherman, 1971b, c). For this reason, and because the work reported in subsequent chapters does not depend closely on the findings reviewed here, the treatment of background factors is abbreviated. This brevity of treatment should not be construed as an indication of the empirical importance of the factors concerned. On the contrary, we would urge that one among these factors represents an extremely significant obstacle to occupational achievement—the factor in question, of course, is membership in a particular "racial" minority group. Aside from demonstrating the severity of the handicap experienced by the individual who is socially classified as "Negro," the analysis shows that all of the measurable influences on achievement are appreciably

50

modified in their effects by membership in this racial category. In statistical terms, race "interacts" with all the other variables in our models. It follows from this that a fully adequate representation of the significance of race would require that all models be separately estimated for whites and blacks—a requirement that cannot be fulfilled for lack of adequate data. In consequence, most of the work in later chapters is based on data for the white population only, with the explicit recognition of the important gap that this leaves in the investigation.

4.1 National Origin

In this section we are using the basic model which was described in the previous chapter, omitting income as an output of the model. Parameters are estimated from the OCG data for native non-Negro men 25–64 years of age with nonfarm background. One way to describe the analysis is to state that national origin has been entered into the model as a background factor in addition to the characteristics of the family of orientation (number of siblings and father's occupation and education). The results are summarized in Table 4.1; intermediate steps and various details are presented more fully in Duncan & Duncan (1968).

Calculations for Table 4.1 derive from Tables 2 and 3 in Duncan & Duncan (1968) and the two-equation recursive Model 4.1,

$$U = \sum_{j=1}^{9} b_{Uj} E_j + b_{UX} X_X + b_{UV} X_V + b_{UT} X_T$$

$$+ b_{Uv} X_v; \qquad \text{(Model 4.1)}$$

$$Y = \sum_{j=1}^{9} b_{Yj} E_j + b_{YX} X_X + b_{YV} X_V + b_{YT} X_T$$

$$+ b_{YU} X_U + b_{Yw} X_w,$$

where X_v and X_w are stochastic disturbances; the E_j ($j = 1 ..., 9$) are dummy variables standing for paternal national origin categories, the coefficients being so scaled that $\Sigma_j n_j b_{jK} = 0$; and variables X, V, T, U, and Y are, respectively, paternal occupation and education, number of siblings, education, and 1962 occupation. The various b coefficients are unstandardized partial regression coefficients.

The first column of Table 4.1 shows the "gross effect" of national origin. This is defined as the deviation of the mean occupational score for a particular origin group from the grand mean in the population under study. (In addition to the origins shown here there is a category of "all other" origins that is too small for analysis.) In the whole population under consideration here, the mean

TABLE 4.1

Effect of National Origin on Mean Occupational Status, for Native White Civilian Men of Nonfarm Background, Age 25–64, with Foreign Fathers: March 1962[a]

National origin	Gross effect[b]	Direct (net) effect	Indirect effect (via education)	Due to social origins[c]
USSR	8.77	2.83	5.94	0.00
Northwest Europe, except Ireland and Germany	5.55	4.32	0.32	0.91
Ireland	1.03	0.66	2.48	−2.11
Canada	0.89	0.07	0.35	0.47
Germany	0.05	2.56	−1.65	−0.86
Europe, except Northwest, Italy, Poland, and USSR	−0.69	1.22	3.27	−5.18
Poland	−4.80	0.28	2.29	−7.37
Italy	−6.03	−1.07	2.25	−7.21
America, except Canada	−14.85	−1.09	−5.12	−8.64

[a] Source: OCG data, as analyzed in Duncan and Duncan (1968: Tables 2 and 3).

[b] Deviation from grand mean for all native civilian non-Negro men with nonfarm background aged 25–64.

[c] Entry in first column less sum of entries in second and third columns.

occupational score is 43.45, with a standard deviation of 24.58. Thus the range of national origin group means is from more than one-third of a standard deviation above the general mean (USSR) to more than one-half a standard deviation below it (Latin America). There are, then, fairly considerable gross variations among origin groups in occupational achievement. Since the data are confined to men with nonfarm background, rural–urban differences can hardly be the source of these variations.

The "direct effect" (second column of Table 4.1) of national origin refers to the coefficient for the particular origin group in a regression of occupational status on education, number of siblings, father's occupation, father's education, and father's country of birth, that is, b_{Yj} for the jth group in Model 4.1. The model assumes additive effects; for example, that the effects of family characteristics on education and occupation are the same for members of each origin group. It will be noted that the direct effects of national origin are in general smaller than the gross effects (the coefficients cluster more closely around zero). Moreover, the ranking of origin groups is not the same on direct effects as on gross effects. On the former criterion, the greatest advantage is enjoyed by men of northwest European origin (other than Ireland and Germany). The fact that the preponderance of coefficients are positive signifies that the status of second-generation immigrant is not, per se, a handicap with respect to occupational achievement. Such handicaps as men in this status do experience are primarily with regard to social origins in the sense of the socioeconomic status of their families of orientation, which is typically lower than that of men with native fathers.

The third column of Table 4.1 shows the effect of national origin on occupational status that operates (indirectly) via education. This is calculated by multiplying $b_{YU} b_{Uj}$, for the jth category.

The sum of the direct and indirect effects of origin represents the influence of origin per se on occupational status, as distinguished from the influence that arises because of the association of national origin with socioeconomic background. The latter, obtained as a residual, is shown in the last column of Table 4.1.

The decomposition of origin effects into those that are direct (that is, net of education as well as family socioeconomic level) and those that are indirect, operating via education, is perhaps suggestive of the mechanisms by which the differentials in achievement come about. The high achievement of men with Russian origin is seen to come about primarily by way of education. By contrast, the northwest European group secures very little advantage by way of superior education (relative to level of social origin), but enjoys comparatively high occupational status relative to its mean educational attainment and socioeconomic background. Men of German and Latin American origin are relatively disadvantaged with respect to education, given their socioeconomic origins, but the German men overcome this handicap while the Latin Americans do not. The latter group is the only one for which both direct and indirect effects are negative; and it is also the one with the least advantageous socioeconomic origins. In these respects it resembles the Negro population, discussed in a later section, although the magnitudes of the effects are much less for the Latin Americans.

The special predicament of the Latin American minority is brought out graphically in Fig. 4.1. Here the direct and indirect (via education) effects of national origin per se are added together into a single component, and the remainder of the variation associated with national origin is treated as a residual due to differences in socioeconomic level of the family of orientation. The two components are plotted on a scatter diagram to bring out any possible correlation between them. It will be observed that there is essentially no such correlation, except that produced by the points for the Latin America minority in the lower-left-hand corner and the USSR group in the upper-right-hand corner.

Some caution should be exercised in detailed pairwise comparisons between countries in view of the sampling variability in the data. Figures for the Latin

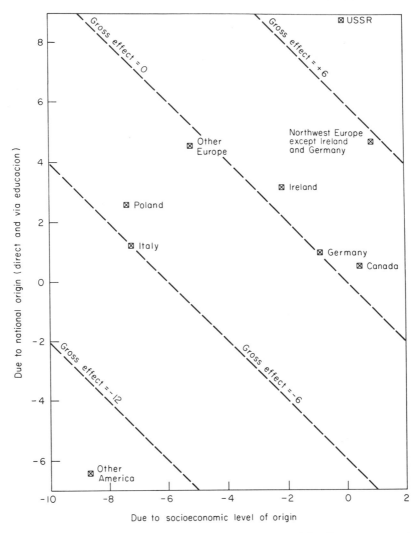

Fig. 4.1 Correlation of two components of gross national origin effects on occupational achievement (see Table 4.1).

Americans, for example, are based on a sample of hardly more than 100 men, while the largest group (Italy) provides a sample of less than 600. In any event, what may be most noteworthy is the comparatively small effects that cannot be attributed to differentials in parental socioeconomic status. It is doubtful that such effects are large enough to sustain complex theories about "national character" or cultural differences in "achievement orientation" (Featherman, 1971c; Duncan & Featherman, 1970). By the same token, the data do not confirm the notion of pervasive discrimination based on national origins. For only one group, as previously noted, are both direct and indirect effects observed which might be taken as evidence for both education and occupational discrimination (if other factors not measured could be assumed equal). In this respect, the situation of white ethnic groups is clearly vastly different from that of the black-American population, as well become apparent presently.

4.2 Race

Two of the separately published reports of this project (Duncan, 1968b, c) deal in detail with differences between blacks and whites in occupational achievement. Only a summary of the results is given here.

It requires no new research, of course, to show that blacks do not enjoy as high a level of occupational status as whites, and that they suffer various disadvantages might constitute part of the explanation for differential occupational achievement. What has been lacking in the considerable amount of research published on this topic is an assessment of the extent to which family background can account for racial differentials in occupational achievement. If it were true that white men with comparable disadvantaged family backgrounds did no better in the pursuit of occupational status than the average for blacks, the racial differential would be "explained" by family background. This, however, is far from being true—a point that has not been fully appreciated by those who diagnose the problems of blacks as being due in large part to a "culture of poverty."

A beginning in acquiring a more realistic assessment of the situation may be made through study of the intergenerational occupational mobility table (see Table 4.2). The size of the OCG sample (roughly 1 in 2170 of the eligible population) is not large enough to permit a great deal of detail in the occupational classification. The basic relationship we wish to bring out, however, is clear even when broad occupational categories are employed. For any given level of occupational origin (father's occupation), the black man is less likely to move into a high status occupation than is a white man with the same level of origin. Thus quite distinct patterns of intergenerational mobility are present in the two populations. From low origins, white men tend (typically) to move up to higher status jobs; given high origins they tend to remain at a high occupational level. For blacks, on the contrary, it happens that men with low origins tend to remain at low occupational levels, while those (few) with higher origins tend to fall to low status levels. The typical destination of blacks, *regardless of level of origin*, is the lower category of manual jobs. The typical destination for whites, on the contrary, depends on where they originate. Thus there is an ironic kind of "equalitarianism" in the way the social structure

TABLE 4.2

Transition Percentages, Father's Occupation to 1962 Occupation (Condensed Classification), by Race, for Civilian Men 25–64 Years Old, March 1962[a]

Race and father's occupation[b]	1962 Occupation[b]						Total	
	Higher white collar (1)	Lower white collar (2)	Higher manual (3)	Lower manual (4)	Farm (5)	NA (7)	Per- cent	Number (000)
Negro								
Higher white collar (1)	*10.4*	9.7	19.4	53.0	0.0	7.5	100.0	134
Lower white collar (2)	14.5	*9.1*	0.0	69.1	0.0	7.3	100.0	55
Higher manual (3)	8.8	6.8	*11.2*	64.1	2.8	6.4	100.0	251
Lower manual (4)	8.0	7.0	11.5	*63.2*	1.8	8.4	100.0	973
Farm (5)	3.1	3.0	6.4	59.8	*16.2*	11.6	100.0	1,389
NA (6)	2.4	6.5	11.1	65.9	3.1	11.1	100.0	712
Total, percent	5.2	5.4	9.5	62.2	7.7	10.0	100.0	–
Total, number (000)	182	190	334	2,184	272	352	–	3,514
Non-Negro								
Higher white collar (1)	*54.3*	15.3	11.5	11.9	1.3	5.6	100.0	5,836
Lower white collar (2)	45.1	*18.3*	13.5	14.6	1.5	7.1	100.0	2,652
Higher manual (3)	28.1	11.8	*27.9*	24.0	1.0	7.3	100.0	6,512
Lower manual (4)	21.3	11.5	22.5	*36.0*	1.7	6.9	100.0	8,798
Farm (5)	16.5	7.0	19.8	28.8	*20.4*	7.5	100.0	9,991
NA (6)	26.0	10.3	21.0	32.5	3.9	6.4	100.0	2,666
Total, percent	28.6	11.3	20.2	26.2	6.8	6.9	100.0	–
Total, number (000)	10,414	4,130	7,359	9,560	2,475	2,517	–	36,455

[a] Source: OCG data set, as presented in Duncan (1968c).

[b] 1, Professional, technical, and kindred workers; managers, officials, and proprietors, except farm; 2, sales workers; clerical and kindred workers; 3, craftsmen, foremen, and kindred workers; 4, operatives and kindred workers; service workers; laborers, except farm; 5, farmers and farm managers; farm laborers and foremen; 6, father's occupation not reported; 7, respondent not in experienced civilian labor force.

allocates blacks to occupational pursuits—they typically go into lower manual pursuits, whatever the status of their family of orientation. In the language of regression and correlation used throughout this report, we may summarize by saying that the slope of respondent's occupation on father's occupation is less steep for blacks than for whites; that the correlation between respondent's and father's occupation is lower for blacks than for whites; and that these differences are superimposed upon the lower mean levels of both black social origins and achieved occupational statuses.

It is convenient to represent this situation graphically in order to bring out a point of some methodological importance for subsequent analysis. Fig. 4.2 portrays the regression of respondent's occupational status on father's occupational status, indicating the distinct regression lines for white and Negro men. It is easy to see that the white line lies above the Negro line throughout the range of the independent variable, father's occupation, here symbolized by X. Thus the conditional value of Y, given X, as predicted from the regressions, will always be higher for white than for Negro men. Of course, the distributions of individual men around these averages will show some overlap. But the regressions make it quite clear that the factor of father's occupation cannot explain the racial difference in occupational achievement. Or, rather, it appears that this factor can explain only a small part of this difference. Our methodological problem arises in attempting to reach a more precise statement.

The regressions indicated that for Negroes, as for whites, father's occupation makes some difference in level of achievement, even though it makes less difference for the former. We also know that the two groups do differ in regard to mean scores on father's occupation: $\bar{X}_N = 16.15$ and $\bar{X}_W = 28.06$. In what measure can we say that this difference accounts for the difference in respon-

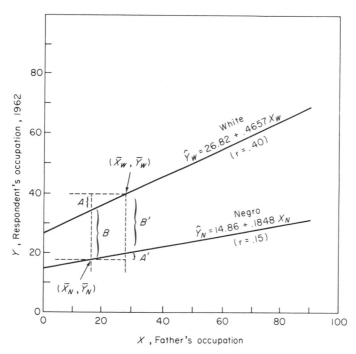

Fig. 4.2. Regression of respondent's occupational status on father's occupational status, for civilian men 25–64 years old, by race, March 1962. (Source: OCG data set.)

dent's occupational status, having observed that $\overline{Y}_N = 17.84$ and $\overline{Y}_W = 39.89$? Taking the difference between the two Y means, 22.05, we have a measure of the "gap" that is to be explained. This gap is represented by the vertical distance between the two horizontal dashed lines in Fig. 4.2 passing through the white and Negro Y means, respectively. In order to see how much of this gap is due to the difference in mean X scores, we proceed in a roundabout way to compute, first, how much of the difference remains after removing the difference in mean X scores.

The difficulty here is that there is no unique answer to the question of how much difference in Y means remains if we look at a selection of black and white men having the same X scores. Because of the difference in regression slope (b_{YX}), which is .47 for whites and only .18 for Negroes, the difference between the Y values expected for a given value of X increases as X gets larger. There are perhaps two special cases, however, that might seem to provide informative comparisons, if not a unique answer to the question. If we let both Negro and white men have an X score equal to the mean for all Negro men, the regressions imply a Y mean of 17.84 for Negroes and one of 34.34 for whites. The difference, 16.50, is represented by component B in Fig. 4.2; it is the amount by which white occupational status exceeds Negro, on the average, standardizing the two populations for father's occupation at the Negro mean on the latter. There is left a residual amount, A, calculated as $22.05 - 16.50 = 5.55$, which represents the part of the total gap which is due to differences in father's occupation. The alternative comparison is to standardize at the white mean on father's occupation. At this value of X, the white regression line implies a Y score of 39.89 while the Negro regression implies 19.85. The difference, labeled as component B' in the figure, is 19.85, leaving $A' = 2.20$ as the part of the observed gap of 22.05 which is attributable to the racial difference in mean father's occupation. As already noted, alternative evaluations of B will differ according to the value of X selected for standardization. We might note, however, that it would not be very meaningful to standardize at a very high X score for two reasons: First, few blacks would be found to have such high scores; and second, the standardization procedure would then put considerable strain on the assumption of linearity of the regressions, although this is not an especially vulnerable assumption in the present case.

In what follows, we shall adopt the first of the two alternatives just illustrated: standardization for background at the Negro mean on background factors. It will be noted that this gives a liberal estimate of the importance of background factors compared to the alternative procedure, given the fact [as is shown in detail by Duncan (1968b)] that slopes of achieved statuses on background factors are in general lower for blacks than for whites. Moreover, the procedure adopted here gives a conservative estimate of the magnitude of the racial difference remaining after standardization. If, as one is tempted to do in certain parts of the analysis, this magnitude is taken as an estimate of racial "discrimination," then it is important to bear in mind that the estimates of discrimination generated here are on the conservative side by comparison with alternative estimates that might seem procedurally equally attractive.

The exercise carried out on Fig. 4.2 in the bivariate context is carried out in the multivariate context in Table 4.3. It should be noted that while the material just discussed pertains to all native Negro and non-Negro (essentially white) men 25–64 years old, the data in Table 4.3 are based only on men with nonfarm background, that is, those not reporting that their fathers (or other persons serving as head of the family of orientation) were farmers or farm laborers.

The model underlying the calculations is the basic model discussed in

TABLE 4.3

Differences in Means between White (W) and Negro (N) with Respect to Number of Siblings, Educational Attainment, Occupational Status, and Income, with Components of Differences Generated by Cumulative Effects in a Model of the Socioeconomic Life Cycle, for Native Men, 25 to 64 Years Old, with Nonfarm Background and in the Experienced Civilian Labor Force: March 1962[a]

Number of siblings	Years of school completed	1962 Occupation score	1961 Income, dollars	Component[b]
(W) 3.85	(W) 11.7	(W) 43.5	(W) 7,070	
−.54	1.0	6.6		940 (A) [Family]
4.39	10.7	36.9	6,130	
−.47	0.1	0.6		70 (B) [Siblings]
(N) 4.86	10.6	36.3	6,060	
	1.2	4.8		520 (C) [Education]
	(N) 9.4	31.5	5,540	
		11.8		830 (D) [Occupation]
		(N) 19.7	4,710	
				1,430 (E) [Income]
			(N) 3,280	
−1.01	2.3	23.8		3,790 (T) [Total]

 a Source: OCG data set.

b Difference due to: A, socioeconomic level of family of origin (head's education and occupation); B, number of siblings, net of family origin level; C, education, net of siblings and family origin level; D, occupation, net of education, siblings, and family origin level; E, income, net of occupation, education, siblings, and family origin level; T, total difference, (W) minus (N) = sum of components (A) through (E).

Chapter 3, with parameters estimated for non-Negro men 25–64 years old. Regression equations in raw score form were computed for these "white" men. Then, Negro means on the explanatory variables were inserted into the white regressions to ascertain what the implied Negro mean on the dependent variable would be if the same regression equation applied for men of both racial categories. This was carried out successively for four dependent variables, number of siblings, educational attainment, occupational status, and income. For each dependent variable, the first estimate equates Negroes and whites for family background (father's occupation and education); then for family background and number of siblings; then for the combination of these plus education; then for all the foregoing plus occupation. We are, therefore, using a sequence of reduced-form regressions to ascertain the contribution of each successive factor to the racial difference in the dependent variable. This procedure provides components of the "racial gap" with respect to each dependent variable.

Let us take as an example the most elaborate computation, that pertaining to income. The entire racial gap, equal to the difference between observed white and Negro means, is $3790. This arises from a white mean of $7070 and a Negro mean of $3280. Equating blacks and whites for the two measures of family socioeconomic level implies that the Negro mean income would be $6130, so that family socioeconomic level accounts for only $7070 − $6130 = $940 of the gap of $3790. This figure of $940 estimates the impact of the "culture of poverty," where the latter is understood as an intergenerational process of status transmission. The estimate (22 percent of the income gap) should give pause to those who cite the "vicious cycle" or the "culture" of poverty as the fundamental cause of the black's lower income. Similarly, equating for both family socioeconomic level and number of siblings implies a Negro mean of $6060; the additional factor accounts for an additional $70 of the income gap. On this estimate, family planning programs would be expected to ameliorate few of the relative economic disadvantages of blacks of equal socioeconomic backgrounds to whites. Whether this implies that family planning programs have few economic consequences for the poor is equivocal since it may be more feasible programmatically to "manipulate" fertility than the socioeconomic status of the family of origin. However, adding the $940 and $70 implies that the maximum effort of equalizing Negro–white fertility and socioeconomic backgrounds will eliminate less than 27 percent of the income gap.

A significant additional component of the income gap, amounting to $520, is contributed by education, for when blacks and whites are equated with respect to family socioeconomic level, number of siblings, and education, the implied Negro mean income is $5540. (The amount of $520, presumably, is an estimate of the net payoff, in dollar terms, to a completely successful effort to equalize educational opportunities.) Adding occupation to the battery of prior factors accounts for a further amount of $830 of the income gap since equalization on this set of factors implies a mean Negro income of $4710. (The component of $830 may be taken as an estimate of what could be accomplished by elimination of job discrimination, given prior equalization of family background, number of siblings, and education.) Finally, there remains an amount, $1430, some three-eighths of the total income gap, which is due to the fact that men in the same line of work, with the same amount of education, the same number of siblings, and the same family socioeconomic background earn different amounts depending on whether they are white or black. This is "economic discrimination" in its purest form. But it should be stressed that the several components are cumulative. If one allows $1010 as the amount of the gap attributable to family socioeconomic status and number of siblings, this leaves a total of $2,780 to be attributed to the combination of educational discrimination, occupational discrimination, and economic discrimination.

The detailed explanation we have given of the last column of Table 4.3 can be carried through for each of the other columns, although there are successively fewer components for the variables that come earlier in the causal sequence.

It should be stressed that there is no absolute significance to the estimates of the components of racial gaps in educational, occupational, and economic achievement. These estimates are relative to the particular model and the particular population considered. A more elaborate model would allocate the components differently, particularly if some powerful intervening variable could be introduced into it. Similarly, if the estimates were made for a different age group, they would, of course, reflect the particular circumstances of the history of that cohort. A slightly more elaborate set of calculations than in Table 4.3 appears in Duncan (1968b, Table 4–4) and is based on an amalgam of several data sets. The addition of the variable, mental ability, does not alter the basic conclusion about the force of discrimination against blacks of equivalent social origins and mental abilities as whites. However, when controlling for mental ability, socioeconomic background, and size of sibship, the gap in educational achievements is virtually closed. Still, this estimate does not reduce the "cost of being a Negro."

It would be possible to offer a lengthy set of comments on the implications of the estimates in Table 4.3. It appears that this set of estimates comes closer than any previously published calculations to an operational representation of the notion of "cumulation of handicaps," as this has frequently been discussed in diagnoses of racial differences in this country. It does not seem appropriate here to engage in a presentation of the policy implications of the estimates (see, however, Duncan, 1968b). Suffice it to say that this demonstration of an extension of our basic model may be one of the most convincing exhibits we can offer of the advantages of adopting a systematic procedure for tracing out the consequences of assumptions as to how a causal process operates.

4.3   Number and Sex of Siblings

There is no need for a lengthy discussion of the influence of size of family of orientation on occupational achievement. Our models suggest that the bulk of such influence, which is in the negative direction, operates via educational attainment as an intervening variable. The effect of number of siblings on schooling has been analyzed extensively elsewhere (B. Duncan, 1965b, 1967; Featherman, 1971b).

As a matter of curiosity, we investigated the possibility that rather than number of siblings as such it might be only the number of brothers or only the number of sisters that has the adverse impact on educational attainment and occupational achievement. The upper diagram in Fig. 4.3 shows results for a model in which the two variables are both introduced into the causal scheme. It will be noted that the path coefficients for number of brothers are just very slightly higher than for number of sisters. If we compute the reduced-form equation with occupation as the dependent variable but with educational attainment eliminated, the path coefficients are $-.10$ for number of brothers and $-.08$ for number of sisters.

The lower diagram in the same figure uses the same data to secure estimates for a model in which number of siblings (brothers plus sisters) is regarded as a background factor. There is really no essential difference between the two diagrams. There is no change in the coefficients of determination or in the path coefficients for the other two background factors. Indeed, the two diagrams can be completely reconciled on the viewpoint that number of brothers and number of sisters depend on number of siblings. The correlation between number of brothers and number of sisters is .39. This correlation is reproduced by the calculation $(.83) (.84) + (.56) (-1.0) (.54)$. The correlation of negative unity between the two residuals reflects the tautology that if number of siblings is fixed, there is a perfect inverse relationship between number of brothers and number of sisters. It will be found that the lower diagram implies the same correlations between number of brothers and all other variables in the system as does the upper diagram; and the same is true for number of sisters.

Inasmuch as the apparent difference in strength of effects of number of brothers and number of sisters is trivial while both can be represented adequately if the sex distinction is disregarded, all our other work with the family size variable simply uses number of siblings.

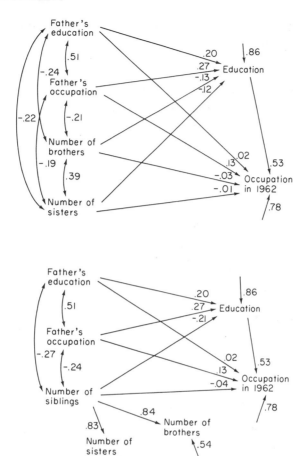

Fig. 4.3. Alternative models representing effects of number of brothers and sisters. (OCG data for native non-Negro men with nonfarm background, ages 25–64).

4.4 Family Stability

Previous research (B. Duncan, 1965b) closely related to this project included a detailed examination of the influence of the stability of the family of orientation on educational attainment. In that research, OCG respondents were dichotomously classified into those who had grown up in an intact family (father and mother both present) and those who had not. When this factor was considered alone, it appeared that "growing up in an intact, rather than broken, family resulted in 1.0 year more schooling for a boy" (p. 50). There was, however, appreciable variation in the magnitude of this effect, depending on age and color of respondent. Part of the gross effect of family stability, moreover, was shared with socioeconomic characteristics of the family of orientation that were correlated with its status as intact or broken. Thus in multiple regressions the net effects of family stability on educational attainment (years of schooling) were as follows, when education of family head, occupation of family head, and number of siblings were taken into account (Duncan, 1967: Table 2):

Age	Total	White	Nonwhite
27–36	0.7	0.7	0.8
37–46	0.7	0.6	0.7
47–61	1.1	1.2	0.4

The differences between older and younger cohorts suggest an increase in the importance of this factor for nonwhites but a lessening importance for whites, although it is difficult to distinguish true changes from sampling and other errors in this analysis.

In view of the well-known vulnerability of Negro families to disruptive forces (Farley & Hermalin, 1971), there has been a widespread suspicion that racial differences in prevalence of family instability constitute an important part of the explanation of racial differences in occupational and other forms of achievement (United States Department of Labor, 1965). Even a cursory analysis, however, suffices to show that no great part of such an explanation can be

TABLE 4.4

Mean Socioeconomic Status Score of Current Occupations Held by Native Non-institutional Males of Nonfarm Background, Aged 25–64, Classified by Race, Family Background and Current Marital Status: March 1962.

	Negro		Non-Negro	
Family background	All	Married, spouse present	All	Married, spouse present
All	19.75	20.00	43.47	44.20
Both parents	20.67	21.80	44.40	45.12
Female head	18.09	17.93	39.25	40.28
Male head[a]	–	–	39.45	40.05

[a] No entry—mean not calculated; base fewer than 150 sample cases.
Source: OCG data set, as reported in Duncan and Duncan (1969, Table 2).

reached through this factor alone. In Table 4.4, based on OCG data for native men with nonfarm background, aged 25–64, we find that Negroes who grew up with both parents had a mean occupational score in 1962 of 20.67 while those growing up in a family with a female head had a mean score of 18.09; corresponding figures for non-Negro men were 44.40 and 39.25. Thus the gross effect of rearing in a female-headed family, relative to rearing in an intact family, was −2.58 points for Negroes and −5.15 points for whites. These unmistakable yet modest effects are to be contrasted with the effects of race, computed from the same data as 23.73 points (44.40–20.67) in favor of whites among men growing up in intact families and 21.16 points (39.25–18.09) in their favor for men growing up in a family headed by a female. The latter contrasts are, of course, free of the influence of differentials in family stability and suffice, therefore, to lay to rest any supposition that racial differences in occupational achievement stem primarily from differing experiences of family stability or instability.

The foregoing summary and Section 4.2 make clear that the primary source of black–white achievement differentials lies elsewhere than in racial differentials in social backgrounds and family composition. With respect to the latter, however, it is family size, rather than family stability, which is more significant as a source of variation in occupational achievement (with caution taken for our ability to measure the effects of stability in the OCG data). Race per se being more important than family characteristics, a more detailed analysis of the relevance of family stability for black and white occupational success is a pursuit of second-order effects rather than of primary influences. Such a detailed examination is reported in Duncan & Duncan (1969), and a brief summary of this work is stated below and in Table 4.5.

As noted previously, rearing in a broken family is associated with an educational handicap, for men of equivalent sizes of sibship and from families with the same occupation and education of family head. If we then inquire as to how schooling is translated into occupational achievement, it turns out that, for Negroes in particular, growing up in a female-headed family seemingly impairs a man's ability to realize the occupational return on his education, even beyond the degree of such impairment associated with race per se. For married males, spouse present (Table 4.5), the net regression coefficient of occupation in 1962 on education is 2.56 points on the occupational scale for Negroes who grew up with both parents as compared with 2.13 for those reared in a family with a female head; corresponding figures for whites are 4.05 and 3.93.

Furthermore, there appears to be differential occupational promotion by entry level (first full-time job after completing schooling) favorable to men reared in intact families within the black population (Duncan & Duncan, 1968, Table 5, p. 282). Finally, the non-Negro female family head contributes to her son's occupational success both by maintaining a regular work-force attachment

TABLE 4.5

Regression Coefficients Describing Relationship of Current Occupation to Social Origin and Education Characteristics for Native Civilian Non-institutional Males of Nonfarm Background, Married and Spouse Present, by Race and Family Background: March 1962[a]

Characteristic	Negro[b]		Non-Negro[b]	
	Both parents	Female headed	Both parents	Female headed
Education	2.56	2.13	4.05	3.93
Number siblings	−0.08	−0.13	−0.24	−0.35
Father's occupation	0.01	–	0.15	–
Head's work status[c]	–	3.58	–	2.09
Head's occupation[d]	–	−0.12	–	0.02
Father's education	0.48	–	0.09	–
Head's education	–	0.08	–	0.11
Coefficient of determination	0.250	0.251	0.387	0.346

[a] Source: OCG data set, as reported in Duncan and Duncan (1969, Table 5).

[b] Unstandardized coefficients.

[c] Net effect of regular work-force participation; dichotomous variable with female family head scored unity if occupation reported, zero if none reported.

[d] Net effect of occupational socioeconomic status, given regular work-force participation.

and by securing a job which ranks relatively high in the occupational structure (last column in Table 4.5). The contribution of the black female family head to her son's occupational success comes not through the kind of work she does but rather through her regular work-force attachment (column 2 in Table 4.5). If our estimates are credible, the magnitude of this net effect in black families headed by females (3.58 points on the occupation scale, as displayed in column 2 of Table 4.5) is nearly as large as the gross effect of broken-family status itself (for Negroes, 21.80–17.93 = 3.87, from Table 4.4). While we view this comparison only as suggestive, we would speculate that a regular work-force attachment on the part of the female head can substitute, in part, for the absent father in providing the son with an orientation to the world of work.

4.5 Summary

In this, the first chapter which extends the basic model of status attainment as outlined in Chapter 3, we have examined the processes of stratification for several population subgroups, as defined by selected background characteristics such as race and national ancestry. In the native white population, national origin (paternal country of birth) is not a major factor in educational or occupational achievement. Only two origin groups show substantial departures from the average: USSR origin is favorable and Latin American origin unfavorable to achievement when all groups are equated for socio-economic characteristics in the families of origin. In both cases cited, origin operates directly on the attainment of schooling, and both directly and indirectly (via education) on occupational status.

Like the Latin American minority, black Americans are disadvantaged both by the low status of their families of orientation and by handicaps to educational and occupational achievement superimposed upon the family factors. The impediments are especially severe for Negroes. Only about one-fourth of the income gap between black and white men can be attributed to the three family characteristics in the basic model (head's education and occupation and family size). Other major components are due to educational discrimination (unequal education attained by men with equivalent family backgrounds), occupational discrimination (unequal occupational achievement for men with equivalent education and family backgrounds), and economic discrimination (unequal earnings for men in the same kinds of occupations, with the same number of years of schooling, and with equivalent family backgrounds).

Number of siblings is, in the basic model as well as in extended models presented later, a consistently negative influence on occupational achievement. It operates mainly via its depressing effect on educational attainment. The effect is equally apparent when either number of brothers or number of sisters is considered. Inasmuch as the sex composition of the sibship seems irrelevant, it suffices to accept total number of siblings as the measure of size of family of orientation.

Rearing in a broken family (headed by a female) is somewhat unfavorable for occupational achievement for both blacks and whites. Contrary to the import of some discussion on this topic, however, family stability is not a major factor in the explanation of racial differences in occupational success. Comparatively, number of siblings is more important than stability of the family of origin in accounting for occupational achievement. However, color alone is the major source of differences in the educational, occupational, and economic achievements of the races, overshadowing in import the color differentials in family size and stability.

We might pause to comment here on a different view of the "powerlessness" of the black male than is implied by some interpretations of the Moynihan Report (United States Department of Labor, 1965). While indeed the proportion of female-headed families is higher among Negroes than whites (Farley & Hermalin, 1971), it is not clear that female domination in family relationships (commonly regarded as a matriarchal structure) characterizes female-headed more than intact families (Kandel, 1971). Whether or not a sense of powerlessness among black men emanates from their experiences in broken families to a greater extent than for white men in such families cannot be ascertained in our data. But such powerlessness as does result thereby is likely to be less than that issuing from pure socioeconomic discrimination against black adult males who are handicapped by color in the competition of the labor market. Again, our data do not speak to this latter kind of powerlessness nor to its relationship (if any) to the intactness of Negro families. We wish merely to point out that efforts directed solely to the "strengthening" of family structure are likely to have substantially less impact on the equalization of racial socioeconomic differentials than efforts applied to the elimination of racial discrimination and the waste of able and talented black citizens.

Chapter 5

Intervening Variables, I: Intelligence

Work with the intervening variable, intelligence, was one of the major pre-occupations of the project, extending over much of its duration. This degree of commitment to the task seemed justified, for one main reason, among others. While there is a widely accepted assumption that mental ability is a primary source of variation in occupational achievement—being built into such bodies of practice as vocational counseling and job placement, for example—there is a surprising and distressing lack of information on how ability actually combines with other determinants of success in the world of work. It is difficult to resist offering the suggestion that the imbalance in the state of knowledge and in the collection of relevant information on the topic is due to the fact that it has been left largely to psychologists and practitioners trained in psychology, who have not been inclined to investigate and discover its social import.

Our work on this topic may be listed as follows: a reconsideration of the conceptual relationship between intelligence and occupational status; a review of sources of reliable evidence on the correlation of measured mental ability with variables implicated in the process of achievement; and the construction of a model to represent the role of intelligence in that process. The final results on the last item are presented in detail in Duncan (1968a) and will only be summarized here; a somewhat lengthier treatment is given of the other two topics and of certain preliminary investigations carried out before constructing the final model.

TABLE 5.1

Barr Rating, Occupation Title, and Description, with Matching Group Socioeconomic Status Score (SES) and NORC Prestige Rating for Occupations Included in Barr Scale (See text for sources)[a]

P.E. Value	Occupation	Description	Group	SES	NORC	Note[a]
0.00	Hobo	–	Omit	–	–	–
1.54	Odd jobs	–	2	–	–	a
2.11	Garbage collector	–	2	–	–	a
3.38	Circus roustabout	Does heavy, rough work about the circus	2	–	–	a
3.44	Hostler	Care of horses in livery, feed and sales stables	2	–	–	a
3.57	R. R. Sec. Hand	Replaces ties, etc., under supervision	2	03	22.20	a
3.62	Day laborer	On street, in shop or factory as roustabout	2	–	–	a
3.99	Track layer	Does heavy work under supervision	2	–	–	a
4.20	Waterworks man	A variety of odd jobs, all unskilled	5	21	–	–
4.29	Miner	Digger and shoveller, etc.	1	10	24.32	–
4.81	Longshoreman	Loads and unloads cargoes	1	11	26.86	–
4.91	Farm laborer	Unskilled and usually inefficient	3	06	21.36	b
4.98	Laundry worker	Various kinds of work in laundry (practically unskilled)	2	15	19.01	–
5.27	Bar tender	–	1	19	19.86	–
5.41	Teamster	–	2	–	–	c
5.44	Sawmill worker	Heavy work, little skill required	2	05	30.75	–
5.59	Dairy hand	Milking, care of stock under supervision	3	–	–	b
5.81	Drayman	–	2	–	–	c
5.87	Deliveryman	Delivers groceries, etc., with team or auto	2	32	–	–
6.14	Junkman	Collector of junk	5	59	–	–
6.42	Switchman	Tending switch in R.R. yards	1	44	32.78	–
6.66	Smelter worker	Metal pourers, casting collectors, etc.	2	18	–	–
6.27	Tire repairer	In general automobile repair shop	5	08	–	–
6.85	Cobbler & shoemaker	Repairman in shoe shop	2	12	–	–
6.86	Munition worker	Average	5	08	–	–
6.92	Barber	Not owner. Has charge of chair	1	17	37.93	–
6.93	Mov. picture operator	Operates machine which projects pictures	2	43	–	–

TABLE 5.1 continued

P.E. Value	Occupation	Description	Group	SES	NORC	Note[a]
7.02	Vulcanizer	Understands the process of hardening rubber	5	22	–	–
7.05	General repairman	Repairs broken articles. Uses wood-working tools	5	19	–	–
7.06	Ship rigger	Installing cordage system on sailing vessels, working under supervision	5	32	–	–
7.17	Telephone operator	–	1	45	40.36	–
7.19	Cook	In restaurant or small hotel	1	15	25.97	–
7.23	Streetcar conductor	–	2	30	–	–
7.24	Farm tenants	On small tracts of land	2	14	21.52	e
7.30	Brakeman	On freight or passenger trains	1	42	34.65	–
7.33	City fire fighter	Handles the ordinary fire-fighting apparatus	1	37	43.81	–
7.39	R.R. fireman	On freight or passenger train	2	45	–	–
7.54	Policeman	Average patrolman	1	40	47.77	–
7.71	Structural steel worker	Heavy work demanding some skill	2	34	–	–
7.73	Tel. & tel. lineman	–	2	49	–	–
7.77	Bricklayer	–	1	27	35.66	d
7.79	Butcher	Not shop owner. Able to make cuts properly	1	29	32.12	–
7.91	Baker	–	1	22	34.18	–
8.02	Metal finisher	Polishes and lacquers metal fixtures, etc.	2	22	–	–
8.04	Plasterer	Knowledge of materials used necessary	2	25	–	–
8.08	General painter	Paints houses, buildings and various structures	1	16	29.78	–
8.22	Harness maker	–	5	32	–	–
8.40	Tinsmith	Makes vessels, utensils, etc., from plated sheet metal	2	33	–	–
8.49	Letter carrier	–	1	53	44.66	–
8.50	Forest ranger	–	2	48	–	–
8.58	Stone mason	–	1	–	–	d
8.75	Plumber	Av. trained plumber employee	1	34	40.58	–
8.89	Gardening, truck farming	Owns and operates small plots	2	–	–	e
8.99	Electric repairman	Repairs elec. utensils, devices and machines	5	27	–	–
9.28	Bookbinder	Sets up and binds books of all sorts	2	39	–	–

TABLE 5.1 continued

P.E. Value	Occupation	Description	Group	SES	NORC	Note[a]
9.37	Carpenter	Knows wood-working tools. Can follow directions in various processes of wood construction work	1	19	37.33	–
9.37	Potter	Makes jars, jugs, crockery, earthenware, etc.	2	21	–	–
9.54	Tailor	Employee in tailoring shop	2	23	–	–
9.72	Salesman	In drygoods, hardware, grocery stores, etc.	2	39	27.13	–
10.11	Telegraph operator	In small town	3	47	–	–
10.21	Undertaker	In small town. Six mo.–yr. special schooling	1	59	53.40	–
10.26	Station agent	In small town. Acts as baggage man, freight agent, operator, etc.	3	60	–	–
10.26	Mechanical repairman	In shop or factory. Keeps machines in condition	2	27	–	–
10.29	Dairy owner and mgr.	Small dairy, 50–100 cows	2	–	–	e
10.53	Metal pattern maker	–	2	–	–	f
10.54	Wood pattern maker	–	2	44	–	f
10.54	Lithographer	Makes prints from designs which he puts on stone	2	64	–	–
10.76	Linotype operator	–	2	52	–	–
10.83	Photographer	City 1000–5000. A few months' training, experience in studio	3	50	–	–
10.86	Detective	Traces clues, etc. Employee of detective bureau	2	36	–	–
10.99	Electrotyper	Prepares wood cuts	2	55	–	–
11.17	Traveling salesman	Sells drugs, groceries, hardware, drygoods, etc.	2	47	41.53	–
11.34	Clerical work	Bookkeepers, recorders, abstractors, etc.	1	51	47.56	–
11.35	R.R. Pass conductor	–	1	58	40.86	–
11.51	Store keeper & owner	Small town retail dealer, general or special store	1	33	46.07	–
11.74	Foreman	Small factory, shop, etc.	1	53	45.05	–
11.78	Stenographer	Writes shorthand and uses typewriter	1	61	43.34	–

TABLE 5.1 continued

P.E. Value	Occupation	Description	Group	SES	NORC	Note[a]
12.02	Librarian	In small institution or public library	3	60	54.58	–
12.06	Nurse and masseur	Graduate	1	46	61.51	–
12.74	Chef	Employed in large first-class hotels	4	15	–	–
12.84	Editor	Small paper, considerable job work	4	82	–	–
12.89	Primary teacher	No college training, 2 yrs. special training	3	–	–	g
12.96	Landscape gardener	–	2	11	–	–
13.08	Grammar grade teacher	Normal graduate expects to make profession teaching	3	72	60.08	g
13.20	Osteopath	Training equal to college grad.	2	96	–	–
13.21	Pharmacist	In town of from 1000–5000 pop.	3	82	60.75	–
13.29	Master mechanic	Thorough knowledge in his field of mechanics	5	27	–	–
13.30	Music teacher	2–4 yrs. special training, not college graduate	4	–	–	h
13.31	Manufacturer	Employs from 10–50 men. Makes simple articles	2	61	65.16	–
13.54	Dentist	Graduate. 2–5 yrs. experience in small town	3	96	–	–
13.58	Art teacher	In high school. 3 or 4 years' special training	4	67	–	–
13.71	Surveyor	Transit man. City or county surveyor	1	48	53.27	–
13.31	Train dispatcher	Must be mentally alert	5	71	–	–
14.45	Land owner & operator	Very large farms or ranches	2	–	–	e
14.70	Musician	Successful player or singer in good company	4	52	14.70	h
15.05	Secretarial work	Private secretary to high state or national officials	4	61	–	–
15.14	High school teacher	Coll. or Normal grad. Not the most progressive	3	72	63.11	–
15.15	Preacher	Minister in town of 1000–5000. College graduate	3	52	68.99	–
15.42	Industrial chemist	Thorough knowledge of the chem. of mfg. processes	2	79	–	–
15.43	Mechanical engineer	Designs and constructs machines and machine tools	2	82	–	–
15.71	Teacher in college	Degree A.B. or A.M. Not the most progressive	3	84	78.26	–

TABLE 5.1 continued

P.E. Value	Occupation	Description	Group	SES	NORC	Note[a]
15.75	Lawyer	In town of moderate size. Income $1000–5000	1	93	75.66	–
15.86	Technical engineer	Thorough knowledge of the processes of an industry	2	–	–	i
16.18	Artist	High class painter of portraits, etc.	4	67	–	–
16.26	Mining engineer	Thorough knowledge of mining and extraction of metals	1	85	61.61	–
16.28	Architect	Training equal to college grad.	1	90	70.52	–
16.58	Great wholesale merchant	Business covering one or more states	5	70	–	–
16.59	Consulting engineer	In charge of corps of engineers	2	–	–	i
16.64	Educational administrator	Supt. city 2000–5000 Coll. or Normal graduate	5	72	67.40	–
16.71	Physician	6–8 yrs. prep. above H.S. Income $5000 and up	1	92	81.55	–
16.91	Journalist	High class writer or editor	4	82	58.83	–
17.50	Publisher	High class magazine and newspaper or periodical, etc.	5	79	–	–
16.81	University professor	Has A.M. or Ph.D., writes, teaches, and does research	1	84	78.26	–
18.06	Great merchant	Owns and operates a million dollar business	Omit	–	–	–
18.14	Musician	(Paderewski)	Omit	–	–	–
18.33	High National official	Cabinet officers, foreign ministers, etc.	Omit	–	–	–
18.85	Writer	(Van Dyke)	Omit	–	–	–
19.45	Research leader	Like Binet or Pasteur	Omit	–	–	–
19.73	Surgeon	(Mayo Bros.)	Omit	–	–	–
20.71	Inventive genius	(Edison type)	Omit	–	–	–

[a] P.E. values for combined titles:

a. 3.09, Odd jobs, garbage collector, circus roustabout, hostler, R.R. section hand, day laborer, track layer (group 2)

b. 5.25, Farm laborer, dairy hand (group 3)

c. 5.61, Teamster, drayman (group 2)

d. 8.18, Bricklayer, stonemason (group 1)

e. 10.22, Farm tenants (gardening, truck farming), dairy owner and manager, landowner and operator (group 2)

f. 10.54, Metal pattern maker, wood pattern maker (group 2)

g. 12.99, Primary teacher, grammar grade teacher (group 3)

h. 14.00, Music teacher, musician (group 4)

i. 16.23, Technical engineer, consulting engineer (group 2)

5.1 Observations on the Concept of Intelligence*

As an entry into the problem, let us summarize an exercise that may have more than an antiquarian interest. At one time there was rather wide use of a scale, purportedly measuring the standing of occupations, which was devised in the early 1920's. The Barr scale is briefly described in Volume I of *Genetic Studies of Genius* (Terman, 1925, p. 66): "Mr. F. E. Barr drew up a list of 100 representative occupations, each definitely and concretely described, and had 30 judges rate them on a scale of 0–100 according to the grade of intelligence which each was believed to demand. The ratings were then distributed and P.E. values were computed for all the occupations. The P.E. values express in the case of each occupation the number of units of intelligence which, according to the composite opinion of these 30 judges, the occupation demands for ordinary success." The listing of the occupations, with their descriptions and P.E. values, is reproduced in Table 5.1. (Note that there are actually 120 titles in the list.)

Socioeconomic status scores (Duncan, 1961a) are available for entries in the list of detailed occupations given in the *1960 Census of Population: Classified Index of Occupations and Industries*. Each occupation has a two-digit score ranging from 00 to 96 which was computed on the basis of 1950 Census data on income and education levels prevailing in the occupations. Prestige ratings are available for a group of occupations included in a 1964 study by Hodge, Siegel, and Rossi (Siegel, 1970) at the National Opinion Research Center (NORC). The NORC list indicates the matching detailed Census occupation title, with an indication as to the quality of the match.

The initial task was to match as many as possible of the Barr scale titles with the Census titles and with NORC titles. No attempt was made to match NORC titles with Census titles directly since NORC had already done this. Having arrived at two sets of titles that were assumed to match, the correlations between the Barr scores and the socioeconomic scores and between the Barr scores and the NORC scores were obtained.

The descriptions included with most of the occupation titles in the Barr scale were not always the most helpful in determining a match with one of the other two listings. In some cases the descriptions were such that no match was possible, for example, "Surgeon (Mayo Bros.)," and these titles were deleted. (One wonders what "ordinary success" as a Dr. Mayo might be.) Of the remaining 112 titles, some were combined using an arithmetic average as indicated in Table 5.1 to facilitate a match. In deciding upon matches, seven descriptions

---

* For a review of the concept of intelligence and of the development of its measurement vis-à-vis performance in modern society, and for estimates of its heritability, see Jensen (1969). An articulation of the role of intelligence in the stratification of contemporary American society and its projected role in the future appears in Herrnstein (1971).

were thought *probably* to bias anyone reading the description so that he would think of only a certain small segment of the workers included under that title, and that this small segment would not be typical. Such an example would be the title "Chef," with the description "Employed in large first-class hotels." A third group of eleven Barr scale titles contained descriptions that were thought *possibly* to bias a person reading a description. For instance, the title "Pharmacist," with a description of "In town from 1000–5000 population," in which case the size of the town was thought possibly to bias a person's judgment as to the amount of intelligence needed to perform the job. There were 64 Barr scale titles for which the description was thought not to influence a person's judgment in a biasing way. These were subdivided into two groups. One group contained 30 Barr scale titles with nonbiased descriptions and with a high quality NORC-Census match; the other group contained 34 Barr titles with nonbiased description but with only a Census match. A final group of Barr scale titles consisted of 14 titles with remote Census matches without regard to the bias effect of the description. Thus five groups of titles were obtained as follows:

Group	Number
1	Thirty titles with good Barr-Census-NORC matches and nonbias descriptions
2	Thirty-four titles with Barr-Census matches and nonbias descriptions but *no* NORC match
3	Eleven titles with Barr-Census matches having *possible* bias descriptions, and which may or may not have an NORC match
4	Seven titles with Barr-Census matches having *probable* bias descriptions, and which may or may not have an NORC match
5	Fourteen titles with *remote* Barr-Census matches which may or may not have NORC matches and/or biased descriptions
Total	Ninety-six titles

An analysis of covariance was made, with the five groups just named as the "treatment variable"; the socioeconomic status scores as the independent variable; and the Barr scale scores as the dependent variable. The five groups of titles were examined to determine if a common slope prevailed, whether the slope differed from zero, and whether one regression line would fit all groups.

The results, seen in Table 5.2, of the three appropriate F tests suggest that there is a common slope, that it is not equal to zero, and that one regression will fit all five groups. Since one regression line will fit all groups, it seems that our worries about bias descriptions and remote matches are without grounds. Thus the five groups can be combined, and the 96 matches obtained can be used in further analysis of Barr-Census comparisons.

TABLE 5.2

F–Tests for Covariance Analysis

Test	N_1 df	N_2 df	Observed F value	P	Table F value for given P	Result
Common slope	4	86	2.20	.95	2.47	Accept
Slope = 0	1	86	143.78	.99	6.94	Reject
One regression line fits all groups	4	90	2.37	.95	2.47	Accept

A similar analysis could have carried out for the Barr-NORC matches as well, but with the conclusions just presented and a look at the scatter plot for the Barr-NORC matches, it was concluded that there was no need for eliminating any of the Barr-NORC matches. In total there are 41 Barr-NORC matches, consisting of the 30 that also have "good" Census matches according to NORC, and 17 additional ones that are thought to have a lower quality match with the Census.

The principal results of the foregoing analysis are as follows: (1) The 96 Barr-Census title matches reveal a correlation between the Barr scale scores and socioeconomic scores of .81. (2) The 47 matches of titles of the Barr scale with NORC titles have a correlation of .91 between Barr scale scores and NORC prestige scores. For these 47 titles the correlation between Barr scores and socioeconomic scores is .90; between socioeconomic and prestige scores, likewise .90.

The purpose of this analysis, of course, was not to ascertain how the "intelligence" of individuals is actually related to the prestige or socioeconomic status of the occupations they pursue. (This topic will be discussed presently.) Instead, we wished to substantiate a point for future reference: The psychologist's concept of the "intelligence demands" of an occupation is very much like the general public's concept of the prestige or "social standing" of an occupation. Both are closely related to independent measures of the aggregate social and economic status of the persons pursuing an occupation. In short, we suggest here, with the intention of elaborating the idea later, that "intelligence" is a socially defined quality and this social definition is not essentially different from that of achievement or status in the occupational sphere. It is not mere coincidence, therefore, when psychologists find that "the kinds of occupational criteria which intelligence tests predict best are measures of the complex status characteristic we call *occupational levels*" (Tyler, 1964, p. 176).

None of these results, of course, resolves the ancient question of what intelligence "really is," or of the degree to which intelligence is actually required for the performance of occupations varying in social status or prestige.

Yet it is surely significant that the preconceptions of psychologists about occupational performance in relation to intelligence—preconceptions which, presumably, are built into conventional intelligence tests—so closely coincide with the public's view of the social worth or standing of occupations. If, as sociologists believe, the occupational role is a central element in the structure of a differentiated society, the abilities required for satisfactory performance of that role must be fairly directly involved in the achievement occupational status.

It is not utterly fanciful to reconstruct the history of intelligence testing in a way that it is seldom presented. As we usually think of the matter, psychologists analyzed mental functions and then abstracted a component, "intelligence," which they took to be a general factor in the relative efficiency of human organisms. They then devised tasks apparently requiring this factor in various degrees and incorporated them into standard sets called "intelligence tests." Once such tests were administered to population samples, it was discovered that they were predictive of the amount of success in school and work people would enjoy.

The reconstruction we wish to suggest is the following. Every society implicitly designates certain key roles in which performance is variable, with the quality of the performance being a basis for the assignment of status. (Other statuses, of course, may depend upon factors besides performance—the so-called ascribed statuses.) Where the society is one with a complex division of labor, many differentiated occupations are pursued, and these occupations are highly salient among the key roles whose pursuit is a basis for status achievement. Adequate performance in a high status occupation is taken by the social group as prima facie evidence of social capability. However, poor performance in a high status occupation leads to uncertain tenure of the status, and performance—whether good, bad, or indifferent—of a low status occupational role is not seen as providing any sizable increment to consensual estimates of a person's value to society. What we call "occupational prestige" corresponds to an unmistakable social fact. When psychologists came to propose operational counterparts to the notion of intelligence, or to devise measures thereof, they wittingly or unwittingly looked for indicators of capability to function in the system of key roles in the society. What they took to be mental performance might equally well have been described as role performance. Indeed, it was clear in the minds of the pioneers of mental testing that they wished to tap capacity to perform well in another social situation—that of the school. For their immediate purposes, it was unnecessary to expand upon the sociological observation that the school is itself (among other things) a primary mechanism for selecting incumbents of occupational roles.

Our argument tends to imply that a correlation between IQ and occupational achievement was more or less built into IQ tests, by virtue of the psychologists' implicit acceptance of the social standards of the general populace. Had the first IQ tests been devised in a hunting culture, "general intelligence" might well have turned out to involve visual acuity and running speed rather than vocabulary and symbol manipulation. As it was, the concept of intelligence arose in a society where high status accrued to occupations involving the latter in large measure so that what we now *mean* by intelligence is something like the probability of acceptable performance (given the opportunity) in occupations varying in social status.

This argument, however, does not imply that the correlation of IQ with occupational status—assuming the latter to be measured on a scale of prestige or (what is nearly equivalent) socioeconomic rank—will be perfect. First, there are many social contingencies (just alluded to by the term "opportunity") which may militate against a matching of capacity to perform occupational roles and actual performance. Second, any test is a small sample of the almost unlimited sorts of personal assessments that could be made; it is thus a fallible basis of inference.

It is an empirically contingent question, therefore, as to how well occupational achievement can actually be predicted from test scores. If our argument were entirely cogent, we might suppose that if all the "social contingencies" bearing upon occupational achievement were properly taken into account, residual variation would be solely due to "intelligence." To accomplish a demonstration of this hypothesis, however, we should require a model that correctly locates intelligence itself in a causal complex and correctly specifies its role in status achievement vis-à-vis the many other contingent factors. One way of stating our purpose in this research is to indicate that we are trying to make progress in this direction. Naturally, we do not expect any such decisive result as that suggested by the statement of the ultimate objective of research.

5.2 Correlates of Intelligence

In a search for psychological data on sizable propulations which could be roughly matched with our demographic data on occupational achievement, we were pleasantly surprised to learn of a very substantial body of information summarized by Byrns and Henmon (1936). They report scores of some 100,000 Wisconsin high school seniors given selected tests of "scholastic aptitude" during 1929–1933. The summary is in terms of ten broad groups of parental occupation and 77 specific occupation titles. Three different tests had been used, so the authors aggregated the results only after making a percentile transformation. Their Table V shows for each of the 77 parental occupations the number of students tested, and the first-, second-, and third-quartile scores of students identified with that parental occupation.

Our interest was in the correlation of students' scores with the *status* of the parental occupation as measured by Duncan's (1961a) socioeconomic index of occupational status. To study this correlation, we had to match the occupation titles given by Byrns and Henmon with the Census titles for which the index is defined. This led us to make certain omissions, such as students whose parents were "retired" or classified in a "miscellaneous" category. We also omitted a few occupations, containing only a small number of students, where the title strongly suggested exclusive application to the female parent, for example, "nurses" and "dressmakers." Altogether, we retained the data pertaining to 88,883 of the original 100,820 students. In some instances we had to make a combination of two titles given by Byrns and Henmon to achieve approximate comparability with a Census category, and sometimes Census titles had to be combined. We ended up with 64 occupation titles for use in our restudy of Byrns and Henmon's data. The process of matching occupation titles is inevitably somewhat arbitrary and subjective, but in the light of our experience it is difficult to believe that the results would have been greatly different in the hands of any knowledgeable investigator. For future use, however, we offer to psychologists the suggestion that their data could be more generally useful if some care were taken to render occupation and other social categories consistent with those employed in official statistical sources.

One further manipulation was required before we could compute the statistics of interest to us. Since Byrns and Henmon used percentiles as their score value, they obtained a roughly rectangular distribution of scores— approximately 10 percent being scored 0–9, 10 percent 10–19, and so on, to 10 percent in the top interval, 90–100 (see their Table I). We assumed that the underlying score distribution was normal, and converted the median percentile scores in their Table V to normal deviates—or, actually, to probits, making use of Table IX in Fisher & Yates (1948). The probit values were then transformed to standard scores with mean 100 and standard deviation 20. For example, Byrns and Henmon report that children of Druggists had a median percentile score of 67.6. In the normal distribution 67.6 percent of the population falls below a score corresponding to .4565 standard deviation units above the mean or a probit value of 5.4565. This probit value multiplied by 20 is 109.13, which (rounded to 109) we took to be the mean standard score of children of Druggists.

Let X_j be the occupational status score of the jth occupation on Duncan's scale, $\overline{Y}_j$ be the mean standard score of children of parents classified in the jth occupation, and n_j the number of such children in the data of Byrns and Henmon, so that $\Sigma_j n_j = N = 88,883$. If Y_{ij} is the standard score of the ith child in the jth occupation category, we have

$$\overline{Y} = \sum_j \sum_i Y_{ij}/N = \sum_j n_j \overline{Y}_j/N = 100.607,$$

differing slightly from 100, presumably because of the omissions noted above and/or errors of rounding. By assumption,

$$\mathrm{Var}(Y) = \sigma_Y^2 = 20^2 = 400,$$

an assumption we cannot check numerically because of the way in which the data are tabulated.

We find that

$$\bar{X} = \sum_j n_j X_j / N = 32.41,$$

a value whose representativeness we shall assess presently; and

$$\mathrm{Var}(X) = \sum_j n_j (X_j - \bar{X})^2 / N = 500.99,$$

whence $\sigma_X = 22.38$, a value likewise subject to an external check.

Finally, we require

$$(\mathrm{Cov}\, Y, X) = (1/N) \sum_j n_j \bar{Y}_j X_j - \bar{Y}\bar{X} = 90.47.$$

From the foregoing, we obtain immediately the regression coefficient $b_{YX} = .1806$, the intercept $a_{YX} = 94.75$, and the correlation $r_{YX} = .2021$, so that $r_{YX}^2 = .041$. We may also compute the squared correlation ratio, $eta_{YX}^2 = .052$, taking each of the 64 occupation titles as a distinct category.

With this large a sample, the difference, eta_{YX}^2 minus $r_{YX}^2 = .011$, is no doubt too large to attribute to sampling error. The scatter diagram (Fig. 5.1), however, gives only the slightest suggestion of curvilinearity: Most of the variation of occupation-specific means from the regression line is simply scatter of particular occupations at comparable status levels.

In view of the uncertainty about the status score for the occupation, Farmer, and the very substantial number of farmers' children in the Wisconsin data, we are pleased to have observed the near coincidence of the actual mean and the regression estimate. The mean standard score for farmers' children is 96. With an occupational status score of 14, the regression estimate for this group comes out at 97.3.

Our correlation $r_{YX} = .20$ may be compared with the result stated by Byrns & Henmon (1936, p. 287): "the correlation between mental ability of the student and the rank of the parental occupation, here discovered, for the entire group of students is only $+.18$." Although we are not quite sure how the latter value was computed, we are reassured by the fact that our manipulations have not resulted in any pronounced distortion of the conclusion originally reached.

In using the foregoing estimates from the data of Byrns and Henmon, one must bear in mind the selectivity involved in their definition of the study population. From the 1930 Census we learn that 53.7 percent of 17-year-old

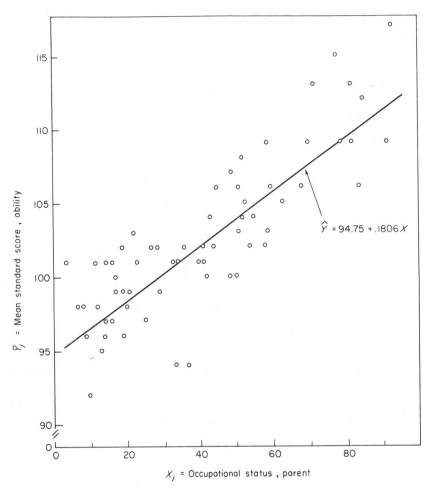

Fig. 5.1. Scatter plot, mean standard scores of ability on occupational status of parent, Wisconsin high school seniors, 1929–1933 (after Byrns & Henmon, 1936).

boys in Wisconsin were enrolled in school. Not all of them, however, were high school seniors, the group covered by the testing program. We probably can secure a better estimate of the coverage of the testing program by considering 1940 Census data on educational attainment of Wisconsin men 25–29 years old, who were, of course, of high school age around 1930. Of these men, 38.0 percent are reported as high school graduates and an additional 4.6 percent as having completed 3 years of high school. In round numbers, therefore, the testing program from which Byrns and Henmon secured their data must have covered about 40 percent of the Wisconsin boys reaching age 18 in the period

1929–1933. The authors give no indication of how far the testing program may have fallen short of covering the target population on account of absences from school and the like.

To evaluate the occupation statistics derived from Byrns and Henmon, we consider national OCG data on native white men 47–51 years old in March 1962 (who were, therefore, 15–19 years old in 1930). For comparability with the population studied by Byrns and Henmon, we exclude those who completed less than 4 years of high school. For this select group of high school graduates we find the mean of father's occupational status is 35.01 (vs. 32.41 derived from the Wisconsin data), with a standard deviation of 23.74 (vs. 22.38). The agreement seems satisfactory inasmuch as we have no reason to assume strict equivalence of the two populations.

Having considered the correlation of mental ability with one important item of socioeconomic background, we turn to the problem of estimating its correlation with measures of achievement. A search of the literature suggests that the best historical data for a general population relating IQ measured at an early age to subsequent educational attainment are those compiled by Benson (1942). She followed up 1989 pupils in the sixth grade of 64 elementary schools in Minneapolis who had been given the Haggerty Intelligence Examination: Delta 2 in April 1923. Records of subsequent achievement (highest grade completed) were obtained for 1680 cases.

Benson reports, "A product-moment coefficient of correlation of $.57 \pm .01$ was obtained between IQ and grade level attained" (p. 164). Her Table I is a cross-tabulation of IQ (10-point intervals) by six levels of attainment. We scored the latter as follows, to conform with our practice in anlyzing OCG data:

3: "Did not enter high school" (but presumably finished at least sixth grade and, for the most part, eighth grade)
4: "Entered high school but did not graduate"
5: "Graduated from high school but did not enter college"
6: "Entered college but did not receive any degree"
7: "Received bachelor's degree"
8: "Took graduate work or received advanced degree"

Using these scores and the midpoints of IQ intervals, we found a correlation of .542 ($r^2 = .294$). The regression of education on IQ was .0321, with an intercept of .99. Mean IQ was 112.4 with a standard deviation of 19.38. (We have ignored the "Stanford-Binet equivalents" also given by Benson; these have a somewhat smaller standard deviation.)

As a rough check on the plausibility of Benson's follow-up data, we looked at 1940 Census data on educational attainment of persons 25–34 years old in Minneapolis. The comparison with Benson's distribution in Table 5.3 is

TABLE 5.3

Percent Distribution by Educational Attainment, for Persons 25–34 Years Old Living in Minneapolis in 1940 and for Sample Studied by Benson

Years of school completed	1940 Census	Benson
Elementary		
None to 5	1	–
6 to 8	20	16
High School		
1–3	23	35
4	36	31
College		
1–3	11	10
4	6	6
5 or more	3	2
Total*	100	100

Source: *1940 Census of Population*, Vol. IV, Part 3; Benson (1942, Table I).
* Excludes attainment not reported.

moderately reassuring. She, of course, missed the 1 percent of children failing to reach sixth grade. The 309 cases not located in the follow-up were known to be negatively selected on IQ. A median of 108 is reported for the 1989 cases originally tested as against 112 for the 1680 cases followed up. We infer that the mean IQ of the 309 lost cases was around 86. Disproportionate numbers of them probably were early dropouts. This fact may help to account for the underrepresentation of persons failing to enter high school in Benson's sample, but it leaves us puzzled at the overrepresentation of those completing 1–3 years of high school. An alternative explanation, of course, is response error in the Census data or lack of comparability between the two sources. In illustration of the latter, it seems likely that many of Benson's respondents who "entered high school but did not graduate" actually dropped out before finishing the ninth grade. In that event, the Census type of question would classify them as Elementary, 8 years, rather than High School, 1–3 years.

Altogether, one can feel considerable confidence when taking a value of .5 or .6 as the correlation between IQ and educational attainment in cohorts completing their schooling during the 1930s. Interestingly enough, this seems to be about the value obtained in correlating IQ scores obtained on adults with their past history of schooling—a point we can check more carefully with the CPS-NORC data and other sources.

We present next some calculations on data summarized by Harrell & Harrell (1945), whose paper shows summary statistics of the AGCT (Army General Classification Test) scores of 18,782 white enlisted men in the Army Air Forces

Air Service Command during World War II. The statistics are classified into 74 previous civilian occupations of these men. The Harrell report contains no information on age, educational attainment, geographic origin, or other social characteristics of the sample. Apparently, occupations infrequently represented in this population were simply omitted from the tabulations. To match Census occupation titles (approximately), it was necessary to combine certain of the Harrell categories. Hence, the present analysis concerns 69 occupation groups.

The AGCT was designed to have a mean of 100 and standard deviation of 20. The Harrell sample as a whole yields a mean of 106.6 with standard deviation 19.1. Evidently, selection into the Air Force enlisted man population involved some screening for intelligence.

When the 69 occupations are scored on Duncan's (1961a) status scale, we obtain a mean of 31.8 and standard deviation of 19.2. These figures suggest that the sample is not highly unrepresentative of civilian occupations of young men. Duncan & Hodge (1963), for example, report a mean of 35.5 with standard deviation 22.1 as of 1940 for a Chicago sample of white men 25–34 years old in that year. The Harrell sample may, therefore, underrepresent men at the extremes of the occupational status distribution.

In Table 1 of the Harrell paper we have the mean and standard deviation of the AGCT scores of men in each occupation. It is, therefore, easy to compute the within-occupation and between-occupation sums of squares; the total sum of squares follows at once. We find eta^2 of AGCT on occupation is .2288. The correlation coefficient of AGCT with occupational status is .4241; hence r^2 is .18. The regression coefficients are .4264 for occupational status on AGCT and .4218 for AGCT on occupational status. In causal models we would probably wish to think of occupational status as a function of intelligence. Hence the former regression is perhaps the more relevant one. The Harrell table, however, shows mean AGCT for given occupation. It is only the latter regression, therefore, that we can inspect for evidence of curvilinearity. The scatter diagram (Fig. 5.2) shows little evidence of systematic departure from a linear relationship.

A second set of Army data for white enlisted men is available in a report by Stewart (1947). A similar collection of data for civilian samples tested with the GATB (General Aptitude Test Battery) will also be studied here (United States Bureau of Employment Security, 1962).

Stewart's data pertain to 81,553 white enlisted men in 227 different occupations. Occupations infrequently represented in her original sample were omitted from the published report. The occupational categories for Stewart's data are, therefore, considerably more detailed than those used in Harrell and Harrell's data described previously.

Some occupations on Stewart's list were discarded: specifically, all titles

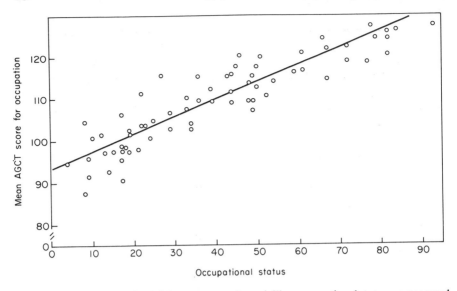

Fig. 5.2. Regression of AGCT score on previous civilian occupational status, as measured by scores on Duncan (1961a) scale.

with a "student" prefix, such as "Student, Medicine," and a few which could not be given a Census code. Stewart reports values of percentiles 10, 25, 50, 75, and 90 for each occupation. We used only the median (P_{50}) values and treated them as occupation-specific mean scores. Since Stewart does not report a standard deviation for her whole sample, we took it to be 20 and used this figure in calculating the variance and sum of squares of AGCT scores. The mean AGCT score for the 62,233 cases included in our calculations is 101.6. The statistics on occupational status in this sample are mean 25.9 and standard deviation 18.6. Thus Stewart's sample has rather lower means on both AGCT and civilian occupational status, but the standard deviation of the latter is quite comparable with the value observed in the Harrell and Harrell material.

The following tabulation compares the regression statistics obtained from the two sources:

	Stewart	Harrell
Correlation, AGCT and occupational status	.446	.424
Regression, AGCT on occupational status	.481	.422
Regression, occupational status on AGCT	.414	.426
Eta^2, AGCT on occupation	.253	.229

In view of the differences in population coverage and the detail of the occupational classification, the similarity between the two sets of results is remarkable. It is difficult to foresee any use for these results where the differences will be of material consequence.

Turning to the civilian data, we consider GATB scores on Aptitude G (Intelligence) collected by the United States Employment Service. Like the AGCT, this score is designed to have mean 100 and standard deviation 20 in the general population. The sample providing data for specific occupations, however, is not a cross-section sample but a collecion of samples of specific occupations obtained in what appears to have been an ad hoc and expedient fashion. While the occupation titles are extremely specific, they do not cover the total occupation structure to the degree that the military data do.

The source publication gives sample size, means, and standard deviation for each of the specific occupations. We deleted a considerable number of occupations the samples for which were predominantly female. The mean for all of the 17,173 cases covered in the source was 100.36; for the 7858 deleted cases it was 90.68; for the 9315 cases studied here it was 108.53. (These figures, of course, are not relevant to the question of general sex differences in intelligence.) Despite the upward bias of this sample's mean, the standard deviation remained 19.99, or effectively 20.

There is likewise an upward bias in the distribution of status scores for the occupations included. The mean for the group studied here is 43.85 with a standard deviation of 21.86.

If the sample for each specific occupation were representative, there would be no bias in the regression coefficient of intelligence (G score) on occupational status. This regression is .504, which may be compared with the regression of AGCT on occupational status of .481 from the Stewart data and .422 from the Harrell data.

The GATB analysis provides a correlation coefficient of .551 between intelligence and occupational status, which is somewhat higher than those obtained from the two AGCT series, .446 and .424, respectively. In view of the (probable) nonrepresentativeness of the occupations covered in the GATB data, one would not accept this as an estimate for the general population.

An interesting feature of the GATB data is the high value of eta^2 for the correlation ratio of G scores on occupation. A value of .490 is obtained, in contrast to .253 and .229 for the two AGCT studies. Yet we have seen that the linear regression of intelligence on occupational status score is not markedly higher in the GATB data than in at least one of the AGCT sets. Evidently, the detailed occupational coding and/or the sampling technique of the GATB study produced a good deal of interoccupation variation in intelligence not captured in the military data. However, this additional variation is not particularly related to occupational *status*.

In consequence, the GATB occupation-specific means show a good deal more scatter around the regression of intelligence on occupation than do the

AGCT means, even though the regression itself is much the same (see Fig. 5.3).

To summarize: Two sets of military and one set of civilian data give essentially consistent indications of the degree of relationship between tested intelligence and occupational achievement. If anything, the civilian data suggest a slightly stronger relationship. The difference, if not due to technicalities solely, could be due to the fact that the military data refer to former civilian occupations of very young men, many of whom had doubtlessly not yet established their occupational career lines at the time of induction.

5.3   Preliminary Models

The information in hand, to this point in the discussion, is summarized in Table 5.4. We wish now to indicate how these data may be used in securing an extension of the basic model of the process of occupational achievement. Figure 5.4 recapitulates one set of estimates on this model from Blau & Duncan (1967, p. 174). For the moment we are taking as the terminal occupational status the "first job" reported in the OCG data, assuming it is the nearest possible approximation to the data on previous civilian occupation given in the

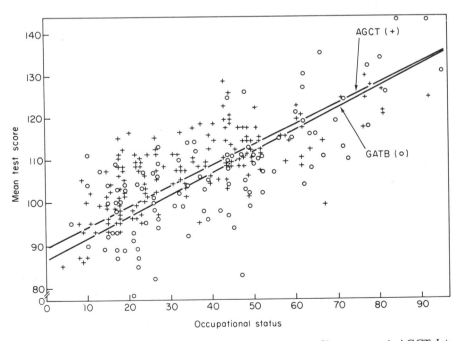

Fig. 5.3. Regression of mental ability on occupational status (Duncan score). AGCT data from Stewart (1947); GATB data from United States Bureau of Employment Security (1962).

TABLE 5.4

Correlations Used in Estimating Path Coefficients in Fig. 5.5[a]

Variable	Q IQ	X Father's occupation	V Father's education	U Respondent's education	W First job
Q, Respondent's intelligence	–	.20	.25	.54	.43
X, Father's occupational status	1	–	.52	.44	.42
V, Father's education	2	5	–	.45	.33
U, Respondent's education	3	5	5	–	.54
W, Status of first job	4	5	5	5	–

[a] Key to sources:
 1. Byrns and Henmon (1936)
 2. Unpublished data of W. H. Sewell (WISC data set)
 3. Benson (1942)
 4. Average of two sets of AGCT data (Harrell & Harrell, 1945; Stewart, 1947)
 5. OCG study, all men 20–64 years old

studies of military mental ability tests. The status of "first job" is represented as being dependent upon educational attainment and status level of father's occupation. Educational attainment, in turn, is taken to depend upon the father's occupational status and his educational attainment—although one might well have used alternative measures of socioeconomic background. Both occupational statuses—the father's (as of respondent's age 16) and the respondent's first job—are scaled on Duncan's socioeconomic status index for detailed occupations. Educational attainment is the number of years of regular schooling completed.

The models are linear causal systems which are hypothesized to account for the observed associations among measured variables. The path cofficients shown for Fig. 5.4 were estimated from data for men 20–64 years of age.

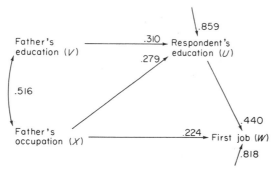

Fig. 5.4. Basic model, with estimates based on OCG data for all men 20–64 years old.

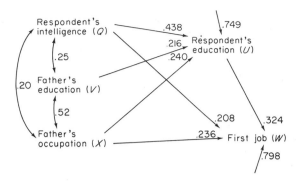

Fig. 5.5. Extended model based on data in Table 5.4.

Slightly different results are obtained in making the estimates for different populations, such as men with nonfarm background, white men, or men in a more restricted age range. Such differences are not at issue here, however, as we have introduced Fig. 5.4 only for illustrative purposes.

The extension we wish to entertain involves considering measured intelligence as a background factor, along with the socioeconomic measures. Thus Fig. 5.5 represents the status of the first job as depending directly upon educational attainment, both directly and indirectly upon father's occupation and respondent's intelligence, and only indirectly upon father's education. Respondent's education, in turn, depends upon intelligence and the two socioeconomic background items. It should be noted that the model requires no assumption concerning the nature of the linkage between socioeconomic background factors and intelligence. Such a correlation could arise on the basis of either genetic or social mechanisms or, more likely, a combination of both. For the purposes of the present model, it suffices to recognize that the correlation exists. A quite different model would be required to represent hypotheses about how the correlation is produced.

The data used in estimating path coefficients for Fig. 5.5 are shown in Table 5.4. At this juncture we are venturing to combine into one model estimates of correlations obtained for several different populations. This tactic will also be followed in our subsequent work. Ideally, we would resort to this procedure only if we had equally representative and reliable samples of the very same population. This condition will seldom be met, and we shall have to assume comparability of data from different sources when there is every reason to believe such comparability does not strictly hold. *From this standpoint, all results obtained on this procedure had best be regarded as hypotheses for ultimate verification upon a single population for which all relevant measures can be obtained.* Even though our procedure is hazardous, it is not actually different from the informal practice of investigators who draw conclusions by comparing information developed in two or more studies. Or, rather, the difference is that we are here undertaking formally what is common in informal practice. Presumably, any liability of the procedure should be more apparent when it is controlled by the formalism of an explicit model than it would be in the absence of such a control.

The importance of taking intelligence explicitly into account is suggested by a comparison of Fig. 5.4 with Fig. 5.5. As far as occupational achievement is concerned, inclusion of intelligence as a background factor does not markedly increase the proportion of "explained" variance in status level of the first job. The residual factor for W (first job status) is .818 in Fig. 5.4 as compared with .798 in Fig. 5.5. Translating these into proportions of variance not accounted for (the square of the residual path), we have 67 percent of the variance of W not accounted for in Fig. 5.4 as against 64 percent in Fig. 5.5. This result dashes any hope that availability of intelligence test scores will enable the investigator to improve markedly the prediction of early occupational achievement as compared with what he can do with education and socioeconomic background factors alone.

However, Fig. 5.5 gives us a rather different interpretation of the nature of the process of status achievement from that implied by Fig. 5.4. A substantial direct path from intelligence to first job must be entered into the system. When this is done, the apparent direct effect of education is diminished, for in Fig. 5.5 education is represented as affecting the first job only insofar as it operates independently of intelligence, as well as socioeconomic background. Phrased otherwise, the apparent effect of education in Fig. 5.4 includes some variation in first job status that is actually due to intelligence, given that intelligence affects educational attainment.

This result assumes a certain importance in view of the current interest in estimating "returns from education" in an economic sense. Conventional Census data reveal that amount of income earned rises with increments to years of schooling. Economists studying the rate of return to education have noted, however, that number of years of schooling partly reflects differences in ability. It has been observed, moreover, that the effect of education on income is transmitted, in considerable measure, via occupational level. At this point we cannot yet include income as a further output of Fig. 5.5, although a model with this feature is presented subsequently. However, we are in a position to look at the respective roles of education and intelligence as determinants of occupational status.

If we look at the gross association of education with occupational status, as measured by the simple (zero-order) correlation between the two, we find the substantial value of .54 (see Table 5.4). Figure 5.4 suggests, however, that education is operating in part to transmit the effect of socioeconomic background so that its direct effect in a model incorporating such background items is reduced to .44. Even this figure is seen to be an overestimate in the light of Fig. 5.5, where with both socioeconomic background and intelligence included in the system, the direct effect of education shrinks to .32. In this model, education is estimated, then, to have a direct effect of .32 and an indirect effect, due to its correlation with antecedent determinants of first job, of .22 (the original simple correlation, .54, less the direct effect, .32). To be sure, the remaining direct effect is still substantial, and its significance is enhanced by the fact that it is measuring the impact of education on occupational achievement independently of some of the obvious determinants of both education and occupation level.

The reduction in the apparent role of education as between Figs. 5.4 and 5.5 contrasts with the lack of change in the direct effect of father's occupation in the two models. Since the correlation between father's occupation and respondent's intelligence is only .2 (according to the estimate used here), inclusion of intelligence in the model hardly affects the estimate of the direct effect of father's occupation; we find it to be .22 in Fig. 5.4 and actually a little higher at .24 in Fig. 5.5. Again, it should be remembered that this is an estimate of the *net* impact of father's occupation on respondent's first job, taking into account its correlation with respondent's intelligence and the fact that it works partly via its influence on education—that is, net of these indirect paths of influence. The net or direct effect of father's occupation is, of course, less than its gross association with first job, which comes to .42 (see Table 5.4).

It will have been noted that no direct effect of father's education on first job is shown in the model. This is the case because such direct effect is very nearly zero and not statistically significant. A version of Fig. 5.4 which included a direct path from V to W yielded a coefficient of .014, rather less than the standard error of the coefficient (Blau & Duncan, 1967, p. 174).

The inclusion of intelligence in the model not only puts a new—and presumably more realistic—interpretation on the roles of education and socioeconomic background factors in occupational achievement; it also leads to a more adequate accounting for the variation in education. In Fig. 5.4, where only socioeconomic background was considered, the residual factor for U is .859, implying that 74 percent of the variance in educational attainment is unexplained. In Fig. 5.5, with the residual path of .749, this figure is reduced to 56 percent. The model, even so, far from exhausts the variance in education.

For advocates of equal opportunity, it may be reassuring that intelligence is clearly more important than socioeconomic background as a determinant of educational attainment. Its direct effect is .438, its indirect effect, due to correlation with socioeconomic background, .102 (the sum of these, .54, being the simple correlation between education and intelligence). However, it is clear that socioeconomic background influences how far boys go in school, quite apart from differences in measured ability. This is apparent from the path coefficients for V and X, father's education and occupation.

To analyze the matter in a slightly different way, we can note that, by itself and including its role in mediating effects of socioeconomic background, intelligence accounts for 29 percent of the variance in schooling (the square of .54, the zero-order correlation between the two variables). In combination, intelligence and the socioeconomic background items account for 44 percent of the variance in education. The increment of 15 percentage points (44–29) is the net contribution of socioeconomic background, as measured by the two characteristics of the father, quite apart from any indirect effects of socio-economic origins operating via intelligence. Whether this net influence amounts to an inequality of "opportunity" or represents inequality in some kinds of social, economic, or psychological resources which a family may bestow upon the child remains to be estimated.* Experiences with models of this kind suggests that inclusion of explicit measures of economic resources, such as family income, would not alter greatly the estimate of the combined impact of all socioeconomic factors on educational attainment. What other kinds of "resources" should be postulated is a separate question. In subsequent discussion, we bring one other suggestive item of information to bear upon this difficult question.

The next complication of the basic model to be considered arises from the introduction into it of a variable reflecting family structure, to wit, number of siblings. For the remainder of this discussion of preliminary models we shall omit consideration of occupational status so that the model presented next has only one output variable, educational attainment. Fig. 5.6 is taken from the work of B. Duncan (1965). Her work was based on data for a subgroup of the OCG sample, consisting of native white males 27–61 years old in 1962. The model happens to include a variable, labeled "intact family," which we shall subsequently ignore; but its inclusion probably has little effect on the path

---

* Estimates of talent loss (under various definitions) for men and women in the WISC data set appear in Sewell (1971) and Sewell, Hauser, and Shah (forthcoming). For young men of equivalent mental ability, there are fewer from lower socioeconomic origins going on to higher education, completing college, and entering postgraduate study than from higher status origins. In the highest IQ quartile, more than 1.5 times as many students from the highest quartile on socioeconomic background as in the lowest socioeconomic quartile go on to post-high-school education. Somewhat greater talent loss is experienced by lowest status, lowest ability Wisconsin students as compared to highest status, lowest ability boys and girls. Sewell and his colleagues interpret their data as demonstrating educational discrimination by social origins (and sex) at all levels of higher education, even in a state with an outstanding record of providing public and private scholarships and low tuition rates in its diverse system of public higher education.

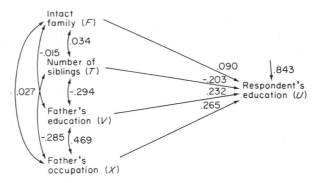

Fig. 5.6. Basic model of educational attainment with estimates for native white men 27–61 years old (B. Duncan, 1965b, Chapter 3).

coefficients for the other determinants of educational attainment since its correlations with them are so low. The intercorrelations among the background variables are shown in the diagram. Their respective correlations with the dependent variable are as follows, $r_{UF} = .087$; $r_{UT} = -.344$; $r_{UV} = .441$; $r_{UX} = .434$. When the population is limited to native white males, father's education diminishes in relative importance (as compared to father's occupation) as a factor in educational attainment of respondents. This is apparent both in the simple correlations and in the path coefficients for Fig. 5.6. An appreciable negative path for number of siblings is estimated, and this factor is itself negatively correlated with the other background factors.

The new interpretation of these data which is required when intelligence is taken into account appears as Fig. 5.7. The crucial item of information is the correlation of intelligence with number of siblings. This correlation is not available in any of the sources from which we have obtained other correlations

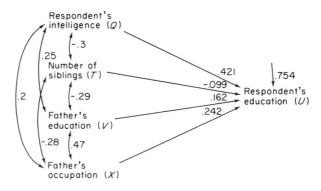

Fig. 5.7. Educational attainment as a function of family background and intelligence.

for intelligence. However, the correlation of IQ with number of siblings has been studied rather extensively (Anastasi, 1956), and there is a sizable and controversial literature on the interpretation of this relationship. The most representative figure for the observed correlation between number of siblings and standard intelligence tests in unselected populations seems to be about $-.3$, and this value has been selected for the purpose of our illustrative calculations. In Fig. 5.7 we are unable to include the "intact family" variable, but as already indicated, it seems unlikely that its insertion into the model would alter the other paths appreciably.

Close comparison between Figs. 5.5 and 5.6 are not warranted since the latter pertains to a somewhat different population from the former. However, there is general resemblance between the two except, of course, for the additional path to education in Fig. 5.6 and the omission from it of the first job. With intelligence and socioeconomic background held constant, number of siblings retains a significant direct effect on schooling. It is interesting, however, to see the extent to which the sibling variable operates via other variables in the system. Its zero-order correlation with educational attainment, noted previously, is $-.344$; with socioeconomic background items held constant, the direct effect shrinks to $-.203$ (in Fig. 5.6); and with intelligence as well included among the background factors there is a further shrinkage to $-.099$. A full interpretation of this outcome would require a considerable elaboration of Fig. 5.7, to "explain" the intercorrelations of the background variables taken as given in that model. Such an explanation would raise complicated issues of "heredity vs. environment," for there is no agreement on the extent to which the inverse correlation of number of siblings and intelligence represents environmental effects on intellectual development as over against dysgenic fertility patterns (Burt, 1947; Nisbet, 1953).

Since Fig. 5.7 includes both intelligence and socioeconomic background, the path coefficient of approximately $-.1$ for number of siblings must represent other influences than these. The most obvious observation is that children in large families enjoy lesser economic resources per head than children in small families, given that the families are at the same socioeconomic level. The same may be true of other resources as well. In a large family, parental aspirations may not be as sharply focused on any one child, designated at random, as in the small family.

An elaboration of Fig. 5.7 on a quite conjectural basis appears in Fig. 5.8. Here we raise the question of how similar the educational outcomes would be for two brothers in the same family. We assume that since the two brothers have the same father and the same number of siblings, values of T, V, and X are the same for them. This is actually a simplification, because for example, father's occupation is specified as of the date the respondent was 16 years old, and two brothers would not have attained that age in the same year, apart from the case

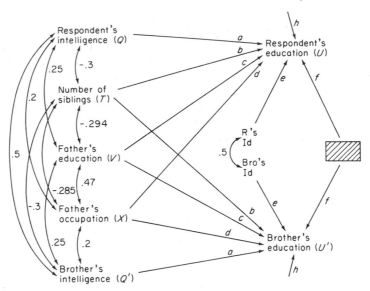

Fig. 5.8. Correlation between siblings in regard to educational attainment, interpreted in the light of Fig. 5.7.

of twins. We assume, moreover, that the socioeconomic background factors act in precisely the same way for the two brothers so that there is only one set of path coefficients applying either to respondent's education or to brother's education. A further assumption is that intelligence of either brother is intercorrelated with background items in the same way as for the other brother and acts in the same fashion on schooling.

Finally, the crucial assumption concerns the correlation between the intelligence scores of the two brothers. This particular correlation has been studied rather extensively. A recent review article instances no less than 35 inquiries into the correlation between siblings in intelligence (Erlenmeyer-Kimling & Jarvik, 1963). Rather widely varying figures, from less than .3 to nearly .8, have been obtained. The median of the 35 correlations is, however, .49. Whether or not this is a mere coincidence, the empirical correlation is very close to the theoretical genetic correlation of .5 between siblings which follows from highly simplified assumptions. Without commenting on the implications of this coincidence, we shall take .5 as the correlation between brothers' intelligence scores.

In Fig. 5.8 it should be noted that educational attainment is not assumed to be directly affected by brother's intelligence so that there is no path from Q' to U or from Q to U'. Such a direct effect would be theoretically anomalous. As we shall see, however, this assumption does not require that the simple correlation between Q' and U or Q and U' be zero.

When either brother is considered separately, therefore, Fig. 5.8 merely repeats Fig. 5.7, and we shall therefore transfer the respective path coefficients from the latter to the former. Hence for the direct effect of intelligence on schooling (for either brother) we have $a = .421$; for the effect of number of siblings, $b = -.099$; for the effect of father's education, $c = .162$; and for father's occupation, $d = .242$. For the moment, let us disregard both the paths labeled e and f. Then the residual path, h, is the same as in Fig. 5.7, or .754, implying that 57 percent of the variance in educational attainment is not accounted for by the model (whichever brother is in question).

If Fig. 5.8, omitting paths e and f, were literally correct, we could derive the correlation between educational attainments of the two brothers, making use of the appropriate theorem from the theory of path analysis:

$$r_{UU'} = ar_{QU'} + br_{TU'} + cr_{VU'} + dr_{XU'}.$$

This expression includes a correlation ($r_{QU'}$) which is not among our empirically given coefficients. But it, too, is readily obtained from the model, assuming the model to be correct:

$$r_{QU'} = ar_{QQ'} + br_{QX} + cr_{QV} + dr_{QT}.$$

We first compute $r_{QU'}$ as .329; inserting this value into the earlier formula (along with the path coefficients and other designated correlations), we secure the implied value $r_{UU'} = .341$.

We are now in possession of a commodity that is all too rare in sociological analysis: a precise quantitative "prediction" from an explicit model. The prediction, of course, does not concern some future event in the real world but the result of an inquiry that might be undertaken to ascertain whether the implied relationship is correct. In this case, however, we shall not have to wait long to test the prediction. The OCG data include readings on the educational attainments of both the respondents and their oldest brothers (for the roughly half of the sample having an older brother and able to report his number of years of schooling). The correlation between respondent and *oldest* brother is not exactly what is called for by Fig. 5.8, which treats the two brothers symmetrically. But it is at least worth considering how well the OCG result for brother's education conforms to the outcome deduced from Fig. 5.8. In fact, the OCG data for all native non-Negro men 25–64 years of age indicate a correlation of .573 between respondent's education and education of oldest brother, which is considerably higher than .341, the value implied by the model. Evidently, the model is incorrect, or else the correlation between respondent and oldest brother is materially greater than the correlation between respondent and a randomly chosen brother (both propositions could hold, of course).

If, for the sake of argument, we take the true value of $r_{UU'}$ to be .573, we shall have to modify the original model. Such a modification—or, rather, two alternative modifications, among many possible ones—are shown in Fig. 5.8.

Let us consider first Fig. 5.8a, a version incorporating additional paths labeled e (omitting paths f). Here were have postulated two mystery variables denoted, respectively, as "Respondent's Id" and "Brother's Id" ("Id" being merely a label for something that behaves in the way to be described). The variable is assumed to have a direct effect, e, on educational attainment, and to be independent of intelligence, number of siblings, and socioeconomic background. Moreover, the correlation between Respondent's Id and Brother's Id is taken as .5. Id, therefore, might be a trait determined by a simple genetic mechanism, independently of any genetic determination of intelligence and unaffected by socioeconomic environment. If the reader cares to think of some unconscious motivational factor arising in such a fashion, he may find some help in the imagery. With this purely illustrative postulate, the model is rendered consistent with our information on the correlation between educational attainments of brothers by inserting an appropriate value for the paths, e. We have already computed the correlation $r_{UU'}$ produced by paths $a, ..., d$ as .341. Since Id is assumed to be uncorrelated with the other background variables, Fig. 5.8a implies that $r_{UU'} = .341 + .5e^2$. Taking $r_{UU'}$ as .573, we can solve for $e = .681$. Moreover, the increment to explained variance in U (or U') amounts to $e^2 = .464$, so that in Fig. 5.8a, the residual, h, is reduced to .323, implying that 10 percent of the variance in educational attainment is unexplained in the model. Evidently, Id is quite a powerful variable, as dynamic psychologists have long suspected!

This "fun with numbers" is not advanced as a serious theory of the determinants of educational attainment. The purpose of the exercise is to illustrate one line of argument and the consequences thereof. We are trying, in effect, to imagine the response of a behavioral scientist to Fig. 5.7 as he seeks to muffle his disappointment with the large unexplained residual. Many such scientists react initially by speculating about variables left out of the model. Here, we have seized upon the remark that a behavioral scientist might have uttered in a seminar discussing Fig. 5.7, and have followed it to its logical conclusion. We imagine him contending that the model omits "motivation," and observing that high motivation and low motivation are found in both lower and middle class youth for reasons that are difficult to apprehend. To translate such a remark into some definite implication we have to specify the formal properties of a model embodying the speculative hypothesis being advanced. Other translations than the one just considered could, of course, be entertained; and the consequences would then be somewhat different. What one would like to see in discussions of empirical results, when they take a speculative direction, is an attempt to make the speculations specific enough that their consequences can actually be confronted.

The consequence in Fig. 5.8a may (or may not) strike the reader as far-fetched. "Id," whatever it may be, turns out to have a greater net effect on schooling than any of the other determinants with which we are familiar. If this is just a way of stating that the region of our ignorance exceeds the area of our knowledge, no harm is done. If it is, on the other hand, a programmatic dictum, then we know we have a hard job ahead in seeking to measure and identify a powerful factor whose source and nature are at the moment entirely mysterious.

In Fig. 5.8b, which includes paths labeled f while omitting those designated e, we consider a slightly different mystery variable to account for the previously unaccounted for correlation between brothers' educational attainments. The mystery variable is now no longer a trait that might be observed in each brother individually but a characteristic of the family or environment which is common to the two brothers. It is designated as a "gray box," whose content will remain unspecified. Here, in contrast to the previous conjecture, we are assuming that the gray box has exactly the same content for both brothers, whereas in Fig. 5.8a the two Id scores were only correlated to the extent of .5. Again, the model permits easy calculation of the unknown path, for $r_{UU'} = .573 = .341 + f^2$, yielding the value of .482 for f. In turn, the residual paths, h, take on the value .580, implying that 34 percent of the variance of educational attainment for each brother is unexplained.

Figure 5.8b, like its alternate, is a highly specialized modification of Fig. 5.7. The gray box is assumed to be utterly uncorrelated with either intelligence or socioeconomic background. This property immediately rules out such candidates for its content as income, "cultural level" of the home, or even such practices as age at weaning and toilet training (which are thought to vary by social class). To be sure, if the critic can suggest a variable like one of these, and if he is willing to specify not only how it affects schooling but also in what degree it is related to background items, we can entertain still another version of Fig. 5.8 to represent this hypothesis. He will, in any event, have to think of a variable with quite a sizeble influence on schooling, for f is the largest path in the diagram; and, if the gray box variable were allowed to be positively correlated with background factors, its correlation with schooling would have to exceed f.

5.4 Ability and Achievement: Final Model

The final model developed in the project is represented in Fig. 5.9a and reduced forms thereof are shown in Fig. 5.9b and in Fig. 5.10. The estimates of path coefficients pertain as nearly as possible to the population of United States white men 25–34 years old in 1964. About half the correlations among the

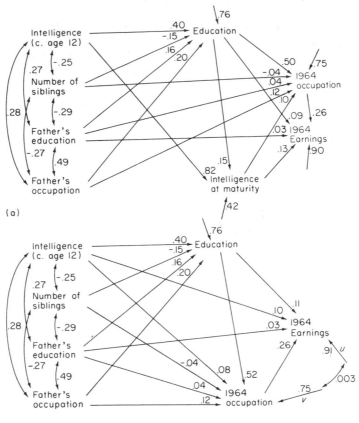

Fig. 5.9. (a) Final model of ability and achievement and (b) semireduced form omitting intelligence at maturity. Source: Duncan (1968a).

eight variables in the model are taken from the CPS-NORC data set. The remainder are either taken from other published sources, such as those discussed earlier, or are derived from the model itself. The details of the estimates, together with some evaluation of them, are given in full in Duncan (1968a).

One important feature of the model is the incorporation of two measures of "intelligence": ability as measured at about age 12 and as measured at maturity. The important work of Bloom (1964) on stability of intellectual traits over the life cycle was consulted in selecting an estimate of .9 as the coefficient of intertemporal stability for intelligence for this segment of the life cycle. The reason why this feature is important is that prior research has left ambiguous the question of the degree to which intelligence measures are contaminated by educational attainment. Thus, in commenting on a Swedish study which

showed that IQ is positively associated with occupational mobility, Lipset &
Bendix (1959, p. 234–235) remarked:

Instructive as these data are, they are vitiated in part by the high correlation
between I.Q. and educational achievement (.82) and between educational
achievement and mobility. Since the intelligence tests were made after the
completion of education—in the course of the process of registering for the
military draft—and since we know that education itself may result in some
improvement of a person's I.Q., the problem of causal imputation is not
resolved. Nevertheless, I.Q. tests do measure (even if they do not isolate)
native ability, and to this extent [the Swedish] data give clear-cut evidence for
the considerable effect of intelligence on social mobility.

In constructing the final model, we explicitly took account of the possibility
"that education itself may result in some improvement of a person's I.Q." The

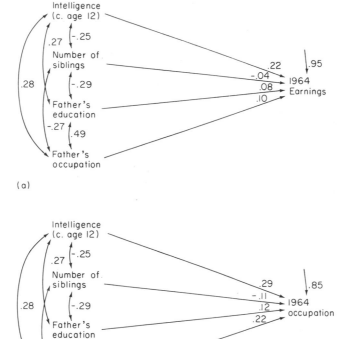

Fig. 5.10. Reduced forms of final model of ability and achievement.

estimate of the magnitude of this effect is a function of (1) the correlation between education and mental ability of mature men; (2) the correlation between mental ability of sixth-grade children and subsequent educational attainment, estimated, as previously described, from the data of Benson (1942); and (3) the assumption as to the stability of mental ability over time, as estimated by Bloom.

Once the model is constructed, we may consider that the data on intelligence at maturity have served their purpose in allowing us to estimate all the coefficients. We may then proceed to eliminate that variable from the model, deriving the semireduced from shown in Fig. 5.9b. If the original model is correct, we can be sure that the semireduced form does not suffer from the ambiguity to which Lipset and Bendix called attention; the variables can be temporally ordered with fairly little error.*

Perhaps the most interesting substantive result is that the bulk of the influence of intelligence on occupation is indirect, via education. The direct path from intelligence to occupation (Fig. 5.9b) is only .08, whereas the indirect path via education is $(.40)(.52) = .21$, or more than twice as large. The sum of the two, $.08 + .21 = .29$, is shown in Fig. 5.10b as the entire effect of intelligence on occupation, apart from joint effects with the other three background variables.

The situation is somewhat different in regard to intelligence as a cause of differential earnings. In Fig. 5.9, it is clear that the effect of intelligence on earnings, net of the effects of education and occupation, is appreciable. Thus men with the same schooling and in the same line of work are differentially rewarded in terms of mental ability. In Fig. 5.9b the direct effect of intelligence on earnings, at .10, is almost as large as the sum of indirect effects via education and occupation, which comes to $(.40)(.11) + (.40)(.52)(.26) + (.08)(.26) = .12$. The combination of direct plus indirect influence, $.10 + .12 = .22$, is shown in the upper diagram of Fig. 5.10 as the entire effect of intelligence on earnings, net of the other three background factors.

5.5   Ability and Achievement: A Replication

As was indicated in the previous section, estimates of coefficients in the "final" model of ability and achievement were derived from data for the population of United States white men aged 25–34 in 1964; but a considerable part of the information used in making the estimates pertains to other popula-

---

* Note that estimates for Fig. 5.9b are computed according to the discussion of semireduced form models with correlated errors (cf. Chapter 2, formulas [2], [6], [7], and [8]). In the case of Fig. 5.9b, eliminating "intelligence at maturity" as an intervening variable in the semireduced form results in a small correlation between the residuals to 1964 occupation and earnings ($r_{uv} = .003$).

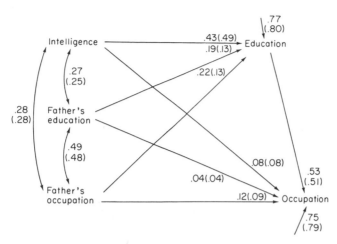

Fig. 5.11. Abridged version of the final model of ability and achievement with path coefficients estimated for two populations. (Figures not in parentheses are based on data summarized in Section 5.4; figures in parentheses are based on DAS data set.)

tions. Access to the DAS data set permits a completely independent replication, although one that does not contain quite enough information to estimate the complete model and one for which the issue of temporal stability of measured intelligence is left unresolved. Fig. 5.11 presents a comparison between estimates secured from the same data used in the previous section and those secured from the DAS data. In the DAS data, the measure of "intelligence" is the "Similarities" subscale of the Wechsler Adult Intelligence Scale. As we have used this scale here, it is interpreted to refer to intelligence as it would have been manifested at some point well before the termination of schooling. That this is a distortion of the probable facts is the main message of the manipulations involved in the work reported in Section 5.4. Yet the results of that work also suggest that the distortion is comparatively minor.

Indeed, the main difference between the two sets of path coefficients in Fig. 5.11 is that the path from intelligence to education is rather larger in the DAS data than in the set of estimates derived from CPS-NORC data and other sources. An exaggeration of this path is precisely what we would expect if a measure of adult intelligence is used as a proxy for childhood intelligence. Apart from this difference, and the corollary reduction in the paths from socioeconomic background factors, the two sets of results exhibit a very nice replication indeed. It appears that the final model of ability and achievement describes features of the process of achievement that are pervasive in American society.

5.6 Summary

Although it is not commonly defined in that way, there is a good argument for conceiving of intelligence as "ability to perform occupational roles." That the pioneers in the measurement of intelligence implicitly proceeded on some such notion is suggested by the very high correlation between the "intelligence demands" of various occupations, as estimated in the Barr scale, and the "prestige" of those occupations as reflected in ratings by the general public. Despite this high correlation, it remains empirically contingent whether particular individuals will find their way into occupations of varying status to a greater or lesser degree on the basis of the kinds of abilities reflected in measurements of intelligence.

Some significant bodies of published data provide estimates of the correlation of parental occupational status with measured intelligence, the correlation of intelligence measured in childhood with subsequent educational attainment, and the correlation of mental test scores of young men with occupations held at an early stage of the career. With appropriate caution, such estimates may be juxtaposed with other data available to the project in the construction of models explicating the role of ability in achievement.

Preliminary versions of this kind of model make it clear that, while intelligence has a substantial influence on amount of schooling, it does not fully explain the correlation of family-background factors with schooling. Moreover, a very substantial correlation between the levels of schooling of brothers can only partly be explained by common family-background factors and sibling resemblance in intelligence.

The work leading to a "final model" of ability and achievement takes explicit account of the possibility that intelligence measured at maturity may be partly a result of amount of schooling. What appears to be an appropriate adjustment for this effect, however, leaves intact the proposition that intelligence has a substantial influence on occupational achievement, apart from its correlation with family-background factors. Much of that influence, however, is mediated by educational attainment. Somewhat similarly, intelligence bears an important relationship to income (net of social origins) for men of equal schooling and occupational statuses. Unlike its relationship to occupational achievement, intelligence affects income directly to nearly the same extent as it influences differential earnings indirectly through schooling and occupational attainment. While the inclusion of intelligence test scores in a model of the process of achievement, therefore, increases appreciably the proportion of variation in occupational status "explained," there remains a very substantial amount of variation still "unexplained."

In Chapter 4 racial differentials in socioeconomic achievements were examined and found to contain a component for which differences in socioeconomic circumstances and structure of the family of origin, and prior attainments, could not account. This residual was interpreted as a handicap, or cost, to some men for being black. Recent commentary on the comparative achievement of whites and Negroes in the United States has suggested that the residual might be explained (in part) as an outcome of racial differences in the distributions of intelligence (Jensen, 1969). We do not wish to comment here on biogenetic, sociogenetic, and other mechanisms by which the documented difference in black–white IQ may have arisen. However, the separation in means by about one standard deviation on a normal IQ scale (about 20 points) does *not* nearly account for the occupational and economic handicaps of Negroes. As reported elsewhere (Duncan, 1968b), little racial variation in schooling remains after equating men for family of origin characteristics and intelligence. Nevertheless, substantial occupational and economic disadvantages accrue to black men, despite their parity with whites in social origins and education, and for constant IQ scores. These supplementary comments are offered to place in perspective the magnitude of the effects of intelligence on achievement and to summarize results from explorations with a more elaborated model not included in this volume.

Chapter 6

Intervening Variables, II: Aspirations and Motives

The general rationale for the class of variables studied in this chapter has been stated by Crockett (1966, p. 281) as follows:

When one asks why, given the presence of certain social structural conditions, particular persons rise, fall, or remain stationary in the status system, personality characteristics immediately become relevant and important. Some sons of laborers become skilled workers, others do not; some sons of professionals descend into slightly skilled white-collar jobs, or into manual occupations, others do not. This variation in mobility among persons sharing similar social positions and influence requires attention to personality factors in mobility.

In this chapter we shall not attempt to construct or maintain a theoretically coherent set of distinctions among such concepts as aspiration, orientation, motivation, ambition, and the like. All such concepts seemingly refer to "dispositions" that are imputed to individuals by themselves or by observers. There is apparently a wide range of variation in regard to dispositions, from those that are more or less transitory, situationally conditioned, and specific to those that are enduring, resistant to change under alteration of conditions, and generalized. Frequently, however, the investigator will wish to argue that a situationally specific intention, such as "college plans," is indicative of a more generalized and persistent orientation that he would call "educational aspiration," or even more broadly, "ambition" or "achievement orientation." Insofar as such arguments are based on general theories in social psychology,

106

the present work will have little to say about their validity—it is no part of our task to make a contribution to theory in that field. Instead, we wish to illustrate how such arguments may become relevant to the interpretation of particular bodies of data on socioeconomic achievement. Our claim is that making the argument explicit in the context of a definite model enables the investigator both to realize its implications more clearly and to ascertain whether these are consistent with the information at hand. In none of the examples considered here is any one interpretation uniquely indicated by the data, although some interpretations that might seem to represent viable alternatives ex ante turn out not to be viable ex post.

6.1 Measurement of Aspirations

Several sociological studies (see literature cited by Haller & Miller, 1963) have dealt with the occupational aspirations of teen-agers. These studies typically relate level of aspiration to indicators of social background. In the absence of longitudinal data, however, they cannot provide information on the degree to which aspirations serve as the mediating link between background and achievement. Even so, we shall review briefly the materials available in certain of these studies. The primary purpose is to suggest that such materials can, in principle, be collected in a form suited for use in models of the kind studied here, although such has not been the practice in the past.

Stephenson (1957) secured data on father's occupation and respondent's occupational plans and aspirations from some 1000 ninth-grade students in four "semi-industrial, medium-sized communities in New Jersey." The responses were classified into the six categories of the Alba Edwards socioeconomic classification of occupations. One table presents the bivariate frequency distribution of occupational plans by father's occupation, and another similarly shows occupational aspirations by father's occupation. Unfortunately, the detailed data are not shown by sex so that the results are a mixture of relationships holding for males and females. Females reporting "marriage" as an occupational goal are excluded from consideration here.

To secure a compact reduction of Stephenson's data, the six occupation categories were assigned integer scores, 1–6, according to the conventional ordering from "unskilled" to "professional." Table 6.1 provides the summary statistics from regression analyses. It is noteworthy that the slope of "aspirations" on father's occupation is much lower than the slope of "plans" on father's occupation. The more realistic the response, the greater is the relationship to background. Moreover, plans are almost a whole step lower on this occupational scale than aspirations, although they are a step higher, on the average, than father's occupation.

TABLE 6.1

Summary of Regressions of Student's Occupational Aspirations and Plans on Father's Occupation, Based on Data of Stephenson (1957)

Item	Aspirations	Plans
Number reporting both aspirations (plans) and father's occupation	812	795
Mean, father's occupation (X)	3.12	3.16
Standard deviation, father's occupation	1.39	1.38
Mean aspirations (plans) (Y)	5.17	4.38
Standard deviation, aspirations (plans)	1.25	1.37
Regression slope, Y on X	.127	.366
Intercept	4.77	3.23
Correlation coefficient	.141	.37
Correlation ratio, Y on X	.154	.382

TABLE 6.2

Empey's Data on Occupational Aspiration, with Derived Statistics

Father's status (X)	Range of scores North-Hatt metric[a]	Range of scores Duncan metric[b]	Level of aspiration (Y)[c] "Preferred" N	"Preferred" Mean	"Anticipated" N	"Anticipated" Mean
10 (high)	88–96	92–96	6	7.83	6	7.83
9	83–87	84–91	12	7.92	8	8.36
8	79–85	74–87	52	7.63	42	7.26
7	77–81	68–80	57	7.26	41	7.32
6	72–76	53–68	174	6.61	132	6.45
5	67–71	37–50	97	6.87	69	6.46
4	58–68	19–40	184	6.47	129	5.99
3	54–60	15–22	115	6.25	87	5.70
2	44–52	7–13	56	6.07	45	5.69
1 (low)	33–46	3–8	11	5.36	6	4.50
–	–	–	764	–	565	–
Summary statistics						
Grand mean						
X			4.86	–	4.89	–
Y			–	6.65	–	6.32
Standard deviation, X			1.83	–	1.86	–
Regression, Y on X			.2329		.3114	
Intercept			5.52		4.80	

[a] Reiss and others (1961, Table II-9, pp. 54–57) *Occupations and Social Status.*

[b] Obtained from North-Hatt scores using transformation shown in the same work, Fig. 1, p. 119 (see also Appendix Table B-1 for comparison of Duncan socioeconomic index and North-Hatt metric).

[c] Source: Empey, (1956), data taken from Table 1 and unpublished listing of occupations

The patterns just noted are likewise present in another body of material. Table 6.2 reproduces data from Empey's study (1956) of occupational aspirations and shows the regression coefficients we computed from these data. Empey asked a sample of seniors in high schools in the state of Washington in 1954 to indicate their occupational aspirations, both in terms of the occupations they would "prefer" to engage in and the ones they actually "anticipated" they would hold. The students also reported their fathers' occupations.

In scaling both father's occupation and student's occupational aspiration, Empey coded occupations to one of ten status levels. These levels were derived by merging the results of the North-Hatt and Smith studies of occupational prestige. From Empey's unpublished listing of occupations in the ten levels, we have estimated score ranges expressed in terms of both the North-Hatt metric and the metric of Duncan's socioeconomic index (which was originally scaled to reproduce the percentage of "excellent" or "good" ratings received by an occupation in the North-Hatt study). Since Empey considered not only the North-Hatt scores but also Smith's ratings, there are some overlaps between ranges of the adjacent levels on his composite scale.

It will be noted that the Empey status levels do not represent equal intervals on either the North-Hatt or the Duncan scale, although this is not necessarily in its disfavor. The more significant question for our purposes is how statistics derived from his data may be compared with other data we are using.

We have no norms for aspiration data, and Empey does not provide distributions or variances of the aspiration scores in any event. We can, however, look at the distribution of fathers' occupations. The mean score of fathers' occupations on his scale is 4.86, which falls in the interval of 19–40 on the Duncan scale. The mean for all fathers in the OCG data is 26.8, while the mean for fathers of men who completed the twelfth grade is 33.8. Although the comparison is necessarily crude, there is no evidence of serious disagreement with the OCG results. One standard deviation below the mean on Empey's scale corresponds roughly to a score of 18 on the Duncan scale and one standard deviation above the mean to about 69. Hence, in this portion of the scale the standard deviation is equivalent to about 20 points on the Duncan scale. In the OCG sample, the standard deviation for all fathers was 21.5 and for fathers of high school graduates, 23.6. We may conclude that Empey's distribution is sufficiently similar to the implied OCG distribution to warrant rough comparisons.

The main statistics of interest are the two regression coefficients. "Preferred" level of aspiration on father's occupation has a slope of .23, "anticipated" level of aspiration a slope of .31. When the means in Table 6.2 are plotted, they lie close to the regression line and show no systematic departure from it. Hence, we infer that a linear regression coefficient is a good summary of the average relationship of level of aspiration to level of origin.

For comparison, we may cite the regression of respondent's actual occupational status on father's occupational status for all men in the OCG sample reporting that their educational attainment was 4 years of high school or more. This coefficient is (computed somewhat roughly as) .325. We may now array the three coefficients:

> "Preferred" aspiration   .23
> "Anticipated" aspiration   .31
> Actual (OCG)   .325

Granted the imperfect comparability of Empey's data with the OCG statistics, the correspondence between "anticipated" slope of respondent's on father's status and the actual slope, is quite remarkable. Evidently, there was more realism in the "anticipations" than in the "preferences."

These results, of course, do not imply that each student anticipated his occupation correctly. Instead, the import is that the aggregate of students implicitly understands fairly accurately the prevailing degree of relationship between origin and achievement.

It is unfortunate that we are unable to study the correlation coefficients for lack of data on the dispersion of the aspirations. One might guess that the standard deviations of the two kinds of aspirations are somewhat less than that of the actual occupations these students were fated to follow. In this case, the correlation between aspiration and father's occupation need not be the same as that between actual occupation and father's occupation, which for the high school graduate segment of the OCG sample comes out at .31. If, as is conjectured here, the standard deviation of aspirations is less than the standard deviation of actual achieved statuses, then the correlation between origin and aspiration would be somewhat higher than .3.

One other comparison between aspiration and reality is instructive. As Table 6.2 shows, the mean of the aspired occupations is rather higher than the mean of social origins. Since there is a net balance of upward mobility in American society, the direction of the discrepancy is realistic. Its magnitude, however, may be exaggerated. The difference between "preferred" occupation and level of origin amounts to 98 percent of one standard deviation of the distribution of origins, and the difference between "anticipated" occupation and level of origin is as great as 77 percent of one standard deviation of the origin distribution. The OCG data show a somewhat more moderate amount of net upward mobility for men who were high school graduates: 58 percent of one standard deviation of the distribution by father's occupational status.

If the OCG experience is prognostic of the outcome for the Washington seniors studied by Empey, a considerable number of the latter are likely to fall short of their aspirations, even though the majority will undergo intergenerational upward mobility. We see that a considerable amount of net upward mobility in a society does not guarantee that the prevailing levels of aspiration will be realized. Indeed, we might speculate that the prevalence of upward mobility tends to generate unrealistic aspirations and, perhaps indirectly, disappointment at failure to realize them.

One other significant set of information on the topic of this section is Turner's (1964) data on occupational aspirations of male high school seniors in selected schools in the Los Angeles area. Both parental occupations and the boys' anticipations of their "life work" were coded in terms of a 9-point scale intended to represent steps on a "prestige-subcultural" dimension of occupational standing. Turner presents (Table 9, p. 50) the median "aspiration" or "occupational ambition" of boys for each category of parental occupation. If this set of medians is assumed to be a set of *means*, we can compute the regression of aspiration on parental occupation, .4695. In Table 5 (p. 36) Turner shows the marginal frequency distributions of aspirations and parental occupations. From these we can compute the mean aspiration score as 5.8 with standard deviation 2.10 and the mean parental occupation score as 4.4 with standard deviation 2.20. Using the ratio of the two standard deviations, we can obtain from the regression slope the correlation between aspiration and parental occupation, which works out to be .491.

The regression of occupational ambition on background is considerably higher in Turner's data than in the data reported by Empey and Stephenson. It is difficult to be sure, however, whether this is due to the way in which the question was asked, the method of scoring occupations, or real differences in the populations under study. Turner (1964, p. 35) was quite explicit that his intention in wording the question on "life work" was to "lessen fantasy and wishful responses." Conceivably, he was simply more successful in this aim than was Empey in asking for "anticipated" occupation or Stephenson in inquiring about "occupational plans."

6.2 Measurement of Plans

In many studies of educational opportunity, high school students are asked in their last year of attendance to state whether they plan to go to college. Such information on "college plans" often has to serve as a surrogate for actual data on post-high-school educational attainment. The available evidence seems to indicate that "college plans" are a somewhat reliable indicator of actual college attendance, but it is obviously desirable to have the actual data on educational attainment in such form that it can be related to ability, family and community background, and like factors. Hence, the WISC data on which Sewell has been reporting are an exceptionally valuable resource. A statewide sample of high school seniors whose plans were ascertained in 1957 were followed up to

1964, at which time their subsequent educational attainment was ascertained. The relevant data for present purposes include measures of the student's family's socioeconomic status, the student's intelligence, his statement in 1957 of plans to go to college, and the actual amount of education completed by 1964 (Sewell & Shah, 1967). Aside from establishing the degree of reliability of statements of college plans, the Sewell study permits analysis of how background factors condition the decision to attend and thereby actual attendance.

For males and females, respectively, college plans correlate .67 and .78 with college attendance, .56 and .58 with college graduation, and .69 and .76 with total educational achievement. Thus plans are by no means a perfect predictor of actual outcome, while the authors' analysis suggests that background factors, in addition to their influence on the student's plan to attend college (as reported), also directly affect educational attainment. This interpretation is conveyed by the diagrams labeled "a" in Fig. 6.1.

The purpose of this discussion is to explore an alternative interpretation of the same data. This alternative interpretation hinges upon the introduction into the causal scheme of a hypothetical variable termed "latent decision." The argument for such a variable is twofold. First, the student's report on college plans may be somewhat unreliable in the sense that for some fraction of students the investigator would have obtained a different report if he had asked the question, say, on Thursday rather than on Monday. It should be noted that in Sewell's data, "College Plans" is the response to a specific question on intentions, in contrast to the somewhat more ambiguous question on "Educational Aspirations" which is sometimes asked in similar surveys. It should, therefore, have higher reliability than the latter. Second, and more important, the actual decision to attend college need not be made at some fixed point in time but can be postponed or accelerated. Moreover, at any given point, some students will not really know their own mind (a familiar example is the "undecided" column in straw vote investigations). We will, in effect, assume that a "true" decision has implicitly been reached by the student at the time he is interrogated about his plans—though not necessarily an irrevocable decision. The calculations we shall offer on this assumption take the diagrams labeled "b" in Fig. 6.1 as the causal model.

The essential property of this model is that the "latent decision," symbolized by X_a, is taken to reflect the background variables (socioeconomic status and intelligence) as fully as one can consistently assume on the basis of the data. The first assumption explored, in fact, was that background affects attainment *only* by way of the "latent decision" to go to college. On this assumption, in model b both p_{61} and p_{62} would be 0. The data do not permit this assumption. However, it is possible to set one of these paths equal to zero while allowing the other to take on whatever value is indicated by the data.

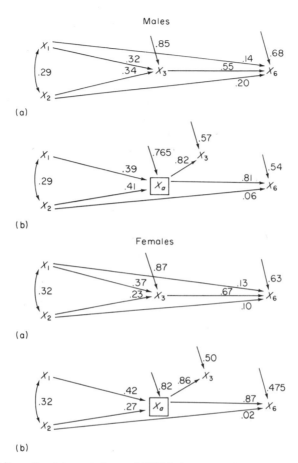

Fig. 6.1. Alternative interpretations of WISC data on college plans. (Variables: X_1 is socioeconomic status, X_2 is measured intelligence, X_3 is college plans, X_6 is educational attainment, and X_a is hypothetical variable, "latent decision.")

While either p_{61} or p_{62} might be treated in this fashion, the interpretation seems easier to maintain with $p_{61} = 0$ as in model b.

Comparison of model a with model b for either males or females indicates the following features of the alternative interpretation. College plans as reported are indeed a fallible indicator of "latent decision." The coefficient p_{3a} is .82 for males and .86 for females. If we were to assume that the only reason for an imperfect correlation between "latent decision" and reported college plans is response unreliability of the latter, we could compute as the reliability coefficient (in the sense of a test-retest correlation) $p_{3a}^2 = .67$ for males and .74 for females. Interpreted as strict reliability coefficients, these are distressingly low. However, our interpretation would be that in addition to sheer response unreliability, the relationship between "latent decision" and college plans is attenuated by lack of crystallization of the latter.

A second observation is that the relative importance of factors in the decision is not altered by replacing X_3 in model a with X_a in model b. For males in both models, intelligence has a just slightly larger influence than socioeconomic status, while the reverse is true for females. In this respect, as in several others, the alternative interpretation requires no revision of conclusions reached by Sewell and Shah.

In model b, the effect of "latent decision" on actual attainment, as measured by p_{6a}, is much greater than the effect of college plans on attainment in model a, as given by p_{63}. By the same token, the residual variation in education attainment is much less in model b than in model a (see the comparisons in Table 6.3). The reader should be neither beguiled nor alarmed by the increases in the

TABLE 6.3

Coefficients of Determination for Models a and b

Model and coefficient	Males	Females
Model a		
$R^2_{6(321)}$	.53	.60
$R^2_{3(21)}$	.28	.24
Model b		
$R^2_{6(a2)}$	.71	.77
$R^2_{a(21)}$	.41	.32

coefficients of determination achieved by adopting model b as an alternative to model a. Even assuming that the construct of "latent decision" correctly represents the function of a fully crystallized plan for further education, the fact that for males 29 percent and for females 23 percent of the variation in attainment remains unexplained is to be understood as allowing a considerable role for contingent factors to come into play after the decision is taken.

Perhaps the most interesting result of the alternative model is that it requires a "sleeper effect" of intelligence to account for the correlation of attainment with background. While small, this effect is not negligible for males. Even for females, the significant point is that the "sleeper effect" for intelligence appears despite the fact that socioeconomic status is more highly correlated with attainment than is intelligence, contrary to the case for males.

This result is, of course, implicit in the diagram used by Sewell and Shah since $p_{62}/p_{61} > p_{32}/p_{31}$ for both males and females. Again, there is no inconsistency between the two models, but model b is useful in bringing out a point that might otherwise have been overlooked. The contrast between the two models, therefore, may serve "to illustrate the process of exploring different points of view which is one of the most useful features of path analysis" (Wright, 1960b, p. 445).

Note on the solution. While model a is merely a recursive regression system, the asymmetrical character of model b requires a somewhat roundabout method of solution. The relevant equations are written out as follows.

Known correlations in terms of unknown path coefficients and correlations are

$$r_{12} \text{ is given} \tag{1}$$

$$r_{13} = p_{3a} r_{a1} \tag{2}$$

$$r_{23} = p_{3a} r_{a2} \tag{3}$$

$$r_{16} = p_{6a} r_{a1} + p_{62} r_{12} \tag{4}$$

$$r_{26} = p_{6a} r_{a2} + p_{62} \tag{5}$$

$$r_{36} = p_{6a} r_{3a} + p_{62} r_{32}. \tag{6}$$

Unknown correlations are

$$r_{a1} = p_{a1} + p_{a2} r_{12} \tag{7}$$

$$r_{a2} = p_{a1} r_{12} + p_{a2} \tag{8}$$

$$r_{a3} = p_{3a} \tag{9}$$

$$r_{a6} = p_{6a} + p_{62} r_{2a}. \tag{10}$$

The solution routine from [4] and [5] is

$$p_{62} = \frac{r_{26} r_{a1} - r_{16} r_{a2}}{r_{a1} - r_{12} r_{a2}}.$$

Substituting $r_{a1} = r_{13}/p_{3a}$ and $r_{a2} = r_{23}/p_{3a}$ from [2] and [3], we obtain

$$p_{62} = \frac{r_{26} r_{13} - r_{16} r_{23}}{r_{13} - r_{12} r_{23}}.$$

Inserting the solution for p_{62} into [4], [5], and [6], we obtain expression of the form

$$p_{6a} r_{a1} = K_1, \quad p_{6a} r_{a2} = K_2, \quad \text{and} \quad p_{6a} r_{3a} = K_3,$$

where K_1, K_2, and K_3 are now known numbers. Straightforward substitutions in [2] through [6] yield solutions for p_{3a}, p_{6a}, r_{a1} and r_{a2}, whence simultaneous solution of [7] and [8] yields p_{a1} and p_{a2}, while [10] gives r_{a6}. The residual paths are computed in the usual manner; for example, for X_a the residual is

$$\sqrt{1 - p_{a1} r_{a1} - p_{a2} r_{a2}} \, .$$

6.3 Measurement of Motivation

For nearly two decades, psychologists and social psychologists have utilized the construct of achievement motivation as both a dependent and an independent variable. In studies of the former approach, achievement-related motivation was viewed as the product of specific child-rearing practices within various socioeconomic categories or as a net resolution of family authority or power relations within the motivational dispositions of children. Investigations which followed the effects of achievement motivation back into the social structure typically involved dependent variables like educational performance or occupational attainment.

In 1962, Harry J. Crockett published his often-cited article which associated achievement motivation with differential occupational mobility (intergenerational) by social class. He hypothesized that the strength of achievement motivation would correlate positively with upward mobility and negatively with downward mobility. Later the substance of his article will be elaborated and assessed. For the moment, however, let us consider the theoretical connection between achievement motivation and its specific behavioral manifestation, that is, occupational mobility.

Atkinson's (1957) theory of achievement motivation provides the theoretical connection. According to the theory, achievement motivation is the product of (1) a basic motive to achieve at tasks involving evaluations of successes or failures (M); (2) the incentive value of the task, that is, its prestige value as perceived by the actor (I); and (3) the complement of incentive value, the subjective probability of success at the task (P). Symbolically expressed, achievement motivation $= (M) \times (I) \times (P)$, where $I = 1 - P$. This representation allows the level of achievement motivation to vary with specific tasks and situations (through factors I and P), as well as with motive strength differentials. The optimal situation for all strengths of M obtains when $P = .50$ and where, by substitution, $I = .50$ as well. Hence for moderately difficult tasks with moderate attraction and a constant motive strength, manifest motivation is maximized.

In speaking of real-life situations which may call out behavioral expression of the achievement motive, Atkinson notes that the occupational structure (seen as a prestige ladder) closely approximates a series of increasingly difficult tasks to perform; in fact, it is similar to a ring-toss game. A person relatively high in the motive to achieve (M) should optimize the incentive value and the probability of success by choosing an occupation of moderate difficulty ($P =$

.50) with respect to his subjective assessment of the occupational structure and his own abilities. Supposedly, persons with higher levels of M are more circumspect about their aspirations than are those lower on this motive and/or higher in fear of failure. At any rate, the achievement motive entails needs to succeed at tasks involving personal evaluation. Such seems to be the situation with occupational choice and advancement.

Crockett's article (1962) based its theory on Atkinson's model. The data came from the Survey Research Center (SRC) of The University of Michigan Project 422 (Modern Living Study) conducted by Gerald Gurin, Joseph Veroff, and Sheila C. Feld in March 1957. The 2460 original respondents comprised a national probability sample of persons 21 years of age or older residing in private households in the United States. As part of the psychodynamic assessment of the sample, TAT protocols were gathered from a random subsample, of which 715 were males; all protocols were scored for achievement (n Ach), affiliation (n Affil), and power (n Power). Crockett eliminated 118 from the 715 males because of inadequate responses, leaving 597 potential respondents. Further deletions included 193 with farm background or residence, 23 unascertained father's occupations, 2 unascertained respondent's occupations, and 11 student respondents, leaving a total $N = 368$. In our analysis of Crockett's data, an additional case had to be dropped because of wild punches on the data card. Our initial working N for Crockett's data was 367.

Crockett and two colleagues coded the occupational responses according to the 1947 North-Hatt prestige scores, reporting intercoder reliability of 80 percent and a correlation of prestige scores of $r = .85$. For analytic purposes, Crockett created four occupational prestige categories based on father's occupation: high (N-H 78–93), upper middle (N-H 69–77), lower middle (N-H 61–68) and low (N-H 33–60). Relating n Ach score on the TAT measure to the percentage of respondents above and below their respective father's occupational score within each of the four prestige categories, Crockett reported that only for the lower middle and low categories was n Ach significantly related to intergenerational upward mobility; in no category did n Ach relate to downward mobility. Similar associations were constructed for n Affil and n Power (scored from the same TAT data). In both cases Crockett concluded that n Ach is the better specific motive for the explanation of occupational mobility, and that the relationship between n Ach and mobility cannot be explained on the basis of a strong, general motivation factor.

Crockett's discussion of his findings pointed to the "sociological naivete" of Atkinson's mobility thesis. Since individuals coming from higher prestige backgrounds (father's occupation) are more likely to attend college or attain specialized training which facilitates upward mobility than are persons from lower status backgrounds, one's upward mobility from middle and upper middle statuses depends *less* on one's psychological traits (n Ach) than does

TABLE 6.4

Frequency Distributions of Respondents' and Fathers' Occupational Statuses, SRC Data Used by Crockett

Occupational status		Whole data		Located data		Not located		After recode (located data only)	
SES code intervals	North-Hatt	Respondent	Father	Respondent	Father	Respondent	Father	Respondent	Father
90+	87–89	8	11	6	9	2	2	8	9
85–89	84–86	12	8	8	5	4	3	2	2
80–84	81–83	22	6	18	6	4	0	17	4
75–79	80	3	1	3	1	0	0	9	5
70–74	78–79	14	5	9	4	5	1	9	9
65–69	76–77	14	6	13	5	1	1	16	10
60–64	74–75	0	0	0	0	0	0	19	21
55–59	73	29	14	26	10	3	4	6	7
50–54	71–72	7	2	7	2	0	0	22	25
45–49	70	0	0	0	0	0	0	16	15
40–44	68–69	129	176	110	152	19	24	28	14
35–39	67	0	0	0	0	0	0	18	25
30–34	64–66	6	5	5	4	1	1	24	24
25–29	62–63	21	9	19	7	2	2	12	15
20–24	59–61	44	47	38	43	6	4	20	21
15–19	54–58	13	14	11	11	2	3	57	63
10–14	49–53	24	22	24	18	0	4	15	15
5–9	38–48	20	41	16	37	4	4	13	14
0–4	20–37	1	0	1	0	0	0	3	16
		367	367	314	314	53	53	314	314

one's upward mobility from lower middle and low statuses. Lacking the sociological advantages of higher strata, the lower strata depend more on their psychology for occupational mobility.

Crockett's thesis at once appealed to our search for psychological components which aid in the transmission of occupational status from one generation to the next. Having secured his data, we ran some preliminary frequency distributions to compare with the OCG sample. The peculiar shape of Crockett's occupational distribution (see Table 6.4, "whole data"), which displayed a prominent overrepresentation in the North-Hatt interval 68–69, provoked two questions: (1) Was the strange distribution of occupations a product of the elimination of cases from the subsample? (2) Was it the product of faulty coding procedures?

To answer these questions, we procured the interview schedules from the Survey Research Center (SRC) storage. Unfortunately, 14 percent of the original Crockett set could not be located, leaving a working $N = 314$. Tables 6.4 and 6.5 summarize the comparison of the located data with the whole set. By inspection one sees a roughly analogous distribution of fathers' and sons' occupations in Table 6.4, while the means and standard deviations of occupational and educational variables in Table 6.5 match closely. On the basis of these comparisons, and in the face of necessity, we used the located set as a representation of Crockett's data.

Proceeding to recode the two occupational items on each schedule, we utilized a modified form of the United States Census coding procedures for occupations. Whereas the Census specifies a fourfold class-of-worker scheme, we collapsed this into a simple dichotomy: self-employed or not self-employed. Apart from this slight change, we followed the Census conventions of using a three-digit code for industry and a three-digit code for occupation. Thus we encoded each response into seven digits and assigned the specific codes for each Census line as listed in the 1960 edition of the *Alphabetical Index of Occupations and Industries.*

Such a coding procedure enabled us to assign Duncan status scores to all occupation titles since a score exists for all Census lines. This technique of using the Census as the basic coding device enlarged the pool of titles to which scores could be assigned directly, rather than through the process of interpolation between titles (as would have been the case had we duplicated Crockett's use of the 90 titles on the North-Hatt list). In addition we translated the derived SES codes into their North-Hatt equivalents, as these are defined by the S-shaped curve reported elsewhere (Reiss, 1961, p. 119). (We also converted Crockett's own North-Hatt codes to the Duncan SES metric, using this same curve.) Finally, to each Census title was attached a 1965 NORC prestige code (Siegel, 1970).

The recoding operations were conducted by personnel of the Population

TABLE 6.5

Means and Standard Deviations of Occupational and Educational Variables

	SRC								OCG^a			
	Respondent				Father				Respondent		Father	
	Whole data		Located data		Whole data		Located data					
Variable	Mean	SD	Mean	SD	Mean	SD	Mean	SD	Mean	SD	Mean	SD
Crockett's coding into 1947 North-Hatt scores	6.74	10.0	67.0	10.0	65.1	9.7	64.8	9.7	–	–	–	–
Transformation of Crockett's coding into Duncan SES metric	42.7	22.7	41.8	22.2	37.3	20.5	36.7	20.2	–	–	–	–
PSC coding into Census and transformation to Duncan SES metric	–	–	41.0	23.8	–	–	36.2	23.1	40.1	24.7	33.1	22.8
PSC coding into Census and transformation to 1965 NORC scores	–	–	40.6	14.6	–	–	39.8	14.5	–	1.7	–	–
Education	4.8	1.5	4.7	1.5	–	–	–	–	4.7	1.7	–	–

^{a} Nonfarm background males, ages 20–64.

Studies Center (PSC) of The University of Michigan. In total, 6 persons were involved in the process, but the great majority of the task was done by just 3 persons. An attempt to evaluate intercoder agreement on assignments indicated a figure of about 85 percent.

Recoding allowed for the following comparisons: (1) We compared Crockett's distribution of occupational SES scores (vis-à-vis his coding procedures) with our distribution of SES scores (vis-à-vis the PSC coding). This comparison helps answer the question of whether the peculiarly shaped occupational distribution of Crockett's sample is a result of his elimination of cases or of his

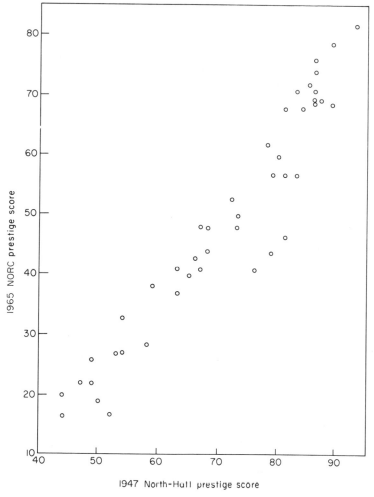

Fig. 6.2. Scatter plot of 1965 NORC on 1947 North-Hatt scores for 44 matching titles.

coding procedures. We have held constant the occupational metric of both coding tasks to examine the effects of independent coding. (2) Analogously, we compared the coding procedures holding constant the prestige metric. While the 1947 North-Hatt and the 1965 NORC metrics are not identical, Fig. 6.2 indicates that the differences are not so great as to jeopardize our comparison. (3) Not without some slippage, we compared the redistribution of occupational scores with the OCG distributions for nonfarm white males ages 20–64 in 1962. This latter comparison speaks directly to the question of the representativeness of Crockett's sample.

Considering the last-mentioned comparison, one finds in Table 6.4 the redistribution of fathers and sons after recoding their occupations (last two columns); the array is more evenly distributed over all SES intervals. Table 6.5 shows that the mean respondents' occupational SES scores for the located Crockett data and the OCG data as 41.0 and 40.1, with standard deviations 23.8 and 24.7, respectively. For fathers, the Crockett data indicate a mean of 36.2 and a standard deviation of 23.1; the OCG equivalents are 33.1 and 22.8.

From these data we conclude that Crockett's elimination of cases from his sample did not appreciably bias the shape of his occupational distributions. Still, why should Crockett have over 200 more fathers and sons in the North-Hatt interval 68–69 than were there after recoding? Whereas Crockett placed 110 respondents and 152 fathers (located data) in the North-Hatt interval 68–69, upon recoding we assigned only 28 respondents and 14 fathers to this interval (see Table 6.4). Table 6.6 shows the redistribution of Crockett's cases which were coded 68 or 69 by him. Only 6 respondents and 8 fathers remained, while the others more or less randomly entered different intervals. Apparently, something rather peculiar occurred in Crockett's coding process.

One possible source of difficulty which Crockett could have encountered was the sheer ambiguity of the responses on the interview schedules. To test this possibility, we classified all responses to occupational items with respect to degree of ambiguity, the latter being determined by the relative amount of information transmitted and the subsequent ability to assign a specific SES code. Three categories were created:

Essentially no ambiguity (regarding SES code assignment)
Appreciable ambiguity
Essentially arbitrary decision required

Table 6.7 indicates that among the located schedules from Crockett's data, about 90 percent of respondents' and 80 percent of fathers' occupational items are codable into SES scores with little ambiguity; nearly 5 percent of respondents' and 10 percent of fathers' items can be scored with appreciable ambiguity, leaving just 5 percent of the respondents' and 10 percent of father's items to be assigned SES scores by some mechanical, arbitrary means. Hence there appears to be no more than a tolerable level of intrinsic ambiguity in the interview data.

TABLE 6.6

Redistribution of Crockett's North-Hatt Codes 68–69 (Located Schedules Only)

Occupational SES intervals	Respondent			Father		
	Total	Code 68	Code 69	Total	Code 68	Code 69
90+	0	0	0	0	0	0
85–89	0	0	0	0	0	0
80–84	1	0	1	1	0	1
75–79	3	1	2	0	0	0
70–74	5	2	3	3	0	3
65–69	6	3	3	5	4	1
60–64	7	2	5	16	2	14
55–59	5	2	3	6	2	4
50–54	8	4	4	10	0	10
45–49	9	8	1	13	8	5
40–44	6	3	3	8	6	2
35–39	8	6	2	14	6	8
30–34	14	14	0	19	13	6
25–29	8	8	0	11	11	0
20–24	5	4	1	7	6	1
15–19	23	21	2	32	30	2
10–14	0	0	0	7	5	2
5–9	2	1	1	0	0	0
0–4	0	0	0	0	0	0
	110	79	31	152	93	59

TABLE 6.7

Distribution of Occupational Response Items in Table 6.6 by Estimated Ambiguity

Degree of ambiguity	Respondent			Father		
	Total	Code 68	Code 69	Total	Code 68	Code 69
Essentially no ambiguity (regarding SES code)	100	70	30	129	81	48
Appreciable ambiguity	5	4	1	10	8	2
Essentially arbitrary decision required	5	5	0	13	4	9
	110	79	31	152	93	59

Another possible source of error might have been scoring procedures by coders. However, Crockett reports an intercoder reliability of about 80 percent in the assignment of North-Hatt scores by 3 sociologists.

Having eliminated sampling, ambiguity, and personal biases as major contributing factors to the sharply peaked occupational distribution in Crockett's data, we suggest that this result may have issued from Crockett's coding manual and from the code itself. The North-Hatt list contains just 90 titles, leaving gaping holes in the occupational structure in which subjective (and often quite arbitrary) placements increase error. While the conventions which coders employ to score nonmatching titles may or may not be specified, surely the Census occupation-industry codes and procedures require and provide more information than the North-Hatt scheme (North-Hatt scoring requires one piece of information while the Census considers three: class of worker, industry, occupation). Clearly, however, the Duncan occupational SES score equivalents to Census lines were not available for Crockett's use. Had they been available and utilized, and given the change in the occupational distributions which were noted, one might ask if any substantive changes would be required in Crockett's thesis about the role of the three motives (n Ach, n Affil, n Power) in intergenerational mobility.

Table 6.8 provides insight into the effects of recoding on the size of zero-order correlation coefficients between mobility variables. Notice that a comparison of variables C_3 and P_{10} as well as of C_4 and P_{11} allows for an assessment of our recoding procedures of sons' and fathers' occupations. Variables C_3 and C_4 take Crockett's coding and transform his assigned North-Hatt scores to the metric of occupational SES codes; variables P_{10} and P_{11} result from our coding of questionnaire items into the Census classification and the transformation of these into equivalent SES codes. Thus the same metric applies across all four variables (C_3, C_4, P_{10}, P_{11}), and any differences in correlations using variable C_3 rather than P_{10}, or C_4 rather than P_{11}, with a second variable are due to the effects of the coding methods employed. Likewise a comparison of variables C_1 and P_{12} as well as C_2 and P_{13} illustrates the coding effect, holding a prestige metric constant (North-Hatt and 1965 NORC).

The correlations between variables C_3 and P_{10} (.64) and C_4 and P_{11} (.62) measure a kind of "intermethod reliability" for sons' and fathers' occupational items. The slightly lower "reliability" with responses to fathers' occupations may mark greater arbitrariness in the assignment of codes. While the difference in the magnitude of correlations is slight indeed, greater ambiguity was noted in responses to fathers' occupation items than to sons' (see Table 6.7). The rather low magnitude of intermethod reliability (holding SES metric constant) does reflect the differences in coding procedures and the nature of the coding schemes as outlined previously. In this connection, see McTavish (1964).

With respect to the intergenerational correlation of occupations of father and son, recoding shows little difference: $r_{3,4} = .284$ and $r_{10,11} = .282$. Other zero-order correlations are affected, however. The correlation of respondent's

TABLE 6.8

Zero-Order Correlation Matrix for 314 Located Schedules

Variable[a]	Variable (see stub)												
	C_1	C_2	C_3	C_4	C_5	C_6	C_7	C_8	P_9	P_{10}	P_{11}	P_{12}	P_{13}
Crockett coding (C)													
C_1 R's occupation (North-Hatt prestige)	—	.250	.972	.264	.367	.097	.105	−.047	.382	.629	.224	.681	.167
C_2 Father's occupation (North-Hatt)		—	.268	.963	.206	.083	.056	−.022	.218	.209	.609	.230	.643
C_3 R's North-Hatt to Duncan metric			—	.284	.383	.107	.099	−.053	.401	.637	.257	.683	.185
C_4 Father's North-Hatt to Duncan metric				—	.208	.085	.042	−.013	.220	.235	.615	.267	.651
C_5 R's Education					—	−.001	−.009	−.134	.977	.529	.322	.450	.194
C_6 R's n Achievement						—	−.057	.020	.001	.122	−.044	.115	−.047
C_7 R's n Affiliation							—	−.088	.014	.063	.029	.094	−.000
C_8 R's n Power								—	−.123	−.022	−.005	.026	.003
PSC coding (P)													
P_9 R's education (OCG intervals)									—	.523	.321	.462	.189
P_{10} R's occupation SES (Duncan metric)									.60[b]	—	.282	.835	.191
P_{11} Father's occupation SES (Duncan metric)									.41[b]	.37[b]	—	.255	.824
P_{12} R's occupation (1965 NORC prestige)												—	.174
P_{13} Father's occupation (1965 NORC prestige)													—

[a] In the body of the text, variables will be denoted by coding and number (for example, C_2, P_{10}); correlations and paths denoted only by number (for example, $r_{1,10}$, p_{56}).

[b] OCG nonfarm age 20–64.

occupational SES with his education (recoded from Crockett to conform to categories compatible with our other research) change from .401 ($r_{3,9}$) to .523 ($r_{10,9}$). Father's occupational SES correlates with sons' education at .220 ($r_{4,9}$) and at .321 ($r_{11,9}$).

These changes in the size of zero-order correlations are attributable in part to the greater variability in the occupational distributions under our coding scheme than under Crockett's. Thus recoding raises the correlation of occupational SES with variables like education and the achievement motive (n Ach); the correlations of occupational variables remain about the same.

Rather than a comparison of zero-order correlations, a better answer to the question about substantive changes in Crockett's thesis is provided by path analysis and path diagrams. Figures 6.3–6.6 illustrate one interpretation of the causal influences on R's occupational status. On the interpretation represented by these path diagrams, son's occupational status (SES) depends directly upon father's occupation, son's education, and his n Ach and indirectly upon each of the latter (taken singly) through each of the remaining two independent variables. Finally, a residual with coefficient u affects the value of respondent's SES, but the model assumes the residual to be statistically uncorrelated with the influences of the three major independent variables.

In Figs. 6.3 and 6.5 the path coefficients derived from the calculations based on the transformation of Crockett's North-Hatt codes into the occupational SES metric (Fig. 6.3) and on our recoding into the Census scheme and the occupational SES equivalents are compared. The multiple R^2 in Fig. 6.4 (.310) indicates that recoding Crockett's data actually allows greater prediction of respondent's occupational SES than Fig. 6.3 ($R^2 = .198$); recoding increases the explained variance in respondent's SES by 11 percent. Although the relative importance of the three independent variables does not change in the process of recoding, the absolute sizes of the path coefficients are noticeably different. In fact the effect of respondent's n Ach increases from .090 to .128, while the influence of father's occupational status declines to virtually the same value (from .206 to .131). Education remains the most important factor in the diagram. The increment in the relative effects of n Ach in the process of status attainment as illustrated in the diagrams can be attributed to the slightly negative correlation between father's occupation and son's n Ach in Fig. 6.4. In Fig. 6.3, $r_{4,6}$ is equally small in magnitude but positive in sign.

Figures 6.5 and 6.6 also illustrate the effects of recoding but they employ the 1965 NORC prestige metric. Parallel results ensue as one moves from Fig. 6.5 (Crockett's coding) to Fig. 6.6 (PSC coding). Again R^2 increases over the two figures, while the relative effects of n Ach surpass those of father's occupational status in Fig. 6.6.

These two sets of figures demonstrate the differences which recoding (or two different coding schemes) introduce in causal diagrams of status attain-

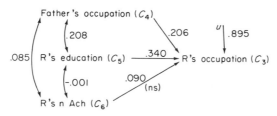

Fig. 6.3. Crockett coding transformed into Duncan occupational SES metric. $R = .445$; $R^2 = .198$.

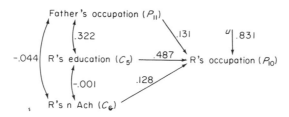

Fig. 6.4. PSC coding into Census and occupational SES metric. $R = .557$; $R^2 = .310$.

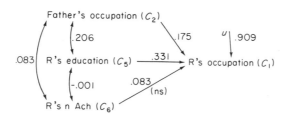

Fig. 6.5. Crockett coding using 1947 North-Hatt prestige metric. $R = .416$; $R^2 = .173$.

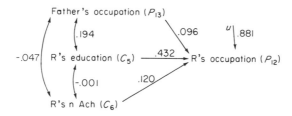

Fig. 6.6. PSC coding into Census and 1965 NORC prestige metric. $R = .474$; $R^2 = .225$.

ment. In fact, our coding scheme increased the importance of n Ach in the process of occupational attainment above the level of importance which Crockett's data (with his coding) could produce. With this in mind we investigated the relative importance of each of the motives in Crockett's study (n Power, n Affil, and n Ach) as they relate to respondent's education and his current occupational status.

Figures 6.7 and 6.8 reveal the differences in causal diagrams which derive from the two methods of coding occupations. Figure 6.7 illustrates the model via a transformation of Crockett's North-Hatt coding into the Duncan SES metric equivalents; Fig. 6.8 shows the process as an outcome of PSC coding in the Duncan metric. The essence of these two figures is that different causal inferences are made as a result of recoding Crockett's data.

While the comparable path coefficients with respect to respondent's education remain the same over the two figures, the paths to his occupational SES contain an ironic finding. If Crockett had employed both the Duncan SES metric and a causal model like these path diagrams, he would have reached different conclusions about the relative importance of the three motives as influences on mobility.

In Fig. 6.7 the paths p_{37} (.099) and p_{36} (.096) denote the *same* relative effect on respondent's occupational SES for his n Affil (C_7) as for his n Ach (C_6). Crockett states that n Ach plays the larger role in mobility and then only in the lower strata of the occupational structure (where the positive effect of father's status is less great). The need for power (n Power) contributes virtually no effect in Fig. 6.7 (p_{38}). Son's education (C_5) and father's occupational status (C_4) are the strong variables in this model ($p_{35} = .343$ and $p_{34} = .200$).

Figure 6.8 (with PSC coding) supports Crockett's conclusions about the greater importance of n Ach over n Affil in occupational mobility. In fact, $p_{10,7}$ and $p_{10,8}$ fail to achieve significance (twice the standard error by convention), illustrating the lesser importance of n Affil (C_7) and n Power (C_8), respectively. The need for achievement (C_6) slightly exceeds father's occupational SES (P_{11}) in influencing son's current occupational status (P_{10}) with $p_{10,6} = .131$ and $p_{10,11} = .126$ while son's education (C_5) clearly remains the dominant variable in the model ($p_{10,5} = .496$). With respect to respondent's education and his SES as dependent variables, the multiple R^2's in Fig. 6.8 are greater than in Fig. 6.7:

$$R^2_{5(4,6,7,8)} = .062 < R^2_{5(6,7,8,11)} = .122$$

and

$$R^2_{3(4,5,6,7,8)} = .208 < R^2_{10(5,6,7,8,11)} = .318.$$

Thus 6 percent more variance in education and 12 percent more variance in son's SES is explained in Fig. 6.8 than in Fig. 6.7. These increases in explained variance accrue as error is reduced (residual paths w reduced from .969 to .937 and u from .890 to .826).

Paradoxically, Crockett may have been correct about the significance of n Ach for occupational mobility. However, if he had employed a causal model

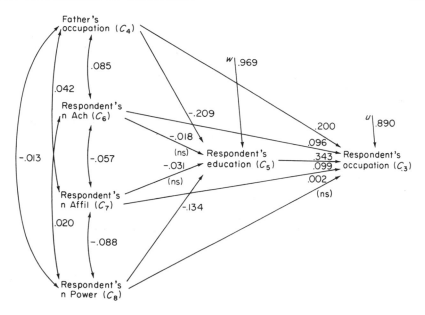

Fig. 6.7. Crockett coding transformed into Duncan occupational SES metric. $R_{5(4678)} =$ .248 and $R^2 = .062$. $R_{3(45678)} = .456$ and $R^2 = .208$.

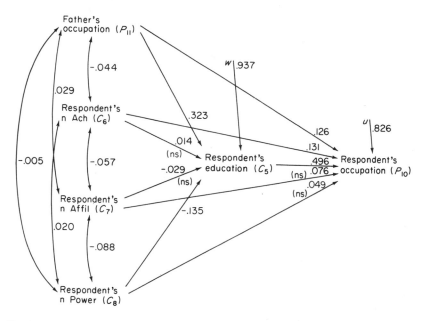

Fig. 6.8. PSC coding transformed into Census and occupational SES metric. $R_{5(678, 11)} =$ .350 and $R^2 = .122$. $R_{10(5678, 11)} = .564$ and $R^2 = .318$.

with *his* coded data (as in Fig. 6.7), his conclusions about the salience of the motivations for affiliation and achievement would have been obscured. Recoding the occupational data (as described previously) enhances the role of a motive component (n Ach) in explaining the process of mobility.

Of course, this conclusion depends on the acceptance of the particular causal scheme of Figs. 6.7 and 6.8. This scheme appears to be as close as one can get to a path diagram conforming to the way in which Crockett originally looked at the problem. There are, however, alternative points of view. For example, given that respondent's current occupation is measured contemporaneously with the projective indicators of motivation, a strong rival hypothesis is that occupational achievement causes motivation (as measured) rather than vice versa.

In conclusion, the method which is employed to code occupations may reshape the inferences (both correlational and causal) drawn from research. This effect is independent of intercoder "reliability" within the method used and of the basic metric of the scoring system used in recoding (although both of the latter can and do influence results in their own right). In applying this observation to a substantial subset of Crockett's motive and mobility data, it was found that his conclusions regarding the role of n Ach in the transmission of status intergenerationally were essentially supported. The latter affirmation holds only when Crockett's occupational data are recoded via Census-like methods so that they can be transformed into Duncan's SES metric, and only when one accepts the kind of causal model that apparently lay behind Crockett's study design.

6.4   Inferences about Motives

As we have just seen, a cross-sectional study of motives and mobility is vulnerable as a basis for estimating causal influences of motivation on occupational achievement. Even if the indicator(s) of motivation that are obtained in such a study are highly valid measures of the *current* motivational state of the respondent, they may not represent at all well his level of motivation at the times when current levels of status achievement actually were attained. At present, we know very little about the persistence of motivational syndromes over time so that a hypothesis like "motivational constancy" is even more hazardous than that of "constancy of the IQ." Moreover, there is a dearth of knowledge as to the degree to which the expressions of motivation at any given point in time may be influenced by contemporaneous situational circumstances as opposed to possibly enduring dispositions or orientations.

In working with Crockett's material, although we are entitled to suspect that motivation, as measured, is contaminated by actual level of achievement, there does not seem to be any convenient way to represent this suspicion formally in a model so as to secure estimates of the degree of contamination or its impact on other relationships. In the analysis of the FGMA data, by contrast, we were able to suggest one possible pattern of relationships among variables that illustrates some of the more salient possible sources of fallibility in measures of motivation. The work of constructing an appropriate model was more than a little arduous, and a presentation in detail is more than a little tedious. The account reported here both summarizes and revises an earlier version of this analysis (Duncan, 1969a); details of measurement of the motivational constructs appear therein.

We begin our analysis by interposing between measures of statuses, with their typical temporal order in the life cycle of an individual, two unmeasured, hypothetical, motivational variables which reflect three psychological indexes as constructed from attitudinal items in the FGMA data. The status variables and their assumed causal ordering are as follows: father's occupation and son's number of siblings are predetermined; education depends upon both of these background variables; and occupation at marriage, income at marriage, current (1957) occupation; and current income (in that order) successively depend upon all temporally prior variables and both predetermined variables.

As described in earlier work on this topic (Duncan, 1969a) the FGMA data contain three motivational indexes of interest: Subjective Achievement, Commitment to Work, and Importance of Getting Ahead. Each index was measured approximately contemporaneously with the collection of information about the statuses (as reported by the men's wives). Consequently, we can only assume that the three motivational indexes reflect states of mind concurrent with the FGMA survey, allowing that these states of mind could have been conditioned by earlier psychological dispositions as well as by intervening and contemporary experiences. In fact, we could argue that (say) Subjective Achievement is an estimate reported about how a respondent evaluates his status attainments in the course of his career to date. This is to say that the measured motivational indexes can be represented as being contaminated by some of the status variables. If we also wish to argue that the motivations reflected in the three indexes are causally antecedent to these achieved statuses, then we are faced with the problem of specifying a model in which the measured indexes are defined as indicators or reflections of unmeasured motivational states and in which the validity (sources of contamination in the indexes) and reliability of measurement are taken into account.

Figure 6.9 is a reduced form of such a model; it specifies that Subjective Achievement is determined by the seven status variables plus a residual. Importance of Getting Ahead and Commitment to Work both are influenced by Subjective Achievement, which transmits the effects of the status variables indirectly; neither of the former has any direct influence from the status variables. However, Importance of Getting Ahead reflects an unmeasured variable,

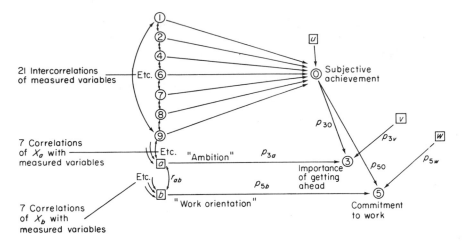

Fig. 6.9. Hypothetical causal scheme for inferring correlations involving theoretical variables "ambition" and "work orientation." (See Table 6.9 for identification of measured variables.) Open circles, measured variables; open squares, unmeasured variables.

"Ambition," a motivation crystallized in youth among the influences of primary family and peers and possibly incorporating congential temperamental traits or emotional capacities. "Ambition" could be regarded as influencing how far an adolescent remains in school and as shaping his occupational plans and orientations. Commitment to Work, however, reflects another unmeasured motivation, "Work Orientation," which possibly comes into play as occupational plans are formulated. While the measured indexes Importance of Getting Ahead and Commitment to Work are not causally connected in our model, we specify in Fig. 6.9 a correlation (r_{ab}) between their unmeasured counterparts. (While this reduced form of our model serves to estimate the correlation r_{ab}, our full model, described subsequently, specifies that "Ambition" is predetermined, along with number of siblings and paternal occupation, and that "Work Orientation" depends upon all three such predetermined variables and is interposed between them and the educational achievement variables.)

At this juncture the reader may wish to consult Duncan (1969a) for a full treatment and definition of these variables as well as for a description of scaling. Suffice it here to say that occupations were scaled by the FGMA investigators according to the 1947 North-Hatt metric. Reliability coefficients were calculated for the three measured motivational indexes from the Kuder-Richardson formula (cf. Duncan, 1969, p. 82), and estimates for the reliabilities of the status variables were obtained from the work of Hodge and Siegel (1968). These coefficients permitted the computation of correlation coefficients

TABLE 6.9

Correlation Matrix for Selected Variables in FGMA Study (Males): Observed Correlations above Diagonal and Correlations Corrected for Attenuation below Diagonal

Variables	1	2	3	4	5	6	7	8	9	10	10a	10b
1. Father's occupation	—	-.134	-.108	.340	.188	.267	.121	.297	.183	.218	.231	.138
2. Number of siblings	-.147	—	.093	-.272	-.061	-.167	-.081	-.203	-.101	-.180	-.192	-.112
3. Importance of getting ahead	-.135	.110	—	-.254	-.004	-.160	-.057	-.216	-.112	-.257	-.199	-.263
4. Education	.379	-.287	-.304	—	.291	.541	.177	.641	.357	.418	.463	.237
5. Commitment to work	.230	-.071	-.005	.342	—	.265	.110	.346	.215	.486	.516	.307
6. Occupation at marriage	.310	-.183	-.199	.604	.324	—	.211	.640	.373	.368	.373	.255
7. Income at marriage	.141	-.089	-.071	.198	.135	.246	—	.165	.547	.194	.165	.178
8. Current occupation	.345	-.223	-.269	.715	.423	.743	.193	—	.356	.407	.412	.284
9. Current income	.214	-.112	-.140	.400	.264	.435	.642	.416	—	.365	.315	.330
10. Subjective achievement[a]	.265	-.207	-.335	.488	.622	.447	.237	.494	.446	—	.914	.832
10a. Level of status satisfaction	—	—	—	—	—	—	—	—	—	—	—	.536
10b. Feelings of economic security	—	—	—	—	—	—	—	—	—	—	—	—

[a] Weighted sum of variables 10a and 10b: see Duncan (1969a). This variable is designated subsequently as X_0.

133

corrected for attenuation, as reported in Table 6.9 along with the uncorrected values.

We now proceed to estimate our model, taking into account both the reliability of measurement and the probable sources of contamination (extent of validity of the constructs) in the measured motivations. The issue at hand is whether and by how much these adjustments and specifications will support the assertion that motivations are "relevant and important" to social mobility.

While we are not concerned primarily with the determination of Subjective Achievement, Table 6.10 contains some data of interest in passing. Either one-

TABLE 6.10

Path Coefficients for Determination of Subjective Achievement
(X_0) by Status Variables

Variable	Uncorrected	Corrected for attenuation
X_1 Father's occupation	.0482[a]	.0517[a]
X_2 Number of siblings	−.0625[b]	−.0691[b]
X_4 Educational attainment	.1761[b]	.1795[b]
X_6 Occupation at marriage	.0823[b]	.0714[a]
X_7 Income at marriage	−.0020	−.0427[a]
X_8 Current occupation	.1410[b]	.1709[b]
X_9 Current income	.2072[b]	.2807[b]
. . . .	. . .	. . .
X_u Residual	.8612	.8081
Coefficient of determination, $R^2_{0(123456789)}$	.26	.35

[a] Absolute value of coefficient exceeds its standard error.
[b] Absolute value of coefficient exceeds twice its standard error.

fourth or one-third of the variation in this index is accounted for by the combination of status variables, depending on whether the uncorrected or corrected correlations are used. By far the most important subset of variables comprises current income, current occupational status, and educational attainment, only these three variables have path coefficients greater than .10. Income at marriage has an anomalous negative coefficient, but it does not reach statistical significance in the uncorrected data and is of dubious significance in the corrected series. The negative influence of number of siblings, though small, is interesting in that one might have expected the influence to be fully accounted for by the intervening variables of achieved socioeconomic status. While father's occupation may have a significant positive effect on Subjective Achievement, its magnitude is surely small. The determinants of Subjective Achievement, in sum, are about what one would expect them to be on the basis of the manifest content of items making up the scale.

The next step is to outline a procedure for calculating the path coefficients and correlations involving the theoretical (unmeasured) variables. The diagram, in the portion which involves these variables, is a very special one; no routine procedure, such as the solution of normal equations in a regression setup, will yield the unknown values. To make the procedure completely explicit, one must write out in full the relevant equations. Each of these equations can be written by studying the path diagram (Fig. 6.9) and applying the basic theorem of path analysis (Duncan, 1966, p. 5).

Equations for known or assumed correlations are as follows:

$$r_{31} = p_{30}r_{01} + p_{3a}r_{1a} \qquad [1]$$

$$r_{32} = p_{30}r_{02} + p_{3a}r_{2a} \qquad [2]$$

$$r_{34} = p_{30}r_{04} + p_{3a}r_{4a} \qquad [3]$$

$$r_{36} = p_{30}r_{06} + p_{3a}r_{6a} \qquad [4]$$

$$r_{37} = p_{30}r_{07} + p_{3a}r_{7a} \qquad [5]$$

$$r_{38} = p_{30}r_{08} + p_{3a}r_{8a} \qquad [6]$$

$$r_{39} = p_{30}r_{09} + p_{3a}r_{9a} \qquad [7]$$

$$r_{51} = p_{50}r_{01} + p_{5b}r_{1b} \qquad [8]$$

$$r_{52} = p_{50}r_{02} + p_{5b}r_{2b} \qquad [9]$$

$$r_{54} = p_{50}r_{04} + p_{5b}r_{4b} \qquad [10]$$

$$r_{56} = p_{50}r_{06} + p_{5b}r_{6b} \qquad [11]$$

$$r_{57} = p_{50}r_{07} + p_{5b}r_{7b} \qquad [12]$$

$$r_{58} = p_{50}r_{08} + p_{5b}r_{8b} \qquad [13]$$

$$r_{59} = p_{50}r_{09} + p_{5b}r_{9b} \qquad [14]$$

$$r_{30} = p_{30} + p_{3a}r_{0a} \qquad [15]$$

$$r_{50} = p_{50} + p_{5b}r_{0b} \qquad [16]$$

$$1 - p_{3v}^2 = p_{30}^2 + p_{3a}^2 + 2p_{30}p_{3a}r_{0a} \qquad [17]$$

$$1 - p_{5w}^2 = p_{50}^2 + p_{5b}^2 + 2p_{50}p_{5b}r_{0b} \qquad [18]$$

$$r_{53} = p_{50}r_{30} + p_{5b}r_{3b} \qquad [19.1]$$

$$r_{53} + p_{30}r_{50} + p_{3a}r_{5a} \qquad [19.2]$$

$$r_{53} = p_{50}p_{30} + p_{50}p_{3a}r_{0a} + p_{30}p_{5b}r_{0b} + p_{3a}p_{5b}r_{ab}. \qquad [19]$$

Equations for certain unknown correlations are as follows:

$$r_{0a} = p_{01}r_{1a} + p_{02}r_{2a} + p_{04}r_{4a} + p_{06}r_{6a} + p_{07}r_{7a} + p_{08}r_{8a} + p_{09}r_{9a} \tag{20}$$

$$r_{0b} = p_{01}r_{1b} + p_{02}r_{2b} + p_{04}r_{4b} + p_{06}r_{6b} + p_{07}r_{7b} + p_{08}r_{8b} + p_{09}r_{9b} \tag{21}$$

$$r_{3b} = p_{30}r_{0b} + p_{3a}r_{ab} \tag{22}$$

$$r_{5a} = p_{50}r_{0a} + p_{5b}r_{ab} \tag{23}$$

$$r_{3a} = p_{3a} + p_{30}r_{0a} \text{ (“validity” coefficient)} \tag{24}$$

$$r_{5b} = p_{5b} + p_{50}r_{0b} \text{ (“validity” coefficient).} \tag{25}$$

Note: Equation [19] is obtained from [19.1], [15], and [22]; the same result is obtained from [19.2], [16], and [23].

The key to the solution of this set of equations is to regard the product appearing as the last term in each of equations [1] through [14] as (temporarily) a single variable. Thus, let

$$q_{3j} = p_{3a}r_{aj} \quad \text{and}$$

$$q_{5j} = p_{5b}r_{bj}$$

for each of $j = 1, 2, 4, 6, 7, 8,$ and 9. These q's are *not* path coefficients but simply arbitrary symbols for the particular products. Now, substitute the expression for r_{0a} given by equation [20] into equation [15], obtaining

$$r_{30} = p_{30} + \sum_j p_{0j}p_{3a}r_{aj} = p_{30} + \sum_j p_{0j}q_{3j}. \tag{15′}$$

The p_{0j} are already known (they are displayed in Table 6.10), as are the correlations r_{3j} and r_{0j} appearing in equations [1] through [7]. Hence those equations together with [15′] comprise a set of eight linear equations in eight unknowns: p_{30} and the seven q_{3j}'s. These are readily solved by standard methods. A parallel calculation based on equations [8] through [14], [16], and [21] yields p_{50} and the seven q_{5j}'s. We find $p_{30} = -.2594$ and $p_{50} = .5820$, with the following values for the q's:

$j =$	q_{3j}	q_{5j}
1	$-.0662$	.0758
2	.0563	.0495
4	$-.1774$	.0580
6	$-.0830$	.0638
7	$-.0095$	$-.0029$
8	$-.1408$	.1355
9	$-.0243$	.0044

These results, like all of the subsequent illustrative calculations, are given only for the set of correlations corrected for attenuation since the corrected values are presumably closer to the "true" state of affairs than the uncorrected.

The model is now seen to be underidentified since we have no way to get from q_{3j} to unique values of p_{3a} and r_{aj} or from q_{5j} to p_{5b} and r_{bj}. Nevertheless, we can get instructive results by computing *conditional* solutions based on *arbitrarily chosen* values of p_{3a} and p_{5b}, for if numerical values of these are assumed, we have

$$r_{aj} = q_{3j}/p_{3a} \quad \text{and}$$

$$r_{bj} = q_{5j}/p_{5b}.$$

The same arbitrary assumptions will lead to conditional solutions for r_{0a} from equation [15], r_{0b} from equation [16], p_{3v} from [17], p_{5w} from [18], r_{3b} from [19.1], r_{5a} from [19.2], and then r_{ab} from [19], which is derived from [19.1], [15], and [22] or, alternatively, from [19.2], [16], and [23]. Finally, we use results thus far assumed or computed to obtain the "validity" correlations, r_{3a} and r_{5b} from [24] and [25]. Note that in all these calculations the only arbitrary assumptions are those concerning p_{3a} and p_{5b}, for all the correlations on the left side of [1] through [19] are known, as are the r_{0j} that appear on the right and the p_{0j} already computed. Moreover, p_{30} and p_{50} have already been obtained, and these values do not depend on assumptions about p_{3a} and p_{5b}.

Although p_{3a} and p_{5b} are to be given arbitrary values, we are not at liberty to assign any values we please. First, the model implies that each has an upper limit. From [15], $p_{3a}r_{0a} = r_{30} - p_{30}$ so that we may rewrite [17] as

$$p_{3a}^2 = 1 - p_{3v}^2 + p_{30}^2 - 2p_{30}r_{30}. \qquad [17']$$

Thus p_{3a} takes its maximum value when $p_{3v} = 0$, and we can compute that maximum as .9452 since we now know the solution for p_{30} and the value of r_{30} from Table 6.9. Similarly, we find from [16] and [18] that $p_{5b} \leqslant .7840$, given the value of p_{50} already obtained.

Lower bounds for p_{3a} and p_{5b} are implicit in the fact that we must select values for both that do not violate mathematical properties of the correlation coefficient and sets of correlations. By virtue of [15], [16], and [19] we may write

$$r_{ab} = \frac{K}{p_{3a}p_{5b}}, \quad \text{where}$$

$$K = r_{53} - p_{50}p_{30} - p_{50}(r_{30} - p_{30}) - p_{30}(r_{50} - p_{50}).$$

Since all the quantities in K are now known, we may compute it once and for all, without regard to assumptions about p_{3a} and p_{5b}. We find $K = .20035$. Since K

is positive, and we shall only be interested in positive values of p_{3a} and p_{5b}, we have $r_{ab} > 0$. But since no correlation can exceed unity,

$$\frac{K}{p_{3a}p_{5b}} \leqslant 1.0.$$

Hence the minimum value of p_{3a} for a given value of p_{5b} is K/p_{5b}.

More restrictive limits can be obtained by considering the partial correlation, $r_{ab.j}$ where $j = 1, 2, 4, 6, 7, 8,$ or 9. This partial correlation is defined as

$$r_{ab.j} = \frac{r_{ab} - r_{aj}r_{bj}}{(1 - r_{aj}^2)^{1/2}(1 - r_{bj}^2)^{1/2}}.$$

This can be conveniently reexpressed in terms of the coefficients q_{3j} and q_{5j} as

$$r_{ab.j} = \frac{K - q_{3j}q_{5j}}{(p_{3a}^2 - q_{3j}^2)^{1/2}(p_{5b}^2 - q_{5j}^2)^{1/2}}$$

where K is the number defined in the preceding paragraph. As discussed by Yule & Kendall (1947, Section 14.25), the condition

$$|r_{ab.j}| \leqslant 1.0$$

must be met for mathematical consistency of the three correlations, r_{ab}, r_{aj}, and r_{bj}. Since in these data the numerator of $r_{ab.j}$ is always positive, we need only consider $r_{ab.j} \leqslant 1.0$ as the consistency condition. This may be rewritten to give the minimum value of p_{3a} for a given value of p_{5b} as

$$p_{3a} \geqslant \left[\frac{(K - q_{3j}q_{5j})^2}{p_{5b}^2 - q_{5j}^2} + q_{3j}^2\right]^{1/2}.$$

It turns out that the functions obtained for $j = 4$ and $j = 8$ define the smallest region of compatible values of p_{3a} and p_{5b}; these functions, plotted in Fig. 6.10, served to delimit the region within which initial arbitrary combinations of p_{3a} and p_{5b} were selected for heuristic purposes. However, certain of the initial selections were found to entail mathematical inconsistencies. This was true of each the points E', F', and G' in Fig. 6.10. When the complete sets of correlations implied by these combinations were computed and merged with the correlations (corrected for attenuation) among measured variables in Table 6.9, correlation matrices (written with unities on the main diagonal) were found to have negative determinants. Accordingly, combinations E, F, and G were selected instead and were found not to imply such inconsistent correlation matrices.

Seven points in the region of permissible combinations of p_{3a} and p_{5b} were chosen as the basis for heuristic calculations. All but one of these points (see Fig. 6.10) represent one or another kind of extreme assumption. For sets A, B,

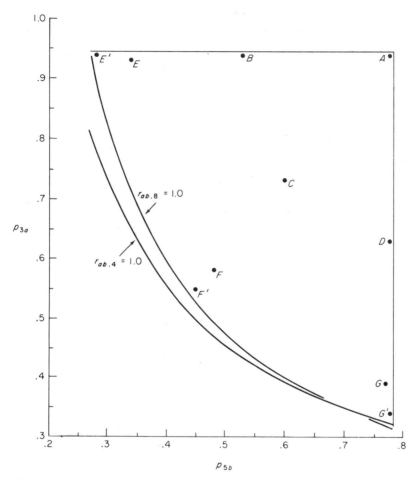

Fig. 6.10. Combinations of p_{3a} and p_{5b} selected to use in illustrative calculations with correlations corrected for attenuation.

and E the assumption is that p_{3a} is near its maximum value (that is, X_3 is close to its maximum validity as an indicator of X_a). For sets A, D, and G, p_{5b} is near its maximum (that is, X_5 is close to its maximum validity as an indicator of X_b). In sets E, F, and G, p_{3a} has nearly the minimum value of p_{5b} (or p_{5b} has nearly the minimum value for the given value of p_{3a}). Set C, which is somewhere in the middle of the region, represents the condition of only moderately high validity of both indicators. Both indicators have almost maximally high validity in set A while both have rather low validity in set F. Table 6.11 shows the values of the various correlations in each set computed on the basis of the formulas and

TABLE 6.11

Correlations Involving Unmeasured Variables, for Diagram in Figure 6.10, Computed under Alternative Assumptions from Correlations Corrected for Attenuation

Coefficient	Set of illustrative calculations[a]						
	A	B	C	D	E	F	G
Assumed							
p_{3a}	.94	.94	.73	.63	.93	.58	.39
p_{5b}	.78	.53	.60	.78	.34	.48	.77
Implied							
r_{1a}	−.07	−.07	−.09	−.11	−.07	−.11	−.17
r_{2a}	.06	.06	.08	.09	.06	.10	.14
r_{3a}	.96	.96	.76	.66	.95	.61	.44
r_{4a}	−.19	−.19	−.24	−.28	−.19	−.31	−.45
r_{5a}	.17	.17	.21	.25	.17	.27	.40
r_{6a}	−.09	−.09	−.11	−.13	−.09	−.14	−.21
r_{7a}	−.01	−.01	−.01	−.02	−.01	−.02	−.02
r_{8a}	−.15	−.15	−.19	−.22	−.15	−.24	−.36
r_{9a}	−.03	−.03	−.03	−.04	−.03	−.04	−.06
r_{0a}	−.08	−.08	−.10	−.12	−.08	−.13	−.19
r_{1b}	.10	.14	.13	.10	.22	.16	.10
r_{2b}	.06	.09	.08	.06	.15	.10	.06
r_{3b}	.24	.36	.32	.24	.56	.40	.25
r_{4b}	.07	.11	.10	.07	.17	.12	.08
r_{5b}	.81	.57	.64	.81	.41	.53	.80
r_{6b}	.08	.12	.11	.08	.19	.13	.08
r_{7b}	.00	−.01	.00	.00	−.01	−.01	.00
r_{8b}	.17	.26	.23	.17	.40	.28	.18
r_{9b}	.01	.01	.01	.01	.01	.01	.01
r_{0b}	.05	.08	.07	.05	.12	.08	.05
r_{ab}	.27	.40	.46	.41	.63	.72	.67
$p_{3v} = r_{3v}$	.10	.10	.60	.70	.17	.75	.86
$p_{5w} = r_{5w}$	.08	.58	.50	.08	.71	.62	.15

[a] Values shown here are rounded, although additional decimal places were carried in subsequent calculations.

assumptions described in preceding paragraphs. These, together with the correlations among measured variables, as corrected for attenuation (Table 6.9), comprise the "data" from which are computed the following illustrative results.

The causal ordering discussed earlier suggests a model comprising a set of recursive regressions. It is important to note that *none* of the numerical results obtained here adjudicates any question as to the validity of the causal ordering, except perhaps insofar as the reader may find these results so implausible as to indicate rejection of that ordering.

TABLE 6.12

Partial Regression Coefficients in Standard Form for Systems Treating Indicators X_3 and X_5 as Perfectly Valid Measures of X_a and X_b, Based on FGMA Observed Correlations and Correlations Corrected for Attenuation

Independent variables	Dependent variable (see stub)						
	4	5	6	7	8	9	0
For Observed Correlations							
1. Father's occupation	.289[a]	.104[a]	.081[a]	.049[b]	.038[b]	.011	.018
2. Number of siblings	−.214[a]	.022	−.019	−.031	−.022	.018	−.070[a]
3. Importance of getting ahead	−.203[a]	.077[a]	−.030[b]	−.011	−.056[a]	−.013	−.179[a]
4. Education	–	.281[a]	.468[a]	.656[b]	.361[a]	.125[a]	.112[a]
5. Commitment to work	–	–	.112[a]	.043[b]	.130[a]	.059[a]	.375[a]
6. Occupation at marriage	–	–	–	.149[a]	.389[a]	.128[a]	.074[a]
7. Income at marriage	–	–	–	–	−.005	.475[a]	−.002
8. Current occupation	–	–	–	–	–	.093[a]	.038[b]
9. Current income	–	–	–	–	–	–	.174[a]
0. Subjective achievement	–	–	–	–	–	–	–
Coefficient of determination	(.21)	(.10)	(.31)	(.06)	(.55)	(.40)	(.40)
For Corrected Correlations							
1. Father's occupation	.315[a]	.121[a]	.079[a]	.052[b]	.025[b]	.002	.005
2. Number of siblings	−.214[a]	.032[b]	−.010	−.032	−.017	.024[b]	−.083[a]
3. Importance of getting ahead	−.238[a]	.111[a]	−.029[b]	−.012	−.064[a]	−.013	−.256[a]
4. Education	–	.339[a]	.519[a]	.038	.356[a]	.119[a]	.096[a]
5. Commitment to work	–	–	.128[a]	.048[b]	.147[a]	.064[a]	.511[a]
6. Occupation at marriage	–	–	–	.183[a]	.462[a]	.133[a]	.094[a]
7. Income at marriage	–	–	–	–	−.021[b]	.559[a]	−.038[b]
8. Current occupation	–	–	–	–	–	.098[a]	−.036
9. Current income	–	–	–	–	–	–	.225[a]
Coefficient of determination	(.25)	(.14)	(.39)	(.07)	(.69)	(.52)	(.58)

[a] Absolute value of coefficient equals or exceeds two standard errors.
[b] Absolute value of coefficient equals or exceeds one standard error.

141

TABLE 6.13

Partial Regression Coefficients in Standard Form for Recursive Model, Based on Correlations in Table 6.11 and 6.9, as Corrected for Attenuation

Set	Independent variables[a]		Dependent variable[a]					
			4	b	6	7	8	9
A	1		$.33^b$	$.08^b$	$.09^b$	$.06^c$	$.03^c$	.01
	2		$-.23^b$	$.09^b$	$-.01$	$-.03$	$-.02^c$	$.03^c$
	a		$-.15^b$	$.30^b$	.02	$.03^c$	$-.06^b$	$.05^b$
	4		–	$.13^b$	$.57^b$	$.06^c$	$.39^b$	$.13^b$
	b		–	–	.03	$-.04^c$	$.12^b$	$-.05^b$
	6		–	–	–	$.19^b$	$.48^b$	$.12^b$
	7		–	–	–	–	$-.01$	$.56^b$
	8		–	–	–	–	–	$.14^b$
		R^2	(.22)	(.10)	(.37)	(.07)	(.68)	(.52)
B	1		$.33^b$	$.12^b$	$.09^b$	$.07^c$	.02	.02
	2		$-.23^b$	$.14^b$	$-.01$	$-.02$	$-.04^b$	$.04^c$
	a		$-.15^b$	$.44^b$	.01	$.05^c$	$-.12^b$	$.08^b$
	4		–	$.18^b$	$.56^b$	$.07^c$	$.37^b$	$.13^b$
	b		–	–	$.04^c$	$-.06^c$	$.21^b$	$-.10^b$
	6		–	–	–	$.19^b$	$.47^b$	$.11^b$
	7		–	–	–	–	.00	$.56^b$
	8		–	–	–	–	–	$.17^b$
		R^2	(.22)	(.23)	(.37)	(.07)	(.70)	(.53)
C	1		$.33^b$	$.11^b$	$.09^b$	$.06^c$	.02	.02
	2		$-.22^b$	$.12^b$	$-.01$	$-.02$	$-.04^c$	.04
	a		$-.20^b$	$.51^b$	.02	$.07^c$	$-.14^b$	$.10^b$
	4		–	$.21^b$	$.57^b$	$.07^c$	$.35^b$	$.14^b$
	b		–	–	$.03^c$	$-.07^c$	$.21^b$	$-.11^b$
	6		–	–	–	$.19^b$	$.48^b$	$.11^b$
	7		–	–	–	–	.00	$.56^b$
	8		–	–	–	–	–	$.17^b$
		R^2	(.24)	(.28)	(.37)	(.07)	(.70)	(.53)
D	1		$.32^b$	$.08^b$	$.09^b$	$.06^c$	$.03^c$	.01
	2		$-.22^b$	$.09^b$	$-.01$	$-.03$	$-.03^c$	$.03^c$
	a		$-.23^b$	$.46^b$	$.03^c$	$.06^c$	$-.12^b$	$.09^b$
	4		–	$.20^b$	$.57^b$	$.07^c$	$.36^b$	$.14^b$
	b		–	–	.02	$-.05^c$	$.15^b$	$-.08^b$
	6		–	–	–	$.19^b$	$.48^b$	$.11^b$
	7		–	–	–	–	$-.01$	$.56^b$
	8		–	–	–	–	–	$.16^b$
		R^2	(.25)	(.22)	(.37)	(.07)	(.69)	(.53)

TABLE 6.13 continued

Set	Independent variables[a]		Dependent variable[a]					
			4	b	6	7	8	9
E	1		.33[b]	.19[b]	.07[b]	.09[b]	−.07[b]	.08[b]
	2		−.23[b]	.22[b]	−.03[c]	.01	−.14[b]	.12[b]
	a		−.15[b]	.69[b]	−.06[c]	.15[b]	−.43[b]	.35[b]
	4		–	.29[b]	.54[b]	.10[b]	.25[b]	.11[b]
	b		–	–	.12[b]	−.18[b]	.58[b]	−.44[b]
	6		–	–	–	.21[b]	.43[b]	.01
	7		–	–	–	–	.04[b]	.53[b]
	8		–	–	–	–	–	.45[b]
		R^2	(.22)	(.56)	(.38)	(.08)	(.81)	(.57)
F	1		.32[b]	.14[b]	.09[b]	.09[b]	−.05[b]	.07[b]
	2		−.22[b]	.15[b]	−.01	.00	−.11[b]	−.11[b]
	a		−.25[b]	.83[b]	.00	.23[b]	−.58[b]	.53[b]
	4		–	.37[b]	.56[b]	.15[b]	.16[b]	.21[b]
	b		–	–	.05[c]	−.23[b]	.64[b]	−.54[b]
	6		–	–	–	.19[b]	.46[b]	−.01
	7		–	–	–	–	.04[b]	.52[b]
	8		–	–	–	–	–	.46[b]
		R^2	(.26)	(.68)	(.38)	(.09)	(.80)	(.58)
G	1		.29[b]	.08[b]	.10[b]	.08[b]	.00	.04[c]
	2		−.19[b]	.08[b]	.00	−.01	−.05[b]	.06[b]
	a		−.38[b]	.88[b]	.13[b]	.25[b]	−.48[b]	.47[b]
	4		–	.47[b]	.63[b]	.19[b]	.14[b]	.30[b]
	b		–	–	−.06[c]	−.21[b]	.45[b]	−.40[b]
	6		–	–	–	.18[b]	.50[b]	.01
	7		–	–	–	–	.03[c]	.53[b]
	8		–	–	–	–	–	.33[b]
		R^2	(.34)	(.64)	(.38)	(.09)	(.74)	(.57)

[a] Variable identification: 1, Father's occupation; 2, Number of siblings; a, "Ambition"; 4, Education; b, Work orientation"; 6, Occupation at marriage; 7, Income at marriage; 8, Current occupation; 9, Current income.

[b] Absolute value of coefficient equals or exceeds two standard errors, as computed from conventional formula, taking hypothetical and corrected correlations as observed values.

[c] Absolute value of coefficient equals or exceeds one standard error, computed as described in footnote b.

To provide a base line against which to evaluate the combined outcome of the several assumptions about reliability of measurements and validity of indicators, Table 6.12 shows results for a recursive model in which the measured variables X_3 and X_5 are used in place of the corresponding theoretical variables

X_a and X_b. This table, therefore, represents the "naive" interpretation of the data. Comparison of the two panels of the table suggests that even the modest step of allowing for differential unreliability of measurements can lead to interesting modifications of the interpretation.

Table 6.13 shows standardized regression coefficients (path coefficients) for the same model, using the theoretical variables, as computed for each of the seven sets of correlations in Table 6.11. Comparisons between Tables 6.12 and 6.13 are described for each dependent variable in turn.

Education (X_4). Only for set G are the coefficients greatly different in the theoretical and the naive versions of the model. In this set the validity of Importance of Getting Ahead as an indicator of Ambition is nearly as low as the model permits. Only on the assumption of such low validity can we attribute appreciably greater importance to Ambition as a (negative) influence on schooling than would be suggested by the observed correlations alone. Indeed, if the indicator of Ambition is assumed to be highly valid (sets *A*, *B*, and *E*), Ambition looks rather less important than its counterpart in a naive model.

Work Orientation (X_b). Here we compare the equation for X_5 in the naive interpretation (Table 6.12) with those for X_b in the several illustrative theoretical interpretations (Table 6.13). The two differ markedly. Each of the seven estimates of p_{ba} is vastly greater than either value of p_{53}. The model, therefore, irrespective of assumptions about degree of validity of the two indicators, forces a moderate to strong positive correlation between the two theoretical variables even though the correlation between the two indicators is virtually nil ($-.005$ with correction for attenuation). The further assumption as to causal ordering leads to the interpretation that high Ambition produces high Work Orientation, although this direct effect is slightly offset by a small indirect effect of opposite sign: p_{ba} is positive while $p_{b4}\,p_{4a}$ is negative. In the theoretical interpretation, education looms less important as a positive influence on Work Orientation than is the case in the naive version of the model. The theoretical interpretation enhances the positive influence of number of siblings, however, making that influence comparable to the one estimated for father's occupation.

Occupation at Marriage (X_6). The role of father's occupation, a modest positive effect, is about the same in the two interpretations. Hence the theoretical variables explain the influence of father's occupational status on son's no better than do the observed variables. In neither interpretation does number of siblings have a significant direct effect. In the naive interpretation, Importance of Getting Ahead has a very small negative coefficient, while the coefficient for Ambition is negative only in set E. The theoretical interpretation enhances rather than diminishes the apparent direct influence of education. In five sets of illustrative calculations the influence of Work Orientation is negligible, unlike the case for Commitment to Work in the naive interpretation. The exceptions are instructive. In set *E*—the only one where Ambition has a significant negative impact—Work Orientation has an appreciable positive coefficient. But in set *G*—where Ambition operates positively—Work Orientation has a negative, albeit small, coefficient. To conclude that either variable has a significant influence, we must assume that one of them has nearly minimum validity. The signs of their coefficients will then be opposite so that the two variables are producing compensating effects, inasmuch as they are positively correlated with each other.

Income at Marriage (X_7). The small and questionably significant positive effect of father's occupation in the naive interpretation reappears in all the sets of theoretical results. Hence that effect, if reliable, is not explained by the operation of the theoretical variables. The direct effect of number of siblings is noteworthy in neither interpretation. In the naive interpretation, Importance of Getting Ahead has a negative though exceedingly small coefficient, whereas in all sets of theoretical results the coefficient for Work Orientation is positive. Its magnitude is appreciable in the three sets (*E*, *F*, and *G*) where one or both indicators of theoretical variables have low validity. Mutatis mutandis, the same thing is noted for Commitment to Work vis-à-vis Work Orientation: The sign changes in going from the naive to the theoretical interpretation, but the coefficient is substantial only where indicators are taken to be distinctly fallible. The two theoretical variables produce compensating effects in view of their positive correlation with each other. Finally, the naive interpretation of the role of occupation as a source of income variation at marriage (with the correction for attenuation) hardly differs from the interpretation involving special assumptions about the theoretical variables. The latter, however, enhances the apparent net effect of education, particularly if the indicators of Ambition and Work Orientation are taken to be quite fallible.

Current Occupation (X_8). In sets *A*, *B*, *C*, and *D* the coefficient for father's occupation is much the same as in the naive interpretation: very small and hardly significant. Even this effect disappears in set *G*, while in sets *E* and *F* the coefficient is negative and ostensibly significant. (Here and elsewhere in Table 6.13 we are probably not justified in placing any strict interpretation on the computed standard errors of the coefficients.) This anomalous result might suggest the advisability of some skepticism about the assumptions underlying the calculations. The negative effect of number of siblings on current occupation, barely suggested in the naive interpretation, is rendered a little more prominent by the theoretical interpretation. The naive and the theoretical interpretations agree in ascribing a negative influence to Ambition (Importance of Getting Ahead) and a positive one to Work Orientation (Commitment to Work). The magnitudes of the respective effects are estimated as modest to large, according to which assumption about validity of indicators is accepted. As before, the lower the validity, the greater the effect; but the effects of the two positively correlated theoretical variables tend to offset each other. The tendency for current occupation to reflect occupation at marriage is hardly affected by any of the manipulations, save for the correction for attenuation itself. The crucial assumption there—one which might well be questioned—is that of independence of errors of measurement in X_8 and X_6. Finally, p_{87} is negligible in all sets of results. Any other outcome would surely be anomalous.

Current Income (X_9). Results for sets E, F, and G suggest that sufficiently extreme assumptions can give rise to significant positive coefficients for both father's occupation and number of siblings, the latter being a reversal of what is noted in the naive interpretation. It is difficult to know what to make of this.

Contrary to what the naive interpretation suggests, Ambition has a positive effect on current income (as on income at marriage), and a substantial one if either of the two indicators of theoretical variables is assumed to have low validity. Similarly, instead of the positive effect suggested by the naive interpretation, the direct influence of Work Orientation on current income is negative in the theoretical results.

The effect of education on current income suggested by the naive interpretation is, if anything, enhanced by the theoretical interpretation. However, the direct effect of occupation at marriage on current income, although it appears in sets A, B, C, and D, vanishes in sets E, F, and G. From the latter result one might argue that the motives represented by Ambition and Work Orientation produce a spurious correlation between current income and occupation at marriage. The cost of this interpretation is the assumption that at least one of the indicators of these theoretical variables has low validity. The stability of income differences over the portion of the life cycle studied here is suggested by the path coefficient p_{97}. Its value is much the same in all the theoretical results as in the naive interpretation, once the correction for attenuation is made. A more anomalous result is the contrast in values for p_{98} between sets A, B, C, and D, on the one hand, and sets E, F, and G, on the other. Mathematically, since the correlation r_{98} is the same in all sets, the larger value of p_{98} in sets E, F, and, G must be required to offset the negative correlation between X_9 and X_8 induced by the fact that both X_a and X_b work in opposite directions on occupation and income. That is, the direct or net effect of Ambition is positive on income but negative on occupation, while the net effect of Work Orientation is negative on income but positive on occupation. Without going into more detail, it is instructive merely to note the value of $p_{9a}p_{8a} + p_{9b}p_{8b}$, which is $-.01$ in set A, $-.03$ in set B, $-.04$ in set C, $-.02$ in set D, $-.41$ in set E, $-.65$ in set F, and $-.41$ in set G.

In summary, perhaps the most striking consequence of the assumptions about how indicators relate to theoretical variables in this model is that we are constrained to recognize that two conceptually distinct motives may be positively related one to the other while in their respective effects on actual achievement they tend to offset each other. Thus an "oversimplified model" may serve to reflect some of the real ambiguity, ambivalence, or intrapersonal conflict in human experience. Unfortunately, this exercise has not yielded an unambiguous verdict on the overall promise of motivational variables as explanatory factors in regard to status attainment. It does, however, afford a basis for some comments on the nature and magnitude of the task of reaching such a verdict. As stated in the introduction, one reason for venturing a frankly speculative causal interpretation is to make explicit the circumstances that currently preclude a firm interpretation.

If motives or dispositions are to be invoked as explanatory factors, the investigator must face the problem of how their effects are to be measured. In models representing empirical processes, estimating the effect of an explanatory variable requires a correlation between measurements of that variable and the outcome variable, or else correlations among indicators of the respective variables whose properties permit an inference as to the magnitude of effect. (The latter strategy of inference, rather than direct measurement of effect, has been exemplified in this discussion.)

In taking measurements on, or in securing indicators of, a dispositional variable, alternative strategies are available. (a) A direct question to the subject is sometimes assumed to elicit a trustworthy indication of the disposition. Thus high school students may be asked to designate the occupation—or, at any rate, the status level of the occupation—to which they aspire. They may be queried directly as to their plans for further schooling. (b) Questions may be put to respondents in such a form that the answers are symptomatic of the presumably underlying disposition, even though the direction or intensity of the disposition is not directly elicited thereby. Such a rationale could be invoked for several of the items in the FGMA scales studies in this work. (c) Subjects may be asked to react to unstructured stimulus material, such as inkblots or ambiguous pictures. The latent content of the responses, as decoded by the investigator, is then assumed to provide a reading on, or at least an indication of, the quality or magnitude of the disposition.

In contrast to these subjective approaches to the measurement of dispositions (so termed because the investigator is seeking access to the subject's conscious or unconscious "state of mind"), there is the theoretical possibility of assaying motives from external information. (d) A disposition may be inferred from the observation of circumstances known or assumed to give rise to it (as in deprivation experiments, where an animal's thirst is indicated by the length of time without water, other relevant conditions being controlled). (e) A disposition may be inferred from the observation of the behavior to which it gives rise (as when a choice is offered between alternatives whose desirability is known or assumed to depend on the motivational state of the organism or value orientation of the person).

Needless to say, strategies d and e are available only if theoretical understanding of a realm of behavior is rather robust. In the absence of adequate theoretical support, inferences of these kinds may merely amount to circular reasoning. With regard to the topic at hand, one would certainly wish to avoid the circularity of the conclusion that occupational achievement is evidence for the "achievement orientations" that he thinks are the causes of occupational achievement. (It is not at all clear that certain discussions of "achievement motivation" have avoided this hazard.)

If the level of sophistication of available theories is too low to permit circumvention of the hazards in strategies d and e, then one would do well to appraise the problems involved in the other three strategies.

Direct ascertainment, method a, would seem to be of rather limited applicability but perhaps fairly reliable within its limited range. Among the limitations, unfortunately, is the circumstance that the dispositions thus reliably ascertained seem to be somewhat volatile or strongly conditioned by transient situational factors. Short-run plans or intentions apparently can be ascertained with reasonable reliability, but in the longer run they change as situations develop. The same is presumably true, though to a degree unknown, of more generalized aspirations.

The asking of "indicator questions," as strategy b may be called, is (like other facets of interrogation technique) still in the prescientific stage; it is an "art" rather than a "method." One reason for this backwardness is that most investigators have remained content to carry out what is here called the naive kind of analysis and have not known how to embed their concepts of how the "indication" mechanism works in an explicit model of the concrete social-psychological process under study. If the present effort stimulates a livelier appreciation of the difficulty of this problem, it will have more than accomplished its objective.

An interesting paradox revealed by a systematic causal interpretation of data secured in this way concerns the possibility of an inverse relationship between the validity of the indicator and the estimate of the relative importance of the underlying theoretical variable. There is a pronounced contrast between sets A and F in Table 6.13 in regard to the path coefficients for Ambition and Work Orientation as determinants of current occupational status. In set F where the respective indicators are assumed to have rather low validity, the two dispositions are of some appreciable consequence. In set A, where their validity is taken to be high, they are rather inconsequential determinants of occupation. This contrast, of course, depends upon other properties of the model and may, therefore, be nothing more than an artifact of unjustified assumptions. Still, it is of interest to speculate upon the question of what assumptions would lead one to prefer set F over set A. (Certainly, it would *not* be that the former gives more weight to motives!)

In set F validity is low because residual determinants of Importance of Getting Ahead (Commitment to Work) account for a sizable part of the variation therein, as compared to the effects of Ambition (Work Orientation) on its indicator. How might such a residual effect come about? The suggestion is that an indicator scale will, almost inevitably, include a number of irrelevant cues which partially account for the responses to questions. (This is a separate problem from that of reliability of measurement. Reliability may be increased by increasing the number of items in a scale, but this will only afford more opportunity for disturbance of response by irrelevant cues.) In the scale of Importance of Getting Ahead, for example, one item refers to "material things, such as a home, car, or clothing, which are at least as good as those of my neighbors and friends." For the man who passionately desires the finest stereo high-fidelity equipment, "clothing" is an irrelevant cue; for the one whose brother-in-law has been conspicuously successful, "neighbors" may be an irrelevant reference group.

It is perhaps impossible to construct indicator questions lacking in irrelevant cues. The main hope must lie in randomizing them with respect to the causal variables under study. If one assumes that the FGMA scales are simply supplied with irrelevant cues but that the perceptions of these are uncorrelated with social origins, achieved statuses, and Subjective Achievement, then he may conclude that set F (where dispositions seem to be relatively important) is closer to the truth than set A (where this is not the case). The price for the claim of theoretical importance is the admission that the indicators are partially irrelevant. Needless to say, no adequate argument has been given here for or against the requisite assumptions so that sets A and F are presented merely as "illustrative" results.

The methodological problems encountered with strategy c, that of so-called projective tests, are not different in kind from those associated with the use of indicator questions. In addition to the points already discussed, it bears emphasis that both procedures are vulnerable to the effects of "contamination." The treatment of Subjective Achievement as a contaminator of two indicator variables in the present volume represents perhaps the simplest procedure that is adequate to deal with the problem. The problem itself may well be much more severe with projective devices than with indicator questions, for in the former case the investigator's presuppositions about the nature of the code linking response to motive may be the strongest contaminator of all. The demonstration of intercoder reliability, where all the coders are trainees of the research worker, is hardly a solution to this problem. Neither, one may rejoin, is the construction of models like that represented in Fig. 6.9. The latter, however, at least has the merit of exhibiting its assumptions for all to witness and, if so inclined, to criticize and to improve upon.

In the spirit of our own invitation to criticize and improve upon causal representations of motivation in the context of mobility, we now can summarize a series of inquiries carried out in the FGMA data after our original project had drawn to its close. We gained access to the second and third panels of the FGMA data which were collected, respectively, in 1960 and during the period 1963–1967. Inasmuch as all the attitudinal data were collected in 1957 (panel I), we were able to assess the long-term direct influences of achievement-related motivations on occupational and income statuses attained over the follow-up period. In addition we could assay the ability of these motivational constructs to account for the zero-order relationships between family of origin status or prior attainments (such as education), on the one hand, and subsequent occupational and economic achievements, on the other. In short, we could measure the extent to which motivations are "key" intervening variables in the process of status attainment. Moreover, with the panel data we could avoid some of the potential contaminations of motivational measures which plague cross-sectional surveys and about which Section 6.4 has been concerned.

The extensions of the FGMA analysis were based on the longitudinal data and on a reconstruction of the original FGMA motivational variables into three new indexes; details of this reconstruction are given by Featherman (1969, Chapter 7). Two of the three indexes were assembled from attitudinal items which conformed to two action tendencies or orientations toward occupational activity, the latter being culled from the corpus of conceptual and empirical writing in the area of achievement-related motivation, wherein a distinction has been made between intrinsic and extrinsic motivation in an achievement situation (cf. Featherman, 1971c).

The first action tendency, Primary Work Orientation, attributes a positive valence to the work or job context. This positive value is noneconomic in quality, and it indicates a preference for work rather than relaxation, a choice of the occupational work role over recreation. The second action tendency is called Materialistic Orientation. Whereas the first tendency refers to the noneconomic incentives of one's occupational role, the second index emphasizes the material goals of the good life, goals achieved through work as instrumental activity.

The third index approximates the former Subjective Achievement variable and was retained for reasons previously given. This new index, Subjective Achievement Evaluation, serves as an indicator of the conscious psychological effects of past and present socioeconomic (up to 1957) achievements which (presumably) have motivational properties (subjective sense of relative deprivation) for an individual's socioeconomic achievements over the duration of the follow-up period. Reliability coefficients for all three indexes are reported in Featherman (1971c), along with the questionnaire items from which the indexes were drawn.

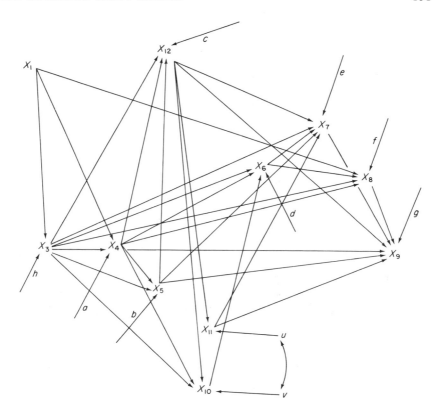

Fig. 6.11. Achievement orientations and status attainment in longitudinal FGMA data (coefficients listed in Table 6.14). Variables: X_1, Father's Occ-NORC; X_3, Education; X_4, Occ-NORC I; X_5, Income I; X_6, Occ-NORC II; X_7, Income II; X_8, Occ-NORC III; X_9, Income III; X_{10}, Index WO; X_{11}, Index MO; X_{12}, Index SA. Definitions of variables appear in Featherman (1969); see also Table 6.14.

Figure 6.11 represents a model which postulates that achievement-related motivation intervenes in the process of status attainment between the socio-economic statuses at panel I (and in the family of origin as well) and those in the follow-up period. The model is recursive and represents the social-psychological argument that achievement-related motivations arise in preadolescence within the matrix of interpersonal relationships of the primary family and are there-after modified by experiences within specific social situations of the later adolescent and adult years.

Estimates for the model represented in Fig. 6.11 appear in Table 6.14. Whether the data are corrected for attenuation or not does not alter the subse-quent summary of results, and so the distinction is ignored for this discussion; detailed analysis appears in Featherman (1969, Chapter 7; 1971c). Several

TABLE 6.14

Coefficients for Fig. 6.11 for FGMA Data Corrected and Uncorrected for Attenuation

Dependent variables[a]	Independent variables		Path coefficients		Residuals			Correlated residuals	
			Uncorrected	Corrected		Uncorrected	Corrected	Uncorrected	Corrected
Education	Fa. Occ-NORC	p_{31}	.339	.378	a	.694	.762	r_{uv} .127	.210
Occ-NORC I	Fa. Occ-NORC	p_{41}	.129	.137	b	.931	.911		
Income I	Education	p_{43}	.593	.657	c	.898	.859		
	Education	p_{53}	.184	.169	d	.596	.417		
	Occ-NORC I	p_{54}	.220	.275	e	.715	.600		
SA	Education	$p_{12,3}$	.138	.118	f	.636	.497		
	Occ-NORC I	$p_{12,4}$	.203	.252	g	.766	.692		
	Income I	$p_{12,5}$	.220	.261	h	.941	.926		
WO	Education	$p_{10,3}$	.135	.098	u	.972	.950		
	Occ-NORC I	$p_{10,4}$	.207	.237	v	.851	.794		
	SA	$p_{10,12}$	.320	.396					
MO	SA	$p_{11,12}$	-.235	-.311					
Occ-NORC II	Education	p_{63}	.251	.170					
	Occ-NORC I	p_{64}	.589	.766					
	WO	$p_{6,10}$	.063	.028					

152

Income II	Education	p_{73}	.141	.160
	Income I	p_{75}	.478	.559
	Occ-NORC II	p_{76}	.154	.137
	SA	$p_{7,12}$	.157	.169
	MO	$p_{7,11}$	.052	.076
Occ-NORC III	Fa Occ-NORC	p_{81}	.086	.087
	Education	p_{83}	.133	.126
	Occ-NORC I	p_{84}	.226	.080
	Occ-NORC II	p_{86}	.450	.662
Income III	Education	p_{93}	.148	.081
	Income I	p_{95}	.101	.076
	SA	$p_{9,12}$	.083	.099
	MO	$p_{9,11}$	.071	.110
	Income II	p_{97}	.252	.309
	Occ-NORC III	p_{98}	.280	.354

[a] Variables: Education coded in years of schooling; occupation, in intervals of 1947 NORC prestige scale; income, in dollars of salaries and wages. SA is subjective achievement evaluation; WO is primary work orientation; MO is materialistic orientation.

conclusions about the role of the motivations in the process of status attainment are apparent in these data. First, social origins (as indexed in the model by paternal occupational prestige) are less important for the direct determination of adulthood achievement motivations than are the more immediate social situational factors; and of the latter, it is education (rather than early career socioeconomic achievements) which more effectively transmits the impact of social origins to the levels of measured motivation.

Second, Primary Work Orientation and Materialistic Orientation have distinctive and empirically separable causal antecedents in the proximal social situation. For example, a materialistic orientation toward work ensues from a negative subjective evaluation of one's status attainments, quite apart from the objective state of affairs, and despite the fact that this subjective evaluation is positively associated with these prior objective achievements. However, Primary Work Orientation reflects both a positive evaluation of prior achievements and also positive, direct influences from education and panel-I occupation which are separate from the former.

Third, achievement orientations have small marginal efficacy (small, positive net effects) in the process of status attainment over the 10-year course of the restudy. The path coefficients for the two work orientations are among the least important (if they are not the smallest in absolute size) of those which represent the determining influences on occupational prestige and income at panels II and III.

Fourth and finally, both work orientations are rather weak intervening variables between paternal occupation and filial socioeconomic statuses, inasmuch as the paths from paternal occupation to the motivations are effectively zero, and since there remains a non-zero path from paternal to filial occupation at panel III. Furthermore, if one computes the indirect effects of paternal occupation on son's occupation and income at panel II (for example), tracing these effects through the variables and paths in Fig. 6.11, one finds that the motivations are less effective as intervening variables than are the son's socioeconomic achievements at panel I.

Featherman (1971c) provides another illustration of this latter conclusion. The achievement orientations were examined for their abilities to account for observed religioethnic differentials in occupation and income at the three panels of the FGMA study. Featherman concluded that the motivational indexes were neither able to account for the gross differentials among the religioethnic categories nor were they as effective as education in transmitting the effects of either religioethnic or socioeconomic background to achievements in adulthood.

In this extension of the FGMA analysis, as in our earlier work with the cross-sectional data, we find little support for the hypothesis that achievement orientations are "highly relevant" to the processes of status attainment in the general population. The indexes of achievement orientations in the FGMA data fail to function as strong intervening variables which are capable of explaining how social origins (or intervening achievements) affect the socioeconomic statuses attained by the middle of the work career. Furthermore, the failure of the motivational constructs as intervening variables does not appear to be attributable to their unreliability.

Such failure could, of course, be a consequence of naive assumptions about the validity of the motivational constructs, as represented in Fig. 6.11. The model specifies that the indexes are rather accurate measures of achievement-related motivations; it does not represent them as "contaminated" reflections of some unmeasured motivations. Under an alternative specification of the model in which the estimated validity of the indexes were lower, one may be forced to revise the conclusions about the "relevance" of motivations as intervening variables (see the previous discussion in this section on the relationship between validity and magnitude of direct effects of motivations). While this is a logical possibility, such alternative specifications regarding validity (for example, Featherman, 1969, Chapter 7) have not suggested the need for such revisions.

6.5 Aspirations as Indicators of Motivation

In Section 6.2, we treated the variable "college plans" in the WISC data set as an indicator of a "latent decision" to attain higher education. Here, a similar technique is employed, but its inspiration is the somewhat different notion that college plans may be interpreted as "educational aspirations," and that expressed aspirations may, in general, be thought of as reflections of an underlying motivational syndrome. To effect an interpretation on this point of view, occupational as well as educational aspirations are brought into the picture.

The seven variables selected from the WISC data set for this exercise are listed in Table 6.15. Some further explanation of the variables may be desired. Socioeconomic status (SES) of the respondent's family of orientation is a composite of six items from the questionnaire filled out by him. Sewell and his collaborators on the WISC project carried out a factor analysis of these items and contrived a factor-weighted score. The mechanics of this procedure are not particularly relevant here, but it may be of interest to indicate the makeup of the composite index. Some relevant information is given in Table 6.16. In view of the fact that in the OCG and other data sets we are limited to only two measures of family SES, father's occupation and education, it is interesting to discover that the composite SES measure in the WISC data is dominated by these two components.

TABLE 6.15

Intercorrelations of Selected Variables in WISC Data Set (Wisconsin Male High School Seniors, 1957, Followed Up to 1964)[a]

Variable name and number		Variable number						
		1	2	3	4	5	6	7
Socioeconomic status of family	1	–	.2929	.4438	.3937	.2177	.4382	.3277
Intelligence quotient	2		–	.4296	.4176	.5320	.4853	.3631
Educational aspiration (college plans)	3			–	.7906	.4215	.6861	.4714
Occupational aspiration	4				–	.4136	.6336	.4641
Grades (high school rank)	5					–	.5046	.3458
Educational achievement (1964)	6						–	.6207
Occupational achievement (1964)	7							–

[a] Source: WISC data set for 4386 senior boys (follow-up sample). These correlations were provided as preliminary calculations, and they differ to some degree from those in Sewell *et al.* (1970, pp. 1018) owing to changes in definitions or scaling of variables in the final analysis of Sewell *et al.*

TABLE 6.16

Components of the SES Index Used in the WISC Data Set[a]

Component	Correlation with SES	Partial regression, standard form, SES on component			
		a	b	c	d
Father's occupation	.790	.442	.554	–	.580
Father's education	.723	.295	.347	–	.457
Mother's education	.590	.210	.245	–	–
Respondent's perception of					
Parents' ability to support college	.633	.253	–	.395	–
Amount of parental support available	.557	.195	–	.279	–
Level of family's economic status	.490	.089	–	.222	–
Multiple correlation (R)	–	1.000	.913	.717	.888

[a] Source: WISC data set for 5004 senior boys (prefollow-up sample), preliminary calculations.

The intelligence quotient (IQ) is the percentile rank on the Henmon-Nelson test used in Wisconsin schools. The category educational aspirations (Ed Asp), so-called in the present discussion, refers to the respondent's statement in regard to "what do you plan to do next year?" Those not planning further schooling at that time are scored 0; scores of 1–4 were assigned for plans to attend schools at various levels, ranging up to university or liberal arts college. The category occupational aspirations (Occ Asp) refers to the "type of occupation" the respondent "hopes eventually to enter." Broad categories are scored on an arbitrary scale roughly similar to the North-Hatt prestige scale or Duncan's socioeconomic scale. School grades were used to compute high school rank (HSR) expressed on the basis of percentiles within the respondent's class.

Educational achievement (Ed Ach) refers to the amount of schooling beyond high school attained by the respondent as of the follow-up survey in 1964; categories include those with no schooling beyond high school, those attending vocational schools, those with some college, those completing college, and those with some postgraduate work. Occupational achievement (Occ Ach) refers to the score on Duncan's socioeconomic scale of the occupation being pursued as of the 1964 follow-up.

Two models were developed to represent the interpretation that aspirations are expressions of an underlying motivational variable; the two are shown together in Fig. 6.12. Substantively, the two models make the same basic general postulate: that expressed aspirations are reflections of an underlying orientation, which may well be a complex of several distinct motives. The difference between the two models arises from the specific assumptions that are required to translate this premise into numerical estimates of parameters. The two models will be described in turn; the basic structure of each can best be brought out by describing the derivation of equations for securing parameter estimates.

Model WISC–1 posits a hypothetical motivation variable M that is allowed to be correlated with the two observed predetermined variables, SES and IQ. Given such correlation, it is assumed that both Ed Asp and Occ Asp depend on M, that neither depends (directly) on IQ, and that only Ed Asp depends directly on SES. The last assumption is reasonable in view of the emphasis in the Ed Asp questionnaire item on definite plans, supposing that plans will somewhat reflect resources for effecting them. Variables $1, \ldots, 4$ and M can be treated as a self-contained system without referring to the remainder of Fig. 6.12a. The basic theorem of path analysis can be used to write the following equations:

$$r_{13} = p_{31} + p_{3M} r_{1M}$$
$$r_{23} = p_{31} r_{12} + p_{3M} r_{2M}$$
$$r_{14} = p_{4M} r_{1M}$$
$$r_{24} = p_{4M} r_{2M}$$
$$r_{34} = p_{3M} p_{4M} + p_{31} r_{14}.$$

From the third and fourth equations, $r_{1M} = r_{2M} r_{14}/r_{24}$. Substitute this into the

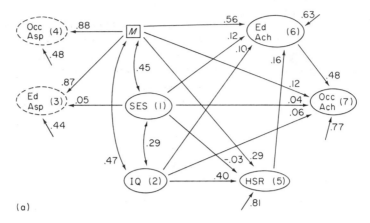

(a)

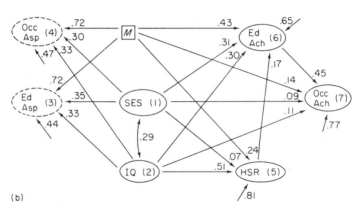

(b)

Fig. 6.12. Alternative models interpreting aspirations as indicators of motivational factor in achievement. (Path coefficients estimated from WISC data set; see Table 6.15.) (a) Model WISC-1; (b) Model WISC-2.

first equation and solve the first two equations simultaneously for p_{31} and the product ($p_{3M}r_{2M}$), obtaining

$$p_{31} = \frac{r_{13}r_{24} - r_{23}r_{14}}{r_{24} - r_{12}r_{14}},$$

and

$$p_{3M}r_{2M} = \frac{r_{24}(r_{23} - r_{12}r_{13})}{r_{24} - r_{12}r_{14}} = K_1 \text{ (say)}.$$

Since p_{31} is known, we have, from the equation for r_{34},

$$p_{3M}p_{4M} = r_{34} - p_{31}r_{14} = K_2 \text{ (say)}$$

and from the equation for r_{13},

$$p_{3M} r_{1M} = r_{13} - p_{31} = K_3 \text{ (say)},$$

where K_1, K_2, and K_3 are now all known numbers. Hence we have the system

$$p_{3M} r_{2M} = K_1$$
$$p_{3M} p_{4M} = K_2$$
$$p_{3M} r_{1M} = K_3$$
$$p_{4M} r_{1M} = r_{14}$$
$$p_{4M} r_{2M} = r_{24}$$

comprising five equations in five unknowns, The system is solved by straightforward substitutions.

Next we consider the relationships of HSR to the three predetermined variables (1, 2, and M) of the model and its correlations with the two indicators of motivation. The model postulates that HSR depends on SES, IQ, and M, and that these relations together with the correlations of the latter three variables with Ed Asp and Occ Asp account for the correlations between HSR and the two aspirations. Thus we secure four equations corresponding to the known correlations involving HSR:

$$r_{15} = p_{51} + p_{52} r_{12} + p_{5M} r_{1M}$$
$$r_{25} = p_{51} r_{12} + p_{52} + p_{5M} r_{2M}$$
$$r_{35} = p_{51} r_{13} + p_{52} r_{23} + p_{5M} r_{3M}$$
$$r_{45} = p_{51} r_{14} + p_{52} r_{24} + p_{5M} r_{4M}.$$

We already have the values of r_{1M} and r_{2M}; and the values of r_{3M} and r_{4M} are implicit in work already done, for $r_{3M} = p_{3M} + p_{31} r_{1M}$ and $r_{4M} = p_{4M}$. Hence we have four equations in the three unknowns, p_{51}, p_{52}, and p_{5M}. As a simple, heuristic device for securing a unique solution, let us add the last two equations together to obtain a set of three linear equations in three unknowns, which are then solved by the usual straightforward routine. This procedure means that the equations do not exactly fit the values of r_{35} and r_{45}, but the fit is very close. Using the three path coefficient obtained by this procedure and the three correlations in the third equation, we obtain the implied value $r_{35}^* = .4216$, which compares with the actual $r_{35} = .4215$. Similarly, the fourth equation yields the implied value $r_{45}^* = .41359$ as compared with the actual $r_{45} = .4136$. (In further calculations on the model we should, for sake of consistency, use the implied rather than the actual correlations, thought it can hardly make any difference in the results.) The close agreement indicates that the model has passed one rudimentary "test" of the suitability of its assumptions, albeit not a very conclusive test.

We now consider Ed Ach as an outcome of the process depicted by the model, assuming that it depends on HSR, IQ, SES, and M but has only indirect linkages with the aspiration variables. It is easy to argue the case for these four influences on Ed Ach. HSR is often used as a criterion for admission to college and, moreover, may represent a pattern of scholastic work habits that should carry over more or less directly into further study. Presumably, IQ represents scholastic aptitude and SES, among other things, the economic means to use in pursuit of further education. Finally, the motivation variable M, although its nature is by no means fully specified by the model, presumably summarizes such tendencies and orientations as need for achievement and persistence. The question left open by this argument is whether these relationships fully account for the correlations of Ed Ach with Ed Asp and Occ Asp. We have five known correlations of Ed Ach with prior variables and the aspiration variables.

$$r_{16} = p_{61} + p_{62}r_{12} + p_{65}r_{15} + p_{6M}r_{1M}$$

$$r_{26} = p_{61}r_{12} + p_{62} + p_{65}r_{25} + p_{6M}r_{2M}$$

$$r_{56} = p_{61}r_{15} + p_{62}r_{25} + p_{65} + p_{6M}r_{5M}$$

$$r_{36} = p_{61}r_{13} + p_{62}r_{23} + p_{65}r_{35}^* + p_{6M}r_{3M}$$

$$r_{46} = p_{61}r_{14} + p_{62}r_{24} + p_{65}r_{45}^* + p_{6M}r_{4M}$$

We note that from earlier work we may compute $r_{5M} = p_{5M} + p_{51}r_{1M} + p_{52}r_{2M}$, so that we have five equations in the four unknown path coefficients. As before, we reduce the number of equations by adding the last two together into one—in effect, giving them slightly less weight in the determination of the solution. Once we have that solution, we can compute the implied values $r_{36}^* = .6687$ and $r_{46}^* = .6510$, which are reasonably close to the actual values $r_{36} = .6861$ and $r_{46} = .6336$. Again, the model passes a modest "test."

The final step is dictated by the assumption that Occ Ach depends on Ed Ach, IQ, SES, and M for more or less obvious and plausible reasons. It is not assumed that Occ Ach depends on school grades, HSR, directly; nor is any direct connection assumed between Occ Ach and Occ Asp or Ed Asp. After noting that the value of $r_{6M} = p_{6M} + p_{61}r_{1M} + p_{62}r_{2M} + p_{65}r_{5M}$ is implicit in previous work, we can write six equations in four unknown path coefficients:

$$r_{17} = p_{71} + p_{72}r_{12} + p_{76}r_{16} + p_{7M}r_{1M}$$

$$r_{27} = p_{71}r_{12} + p_{72} + p_{76}r_{26} + p_{7M}r_{2M}$$

$$r_{67} = p_{71}r_{16} + p_{72}r_{26} + p_{76} + p_{7M}r_{6M}$$

$$r_{37} = p_{71}r_{13} + p_{72}r_{23} + p_{76}r_{36}^* + p_{7M}r_{3M}$$

$$r_{47} = p_{71}r_{14} + p_{72}r_{24} + p_{76}r_{46}^* + p_{7M}r_{4M}$$

$$r_{57} = p_{71}r_{15} + p_{72}r_{25} + p_{76}r_{56} + p_{7M}r_{5M}.$$

We add the last three equations into a single one so that a unique solution is obtained for the four path coefficients. We may then check the implied values, $r_{37}^* = .4767, r_{47}^* = .4632,$ and $r_{57}^* = .3414,$ against the actual values, $r_{37} = .4714,$ $r_{47} = .4641,$ and $r_{57} = .3458.$ All discrepancies are in the third decimal place so that the final set of assumptions in the model passes its modest "test."

Comments on the numerical results with model 1 are reserved until model 2 has been described. In terms of the structure of relationships, the two models differ only in the assumptions used to relate the indicators Ed Asp and Occ Asp to the hypothetical motivation variable M. In model 2, M is assumed to be uncorrelated with IQ and SES. To see how this assumption is used, consider variables 1, ..., 5, and M as a self-contained system with reference to variables 5 and 6. Essentially, M is taken to explain such intercorrelations of HSR, Occ Asp, and Ed Asp as are not explained on the assumption that each of these variables depends on both SES and IQ. The procedures is to compute the regressions of HSR on SES and IQ, of Occ Asp on SES and IQ, and of Ed Asp on SES and IQ, thus obtaining the path coefficients $p_{51}, p_{52}, p_{41}, p_{42}, p_{31},$ and $p_{32}.$ Our assumption that M is the common factor in HSR, Ed Asp, and Occ Asp which accounts for their residual intercorrelations allows us to write

$$r_{34} = p_{3M} p_{4M} + p_{31} r_{14} + p_{32} r_{24}$$

$$r_{35} = p_{3M} p_{5M} + p_{31} r_{15} + p_{32} r_{25}$$

$$r_{45} = p_{4M} p_{5M} + p_{41} r_{15} + p_{42} r_{25}.$$

Since the correlations are known and we have obtained values for $p_{31}, p_{32}, p_{41},$ and $p_{42},$ these equations take the form

$$p_{3M} p_{4M} = C_1$$

$$p_{3M} p_{5M} = C_2$$

$$p_{4M} p_{5M} = C_3$$

and are easily solved by straightforward substitution.

The remainder of the model generates the same two sets of equations obtained at the corresponding juncture in the work with model 1. A different solution routine was used, however, for the sake of variety if for no other reason. Of the five equations for known correlations with Ed Ach, only the four corresponding to $r_{16}, r_{26}, r_{46},$ and r_{56} were used to solve for the unknown path coefficients. The fifth equation, therefore, supplies an implied correlation, which works out as $r_{36}^* = .6513,$ as compared with the actual $r_{36} = .6861.$ Thus, although Ed Asp is not assumed in the model to influence Ed Ach, and although the correlation between these two variables is not used in estimating the parameters of the model, these estimates imply a value of r_{36} that is within .035 of the actual value.

In similar fashion, in the last set of six equations are two, those for r_{37} and r_{47}, that were ignored in solving for the four path coefficients. Given the estimates of the latter, we have the implied values $r_{37}^* = .4912$ (when the implied value, r_{36}^*, is used in the calculation) and $r_{47}^* = .4870$. These are to be compared with the actual values, .4714 and .4641, respectively.

As far as such "tests" may be considered relevant, there is little basis for choosing between the two models. Indeed, there is nothing in the numerical results to afford a basis for such a choice, unless one has strong preconceptions such that one set of results seems more reasonable than the other. No claim can be made, moreover, that the two models exhaust the logical possibilities with respect to models that treat aspirations as indicators of motivation.

In one respect, the models hardly differ (and this trivial difference may reflect variation in the estimation procedure as well as the structure of the models), that is, in regard to the direct determinants of occupational achievement. Corresponding paths to Occ Ach are very similar in the two models, and neither has an advantage with respect to "explained" variation. By contrast, model 1 gives heavier weight to M as a direct influence on Ed Ach and lesser weights to IQ and SES, while HSR has about the same modest weight in both models. Evidently, the reason for this contrast is that in model 1 M is allowed to be rather substantially intercorrelated with SES and IQ. In model 2, however, the paths from SES to Ed Ach and IQ to Ed Ach are not affected by the inclusion of M. Hence this model gives an immediate impression of what is gained in a formal explanatory sense by inclusion of M along with SES and IQ as predetermined variables of the model. Model 2, however, makes equally good use of this additional information since the residual for Ed Ach is about the same as in model 1.

The differences between the two models in regard to the paths to HSR are surprisingly small, given the ostensibly different logic on which they are obtained in the two cases. In model 2, HSR is, in effect, itself regarded as an indicator of motivation, along with Ed Asp and Occ Asp, and the treatment of the three variables with respect to SES, IQ, and M is completely symmetrical. In model 1, however, HSR does not come into the picture until interrelations of the two aspirations and the three predetermined variables are established. The main difference, numerically, between the two models, is that model 2 shows IQ and SES as somewhat more important determinants of HSR than does model 1. Indeed, in the latter there is an anomalous, though numerically negligible, negative path from SES to HSR.

The two models evidently entail a somewhat different conception of how motives, intellect, and family circumstances combine to give rise to aspirations, as these may be expressed in response to direct interrogation. In model 1 aspirations are taken to be relatively "pure" measures of motivation, but the motivation variable is intercorrelated with SES and IQ. The model does not attempt to specify how such intercorrelation arises—whether high IQ leads to high motivation or vice versa, for example, or whether both have some common cause in the genes. Hence it can only be stipulated that M in model 1 must be assumed to be determinate only after any causal relationships giving rise to such correlation have done their work. In arguing for model 2, however, one might insist that M represents an innate or congenital disposition pattern that is uninfluenced by intellectual traits or socioeconomic circumstances but that combines with the latter in producing such manifestations as aspirations and in affecting such behavioral outcomes as school grades, educational attainment, and occupational achievement. Perhaps enough has been said to suggest that there is no intention here of making a contribution to the theory of motivation. The much more modest goal of making some plausible assessment of how motivation may influence achievement is elusive enough.

A reconciliation, or at least a clarification of the differences between the two models, may be facilitated by a study of their respective reduced forms, as depicted in Fig. 6.13 and 6.14. This comparison, as well as the one afforded by Fig. 6.12, makes it clear that there is no difference in overall "explanatory power" between the models to suggest a choice between them. Parenthetically,

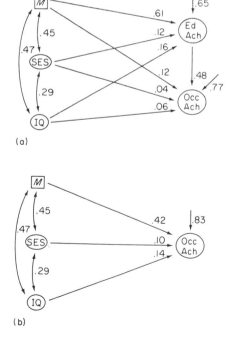

Fig. 6.13. Reduced forms of model WISC-1.

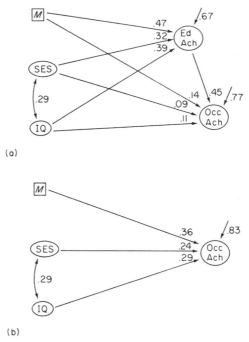

Fig. 6.14. Reduced forms of model WISC-2.

we might note that neither model represents an improvement, in this purely statistical respect, between a straight regression of variable 7 on variables 1, ..., 6, ignoring the construct *M*.

In model 1, motivation looms larger as an influence on Ed Ach and Occ Ach than in model 2, reflecting the assumption in the former that motivation is correlated with SES and IQ. One might elect to state the matter this way: Model 2 depicts a conception of "motivations" that tends to locate it in sources independent of socioeconomic influences and intellectual ability. Perhaps *M* in model 2 is simply the earlier, more nearly innate basis of what is seen as *M* in model 1. In model 1 we are observing (actually, of course, constructing) the motivation variable after it has emerged from a process of organism–environment interaction that sets up correlations between *M* and both SES and IQ.

Suppose one held to the view that *M*, as it operates in model 1, is actually a "socialized motivation" that represents the resultant of a combination of three factors: some congenital, perhaps temperamental, basis of motivation—(call it *M'*); intelligence; and socioeconomic environment. Then we might regard *M* as caused by (dependent on) *M'*, SES, and IQ. This hypothesis is represented by

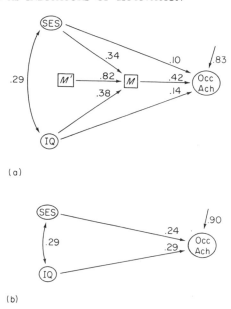

Fig. 6.15. Modification of model WISC-1 to treat *M* as dependent on SES, IQ, and earlier motivation (*M′*) and reduced form of modified model.

Fig. 6.15a, in which the assumption is made that *M* is completely determined by the three identified factors. If we now compute the reduced form of this modified model, as in Fig. 6.15b, we obtain the same coefficients for SES and IQ that we had in the reduced form of model 2 (Fig. 6.14b). The latter, however, shows *M* as an influence on Occ Ach, operating independently of SES and IQ. On the hypothesis just stated this must be, in actuality, *M′*, that is, the postulated early or congenital basis of motivation.

Whatever the details of the argument, therefore, we reach much the same general conclusion on the basis of either model: If aspirations are conceived as indicators of motivation, then the data allow us to claim that motives play a significant role in the process of achievement, either as intervening variables transmitting the effect of socioeconomic background and intelligence or working independently thereof, or in both ways. The data do not permit a choice among these possibilities, nor do these exhaust the possibilities that might be considered. A further examination of several hypotheses about indicators of motivation is available in the DAS data, as reported in Duncan & Featherman (1970). The latter exercise should be interesting to the student of stratification in that it entertains a model in which both a measure of intelligence and some indicators of motivation are included.

6.6   Conclusions

A wide variety of concepts and approaches to measurement can be subsumed under the heading of "dispositions." We have not sought to adjudicate conceptual issues but rather to point up some problems in measuring dispositions and in interpreting the results of such measurement in the light of hypotheses concerning their operation.

Both occupational "aspirations" and occupational "plans" are correlated with family background. The slope of the regression on father's occupational status is higher, however, to the extent that the stimulus question emphasizes realistic prospects (as against fantasies or desires) for occupational achievement. With such an emphasis, the slope of occupational plans on father's status is about the same as the slope of actual achievement on father's status. However, the mean level of aspirations is higher than the mean level of achievement. This suggests that, despite pervasive intergenerational upward mobility, many men fall short of realizing the aspiration of their youth.

Educational plans can be reported rather realistically when the questions designed to elicit them are appropriately phrased. Nonetheless, one can entertain the hypothesis that at any given time not all respondents will have made plans that are equally well crystallized. Hence, plans as measured may be interpreted as an indicator of "latent decision" to pursue further education. On this interpretation, very little influence of family background carries over into a *direct* effect on educational attainment, for the hypothetical construct latent decision can be so formulated as to take background factors fully into account.

Use of a projective test to infer level of achievement motivation has been strongly advocated, and the well-known study of Crockett (1962) used achievement motivation so measured as an independent variable influencing occupational mobility. We reworked Crockett's material to accomplish two things: (1) to render the coding of occupations in his material comparable to that used in the remainder of this project and (2) to put the relevant variables into a format suited to the type of model developed here. When this is done, we find that the projective measure of need achievement has a significant association with achieved occupational status, to that extent supporting Crockett's original conclusion. However, inasmuch as this measure is *negatively* correlated with father's occupation (though perhaps not significantly so) the need-achievement score does not turn out to be an especially informative intervening variable. Its inclusion in a model does not help to explain the intergenerational correlation of occupational statuses.

In research on social processes operating in real human populations we shall often, if not always, be in the position of *inferring* motives from one or another kind of indicator rather than measuring them directly. In this event we must make explicit the conceptual scheme upon which the inference rests as well as that containing the hypotheses concerning how motives operate. One of our most elaborately constructed models provides a paradigm for the problem in which it must be assumed that the indicators of motivational factors are contaminated by the very outcomes that the motives presumably help to explain. On certain postulates about how the contamination is effected, it becomes possible to derive rigorously an interpretation that departs in several significant particulars from one that merely interprets indicators naively. While this particular exercise is perhaps most interesting for its suggestions about method, it does lead to the suggestion that motives which are positively intercorrelated may nonetheless have opposing influences on achievement outcomes.

We had access to one body of longitudinal data (WISC), including indicators of motivation (if educational and occupational aspirations are so interpreted) measured at a time well before the achievements they presumably influenced. We explored the consequences of postulating an unobserved motivational factor underlying the expressed aspirations. One model developed along these lines suggested that motivation, as crystallized by late adolescence and as indicated by adolescents' aspirations, is indeed a significant factor intervening between family socioeconomic background and intelligence, on the one hand, and occupational achievement, on the other. The two prior factors, nevertheless, appear to retain significant direct (unmediated) effects, and inclusion of the motivational factor in the causal scheme did not result by any means in an approach to complete "explanation" of the outcome.

Somewhat less significance could be assigned to achievement-related motivations when measured by the attitudinal statements of adults (FGMA panel data). In this case, motivations could account for only a small portion of the effects of background on achievement, although they had positive, nontrivial effects on attainments some 10 years later. The differences in conclusions drawn from the WISC and FGMA exercises are a matter of degree and not substance, but they do point up the possibility that motivations (and their indicators) may express their effects on achievements at specific points in the life cycle. If this speculation were supported in future research, it would suggest the need for a development theory of achievement motivation which would explain how one dimension of the total tendency to achieve (say, that indicated by adolescent aspirations) gives issue to another dimension (as indicated by the achievement attitudes and values of adults) and why its effect is linked to a specific stage in the socioeconomic life cycle.

Finally, in several of the models in this chapter, the data have been shown to be consistent with—that is, they cannot be used to disprove—an interpretation that treats underlying but unobserved motivational factors as relatively important determinants of occupational achievement. At the same time, these models do not begin to approximate a "complete explanation" of achievement, nor would we want to assert that motivational variables are "key" ones in the processes of status attainment as represented here. Moreover, the attribution of considerable importance to motivational factors is carried through consistently *only* by the simultaneous acceptance of the assumption that the available indicators of motives are exceedingly fallible.

Chapter 7

Intervening Variables, III: Social Influences

The concept of "social influences" in this chapter is that of other individuals or groups who may have an impact on a given indvidual's socioeconomic achievement. Parents, neighbors, friends, teachers, classmates, and spouses are some of the categories of significant others whose influence is often perceived by individuals themselves or alleged by observers. What form the influence may take is itself problematic: It may issue from direct interaction between the individual and the other(s), or it may be that the latter in effect define existential conditions for the individual, apart from direct interaction. The influence of the family of orientation, insofar as this may be inferred from the correlation between level of social origin and level of achievement, is, of course, assumed throughout this study. In the present chapter, parental influence means something a little more specific; the relevant indicators are those that purport to tell whether the individual is subject to patterns of personal interaction with parents that lead to a stress on achievement. Although this variable has received a good deal of emphasis in the literature (Kahl, 1953; Bordua, 1960), the study remains to be executed in which the long-run influence of parents' ambitions for their children can be assessed. A few interesting clues turn up in our effort to include this type of variable in partial models of the process of achievement.

Indeed, it would be more accurate than modest to concede that "a few interesting clues" are primarily what we have to exhibit with regard to the influence of wives, friends, and classmates. Yet, we feel that the problem of incorporating such influences into models of the achievement process is sufficiently important that it should be carefully studied even in the absence of wholly ideal data. The effort to make such extensions of the basic model has proved to be most interesting in its own right.

7.1 Wives and Mothers

This section describes an investigation of the relationships (a) of characteristics of wives with the occupational status of their husbands and (b) of selected psychological and background factors of mothers with their expressed desires for their children to attend college. One question raised for discussion centers on the role of the wife in shaping the career of her husband via the influence of such factors as her intelligence, achievement motivation, drive to get ahead, education, and social origins (occupational status of her father). The other issue poses the question of the effects of psychological characteristics of the mother in forming the aspirations she entertains for her children to attend college. Hence, at the core of both problems lies the whole issue of the interaction of demographic and psychological variables within the general context of the process of occupational achievement.

That wives may spur their spouses upward occupationally is expressed by the stereotype of the ambitious social climber. Realistically, one might well expect wives to assist in molding the occupational careers of their husbands, at least in a statistical sense. The latter qualification underscores the issue of assortative mating. Marriages are made in social reality and not in heaven, and the woman brings a social and psychological dowry to the union. That this dowry is selected rather than randomly assigned is the crux of selective mating.

To explore the roles of wives and mothers in mobility patterns, we used the FGMA data set. The unique characteristics of these data require description since they bear upon any analysis and interpretation derived from them.

Westoff and his collaborators (1961) sampled in the eight largest standard metropolitan areas (populations of 2 million or more) in the United States in 1956, excluding Boston; these areas included New York, Chicago, Los Angeles, Philadelphia, Detroit, San Francisco–Oakland, and Pittsburgh. Since fertility patterns constituted their main dependent variable, the investigators selected only couples whose second child was born during September of 1956. In addition, the couples resided at birth as well as at the time of interview in one of the eight SMA's; both spouses were white, married once, and currently living together. Respondents ranged in age from 20 to 30 years; husbands employed in farm categories and/or spouses residing in institutions were excluded. Initial interviews produced 1165 usable responses, one for each couple. The interviewers left a psychological questionnaire supplement with each partner to be completed and mailed to the investigators; 961 females and 941 males returned completed schedules. At least part of the psychological questionnaire included items from the Personality Research Inventory, designed by David E. Saunders of the Educational Testing Service at Princeton.

These specific features of the sample might raise doubts about its utility for research of a more general type. However, if one reasons that the couples in the FGMA study represent a common type of American family (young adults between 20 and 30 years of age, parents of two children, and residing in one of eight largest SMA's), then the peculiarity of the data is mitigated somewhat. As an external check, national statistics from the OCG data (for men 20–64 years old residing in urbanized areas of 1 million or more inhabitants) were compared with the FGMA data. The frequency distributions of male respondents by their own occupations and their fathers' occupations in the two samples are shown in Table 7.1. Looking at the proportions of the respective column totals contributed by each occupational category for both samples, one sees that the two bodies of data neither compare exactly nor deviate suspiciously from each other. Hence, for the purposes of the analysis at hand, there is no apparent bias in the FGMA data.

Before embarking upon the empirical analysis of the data, some remarks are offered concerning the validity and reliability of several of the indexes of psychological traits in the FGMA data. To measure the intelligence of female respondents, a twenty-word verbal IQ test was administered as part of the initial interview. This measure of intelligence, drawn from the work of Thorndike, comprises a short, verbal measure of intelligence which reliably reflected IQ in a survey setting. Thorndike (1942) assessed the validity of this measure in a published article; and Thorndike and Gallup (1944) applied the technique in an American survey. The results of these discussions of the verbal measure of intelligence cast no serious doubts on its use in the present context.

To measure wife's drive to get ahead, the FGMA investigators chose a device to discriminate "which values would be sacrificed to get ahead." Respondents were asked, for example:

In order to get ahead, would you be willing to become more active in community organizations and clubs not of your own choice?

Would you be willing to leave your friends?

Would you be willing to postpone having a child?

Would you be willing to keep quiet about your religious views in order to get ahead?

Would you be willing to have your husband take a chance on a job that he might be less certain of holding, if it had better opportunities?

The greater the number of "sacrifices" the woman said she was willing to make, the greater was the drive to get ahead, scoring 1 (low) to 9 (high). This method of measuring the drive to get ahead, while it is not new with the FGMA study (see Reissman, 1953), poses a problem of validity. The instrument

TABLE 7.1

Comparison of Occupational Distributions of Fathers and Sons in FGMA Data and OCG Sample of Urbanized Areas with Populations of 1 Million or More

Duncan's occupational SES	North-Hatt scores[a]	Frequency and proportional distributions							
		FGMA data				OCG data			
		Fathers		Sons		Fathers		Sons	
		Frequency	Proportion	Frequency	Proportion	Frequency	Proportion	Frequency	Proportion
0–4	33–38	59	.052	97	.083	453	.038	1013	.079
5–9	39–48	160	.141			960	.080		
10–14	49–54	77	.068	85	.073	2109	.175	647	.051
15–19	55–58	52	.046	76	.065	2081	.172	2087	.163
20–24	59–61	210	.185	254	.218	1327	.110	1539	.120
25–29	62–64								
30–34	65–66			226	.194			2658	.207
35–39	67	138	.122			2038	.169		
40–44	68–69								
45–49	70–71			195	.167			1461	.114
50–54	72	296	.261			1256	.104		
55–59	73–74								
60–64	75								
65–69	76–77	88	.078	81	.070	1036	.086	1876	.146
70–74	78–79								
75–79	80–81	34	.030	111	.095	566	.047	1174	.091
80–84	82–83								
85–89	84–86	20	.018	40	.034	248	.021	367	.028
90+	87–96								
		1134	1.001	1165	0.999	12,074	1.002	12,822	0.999

[a] North-Hatt equivalents given to Duncan SES code. Westoff used 5-point intervals of the North-Hatt scale. Therefore, even though the North-Hatt equivalents have been clustered to approximate Westoff's grouping of his intervals, the match is not perfect.

purports to measure the *amount* of the drive or perhaps the intensity of desiring change by counting the *number* of "sacrificed" values. The burden of justification of the method falls on the theoretical structure of the questions themselves. First, in counting the *number* of sacrificial answers and comparing respondents on the basis of relative sacrifices (strength of drive) it is assumed that each person has an equal chance of sacrificing any of these values. Put in another way, each statement (value) should have an equal probability of being sacrificed if all persons were equal in drive to get ahead. In fact, however, it is hard to establish equivalence (in a "sacrificial" sense) in all the value statements. For example, does one require the same, more, or less drive in leaving one's friends as opposed to sending one's children to a less satisfactory school in order to get ahead? If there is a difference in drive in each case (an empirical proposition), then counting the number of sacrificed values gives a false estimate of the strength of the drive itself. Further, even if each value involves the same amount of drive, does each question on the schedule include only *one* value to be sacrificed? Similar questions arise with virtually any psychometric approach to personality. Here, as in all research making use of such instruments, there is a need for caution in interpreting both what is meant by the drive to get ahead as it is used in the present data and what can be concluded about the relationship of its content to other variables in an analytical sense.

Another conception used in the FGMA research involves the mother's aspirations for her children's college education. Remembering the time in the life cycle of these women and children when the interview was conducted, one is discussing aspirations for two children who are quite young (the younger actually is less than 1 year old). The utility of assessing the mother's aspirations at this juncture lies in being able to partial out any confounding influences of child's college suitability (intellectual capacities and personal interests being still unascertained) on the kind and quality of maternal aspirations. One might expect, however, that the correlation between current expressed aspirations and later ones, based in part on the mother's assessment of the child's college suitability, would be less than perfect (see the discussion of this point in Section 7.2). Further, since our main interest in these aspirations is as contextual elements of a child's occupational career, the fact that the child's abilities and personal preference still are unknown does bear upon the predictive strength of mother's aspirations measured at this time.

The specific nature of the aspirational questions also should be mentioned. Four items, two multiple-choice and two open-ended, are used to elicit mother's educational aspirations for her children:

Do you *expect* to send your children to college?

How do you expect this college to be paid for?

Would you send a *daughter* of yours to college even if it meant serious financial hardship?

Would you send a *son* of yours to college even if it meant serious financial hardship?

Respondents were scored low to high (1–7) on the criteria below:

1. Do not expect to send children to college
   If it meant serious financial hardship:
2. Wouldn't send either son or daughter
3. Not send daughter; depends or don't know for son
4. Depends or don't know for both
5. Not send daughter; send son
6. Depends or don't know for daughter; send son
7. Would send both

Again the problem of the quantification of the categories can be solved in only an arbitrary way. That sending a son to college and not the daughter in times of financial stress indicates that a woman has *higher* (directional and quantitative) educational aspirations for her children than a woman who would send the daughter and not the son is an ad hoc assumption which, although plausible, could be debated either way.

The final conceptual problem centers on the construct called "need achievement," or the woman's need to achieve. To measure this psychological quality, the FGMA questionnaire included several multiple-choice questions, some of which follow:

9. Can you always be counted on to try to do your best job regardless of how hopeless it may be?

20. Which do you do? Just what comes along as most of the crowd does or set yourself a goal of attainment that is quite hard?

42. Do you usually like work that requires accuracy in fine detail?

64. What kind of goals do you usually set for yourself? Low enough so that you can reach them without too much effort or too high for you to reach without a lot of effort?

If what the FGMA investigators meant by "need achievement" is what psychologists like McClelland and Atkinson mean when they speak of the need to achieve, then the measurement instruments appear to fall short of eliciting the same motivational components.

How do McClelland and Atkinson define achievement-related needs? Without becoming too mired in the jargon of psychology, one can describe the achievement motive by analogy. As a motive, the need to achieve is like the hunger motive, which also is a "need," although more biologically specified. The domain of the achievement motive, however, consists of only those instances "when an individual knows that his performance will be evaluated (by himself or by others) in terms of some standard of excellence and that the consequences of his actions will be either a favorable evaluation (success) or an unfavorable evaluation (failure). It is, in other words, a theory of *achievement-*

oriented performance" (Atkinson, 1964, pp. 240–241). Further, the achievement motive might be conceived as a *"capacity for taking pride in accomplishment* when success at one or another activity is achieved" (p. 241).

Atkinson has developed a theory of achievement motivation which further qualifies the phenomenon. He states that in addition to the persistence of an enduring motive component, achievement motivation is associated with two situational factors or products of individual experience—the expectancy of success and the value of incentive. In further qualifying achievement motivation, McClelland (1961) indicated the importance of the person's feelings of responsibility for outcomes, of his explicit knowledge of results, and of the existence of some degree of risk. In the context of these criteria, Atkinson's notions about expectancy of success take account of the person's subjective evaluation of success at a given task. Further, the person appraises a given task in terms of the reward he may enjoy should he complete it successfully or of the chagrin he may feel if he fails; hence for some tasks the incentive is greater than for others.

In terms of all three components of achievement motivation, Atkinson posits that the tendency to achieve success is a product (multiplicative model) of the motive to achieve, the expectancy of success, and the incentive value of success at a given task. The latter two components vary from task to task, while the motive itself endures as part of the personality. For a given task, the incentive value is the complement of the perception of success ($I = 1 - P$). Tasks with no or little probability of failure (high probability of success) offer small reward for successful completion. Likewise, extremely difficult tasks (low probability of success) promise almost certain failure and inspire few bold adventurers. From these general propositions, Atkinson (1964, pp. 240–247) deduces that where the motive to achieve (motive component) is relatively strong, one would expect that the person will select a task of *intermediate* difficulty (medium risk) so as to optimize both success and reward.

To measure achievement motivation, McClelland and Atkinson maintain that Henry Murray's TAT pictures best allow a respondent to project his motive-related imagery. Any other method of eliciting achievement-related motives fails to encompass these themes in a contextual, holistic fashion and may not generate comparable measures of the need to achieve. Because of their partial effectiveness, questionnaire items may deal with one aspect of achievement need which, taken by itself, has no unitary significance. For example, FGMA question 9, cited previously, may evoke a person's persistence independently of his need to achieve. Question 20 asks about setting "hard" goals, while Atkinson's theory of n Ach deals with *moderately difficult, realistic goals*. Similar criticisms could be made of other FGMA items.

This digression into the limitations of the FGMA measure serves no other purpose than to warn the wise that all who need do not achieve. The FGMA instrument may well have measured some internally consistent achievement syndrome (as indicated by a factor analysis), but that it taps the achievement motive in the McClelland and Atkinson sense is doubtful; only correlational analysis of projective and questionnaire results from the same population can dispel the doubt. For the analysis which follows, the label, need to achieve, abbreviated as n Ach, will be used for convenience without assuming correspondence with McClelland and Atkinson.

Having qualified the data, we may proceed with the analysis. Our basic model suggests the treatment of father's occupational status (X), father's education (V), education of respondent (U), and respondent's first job after completion of education (W) as determinants of current occupational status (Y). From the FGMA data, correlations among X, U, W, and Y were obtained and are compared in Table 7.2 with those for males, age 25–34, in the OCG

TABLE 7.2

Comparison of Zero-order Correlations of Mobility Variables in FGMA Data and for OCG Males, Age 25–34, Nonfarm Background

	Variables*							
	X		U		W		Y	
	OCG	FGMA	OCG	FGMA	OCG	FGMA	OCG	FGMA
X	–		.411	.340	.380	.267	.366	.297
U			–		.574	.541	.657	.641
W					–		.584	.640

* X, Y, and W measured on North-Hatt scale for FGMA, on Duncan's occupational status scale in the OCG data. W is occupation at marriage for FGMA, first job after completion of education for OCG.

data. Actually, this age group in the 1962 OCG study is roughly the same cohort studied in FGMA 5 years earlier, when the men were 20–30 years old. However, the size of place, marital status, and fertility specifications of the FGMA sample may account for some of the larger discrepancies in the size of the correlation coefficients. For example, the closer association between W and Y in the FGMA data may reflect the effects of marriage and children in preventing a man from leaving the occupational status he occupied at marriage. Then, too, some of the discrepancies reflect the different methods of scoring occupations in the two studies. The OCG study used Duncan's occupational status code, and FGMA used the North-Hatt prestige scores. Variable W in the OCG study represented first job after completion of education; for FGMA it was the job at marriage. Naturally, coding errors and lack of reliable respondent reporting also render complete corroboration impossible. In short, while the specific results seem somewhat dissimilar, the general pattern of the relationships appears analogous.

Figure 7.1, which is compatible with our basic model, represents occupational achievement (to the date of the survey) as a function of the husband's own background and prior achievement. If, hypothetically, one were to suggest that husband's achievement depends only on the wife's characteristics, the best estimate of the degree of such dependence obtainable from the FGMA data is shown in Fig. 7.2. Of the two sets of predictors, the husband's characteristics are evidently the more powerful:

$$R^2_{Y(WUX)} = .534 \quad \text{vs.} \quad R^2_{Y(NQDSZ)} = .251.$$

This unsurprising result, however, does not answer our main question, to wit: If one knows (for example) wife's IQ, n Ach score, strength of drive to get ahead, origin status (her father's North-Hatt score), and education, how much additional variation do these variables explain *after* X, U, and W have exerted

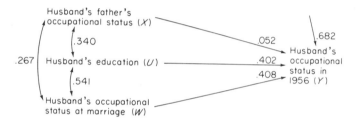

Fig. 7.1. Path diagram showing husband's characteristics as determinants of husband's occupational status (FGMA data). $R^2 = .534$; $N = 1165$.

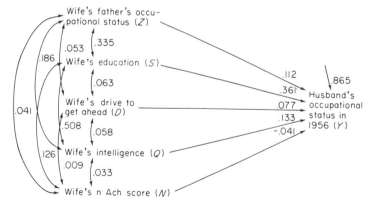

Fig. 7.2. Path diagram representing husband's occupational status as depending on wife's psychological and background characteristics (FGMA data). $R^2 = .251$; $N = 941$.

their influence? Before examining the evidence, one might be reminded that to enlarge appreciably the amount of explained variation, the new variables should operate somewhat independently of W, U, and X and correlate only moderately with each other.

Computing the multiple regression of Y on both the husband's background variables (W, U, and X) and the wife's background and psychological variables (Z, S, D, Q, N), we obtain the multiple $R^2 = .538$. Hence, the adding of wife's background and psychological variables to the husband's factors only increases the explained variance of Y by .004

$$(R^2_{Y(WUXZSDQN)} - R^2_{Y(WUX)}).$$

In addition, all *beta*-coefficients for wife's characteristics, except education, fall below two times their standard errors.

Adding wife's education (S) to the path diagram for the husband's factors (Fig. 7.3) confirms that whatever influences the wife contributes to changes in Y operate mainly through her education, inasmuch as $R^2_{Y(SWUX)} = .536$. Note that S relates slightly more importantly to Y than does X in this diagram.

These results confirm the conclusion of Blau & Duncan (1967, pp. 341–346) that characteristics of wives have little effect on husband's occupational achievement, independently of the characteristics of the husbands, given the moderate to strong patterns of assortative mating on socioeconomic characteristics found in American data. The special interest in the present result stems from the fact that the FGMA data include some measures of the wife's psychological traits that might have been supposed (before the fact) to have strong and independent bearing upon the course of the husband's career even if her socioeconomic background does not. The data do not support such an hypothesis.

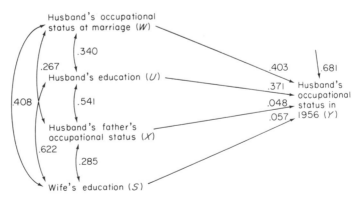

Fig. 7.3. Path diagram representing husband's occupational status as a function of his background and wife's education (FGMA data). $R^2 = .536$; $N = 1165$.

While wives apparently contribute little directly to their husbands' careers—at least by way of their socioeconomic characteristics and personality traits—perhaps in their capacities as mothers they supply some impetus for the mobility of offspring, specifically in terms of children's education. McClelland (1961) and Rosen & D'Andrade (1959) have stated independently that mothers high in need achievement motivate their children similarly, especially through early mastery (achievement) training, few negative sanctions, and positive physical affection. Granting this hypothetical relationship, one might expect a positive association between a mother's n Ach and her aspirations for her children's college education. It was assumed that certain other variables should also be connected with these educational aspirations; such linkages are illustrated in Fig. 7.4. Notice that the model involves all possible paths leading from antecedent variables.

The rationale for the arrow from N to A has been justified conceptually. Arrows also lead from S to A and Z to A. It seemed logical that some tie might bind the length of mother's own educational experience with the aspirations she entertains for her children. Further, maternal education itself can be understood as partly a function of scholastic aptitude or IQ, as partly determined by the motivations called out for the educational experience (N), and as somehow influenced by the differential distribution of educational values and motivation within various occupational strata (Z) (Hyman, 1953). That these stratum-linked values may directly shape the mother's aspirations, apart from the indirect relationship through education, is noted by the arrow from Z to A. Two arrows run to N, one from Z and one from Q. McClelland *et al.* (1953, pp. 63–66) make the case that IQ might be a factor in need achievement, although the precise nature of that connection remains unexplored. Since child-rearing practices often mold achievement motivations, and since the

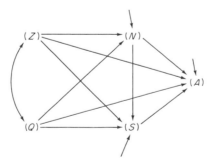

Fig. 7.4. Initial path diagram for explaining mother's aspirations for her children's education. Z, Mother's status origins (her father's occupational status); Q, Mother's intelligence; N, Mother's n Ach score; S, Mother's education; A, Mother's aspirations for children's education.

optimal "achievement-rearing" norms appear stratum-linked (Winterbottom, 1958; McClelland, 1953; Rosen & D'Andrade, 1959), the arrow from Z to N is drawn. The unanalyzed correlation of Z and Q arises from several pieces of literature, citing a correlation between origin status and IQ scores (see Section 5.2). To complete the diagram, three residual arrows are included.

Path coefficients were computed by a multiple regression routine. Noting that many of the initially assumed paths failed to achieve acceptable size (twice the standard error), a new diagram was constructed as Fig. 7.5. According to the revised model, only two direct paths extend from the mother's background and personality to her aspirations for her children's education. Two variables, maternal education (S) and n Ach (N) account for 5.7 percent of the variation of maternal aspirations (A). The larger magnitude of the path for S denotes the greater relative importance of mother's education for her later educational aspirations (child directed). In fact, all prior factors (including a portion of n Ach) appear to exert their influences indirectly or jointly through maternal education (primarily) and n Ach (secondarily). For complete arithmetical consistency Fig. 7.5 would have to show the residual factor in A as correlated to the extent of .046 with Q and .018 with Z, but these are neglected in the interest of simplicity.

From the model in Fig. 7.5, if its present form is accepted, one concludes that mothers may play a role in the occupational careers of their children via their educational aspirations for them. In terms of the influences on the aspirations themselves, background and psychological factors work through maternal education and n Ach, particularly the former.

Let us now consider an extreme hypothesis: that characteristics of a child's family affect his education *only* via his mother's educational aspirations for him. Figure 7.6 illustrates the situation where the father's occupational status (Y), his education (U), and the mother's education (S) do affect the son's educational attainment (U') not directly but only indirectly through the mother's aspirations for her child (A); the only direct effects are from the mother's aspirations themselves.

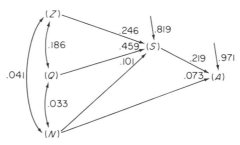

Fig. 7.5. Revised causal model of mother's aspirations for children's education. $R^2_{A(SN)} = .057$; $R^2_{S(ZQN)} = .328$; $N = 941$. See Fig. 7.4 for definition of symbols.

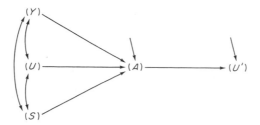

Fig. 7.6. Hypothetical model: background influences on son's education through mother's aspirations only. Y, child's father's occupational status; U, child's father's education; S, child's mother's education; A, mother's aspirations for child's education; U', child's potential education.

The zero-order correlations for $r_{YU'}$, $r_{UU'}$, and $r_{SU'}$ for Fig. 7.6 each can be expanded and expressed as the product of two correlations:

$$r_{YU'} = r_{AU'} r_{AY} \qquad\qquad [1]$$

$$r_{UU'} = r_{AU'} r_{AU} \qquad\qquad [2]$$

$$r_{SU'} = r_{AU'} r_{AS}. \qquad\qquad [3]$$

The FGMA data do not permit computation of $r_{YU'}$, $r_{UU'}$, $r_{SU'}$, and $r_{AU'}$. However, the OCG tabulations for nonfarm men between the ages of 25 and 34 can be used as substitutes for two correlations ($r_{YU'} = .41$ and $r_{UU'} = .42$). Taking these two correlations along with those in FGMA, one can solve the above three equations for $r_{AU'}$ and $r_{SU'}$. Note, however, that equations [1] and [2] contain separate solutions for $r_{AU'}$. If these two solutions are dissimilar, then one must reject Fig. 7.6 as drawn on the basis of its mathematical inconsistency. The correlations (see Table 7.3) can be substituted into equations [1] and [2] as follows:

$$.41 = r_{AU'} (.19)$$

$$\frac{.41}{.19} = r_{AU'}$$

and

$$.42 = r_{AU'} (.29)$$

$$\frac{.42}{.29} = r_{AU'}.$$

One can see that in both equations $r_{AU'}$ exceeds 1.00.

These computations indicate that Fig. 7.6 cannot be accepted; mother's aspirations for her child's education cannot *by themselves* transmit the effects

TABLE 7.3

Zero-Order Correlation Matrix for FGMA Data

Variable[a]	X	U	W	Y	Z	S	D	Q	N	A
X	–	.340	.267	.297	.226	.285	.109	.188	.056	.106
U		–	.541	.641	.280	.622	.112	.434	.018	.228
W			–	.640	.263	.408	.091	.299	.039	.139
Y				–	.260	.466	.113	.340	.014	.191
Z					–	.335	.053	.186	.041	.093
S						–	.063	.508	.126	.228
D							–	.058	.009	.095
Q								–	.033	.158
N									–	.100

[a] Key: X, Husband's father's occupational status; U, husband's education; W, husband's occupational status at marriage; Y, husband's occupational status in 1957; Z, wife's origin status (wife's father's occupation); S, wife's education; D, wife's drive to get ahead; Q, wife's IQ; N, wife's n Ach; A, wife's aspirations for her children's education.

of father's occupation and education and mother's own education to a son's educational attainment.

While Fig. 7.6 clearly must be rejected, could some modification be made which would allow a consistent solution to the diagram? One possible modification appears in Fig. 7.7, which adds a direct effect of Y on U' to the other direct effect of A on U'. One can expand the three correlations again as follows:

$$r_{YU'} = p_{U'Y} + p_{U'A} r_{AY} \qquad [1]$$

$$r_{UU'} = p_{U'Y} r_{YU} + p_{U'A} r_{UA} \qquad [2]$$

$$r_{U'S} = p_{U'Y} r_{YS} + p_{U'A} r_{AS}. \qquad [3]$$

Similarly, one can expand the three correlations containing A:

$$r_{AY} = p_{AY} + p_{AU} r_{UY} + p_{AS} r_{SY} \qquad [4]$$

$$r_{AU} = p_{AU} + p_{AY} r_{YU} + p_{AS} r_{SU} \qquad [5]$$

$$r_{AS} = p_{AS} + p_{AU} r_{US} + p_{AY} r_{YS}. \qquad [6]$$

Equations [1], [2], and [3] give solutions for $p_{U'Y}$, $p_{U'A}$, and $r_{U'S}$; equations [4], [5], and [6] solve for p_{AY}, p_{AU}, and p_{AS}:

$$p_{U'Y} = .232 \qquad p_{AY} = .057$$

$$p_{U'A} = .936 \qquad p_{AU} = .111$$

$$r_{U'S} = .38 \qquad p_{AS} = .134.$$

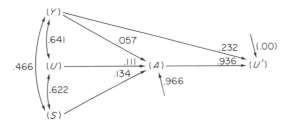

Fig. 7.7. Hypothetical model modified. See Fig. 7.6 for definition of symbols.

If one accepts the *logic* of Fig. 7.7, then one cannot reject the model on the basis of either logic or mathematics. Accepting the algebra allows one to calculate the correlation $r_{AU'}$ (unobserved in either OCG or FGMA data) as follows:

$$r_{AU'} = p_{U'A} + p_{U'Y} r_{YA}$$
$$= (.936) + (.232)(.19)$$
$$= .940.$$

One may question the magnitude of $r_{AU'}$ as calculated from the model. However, since the model is drawn to represent a logical conception of how mothers influence their sons' educational attainment, to question the correlation is to question the present representation of the relationships. Certainly, one can make a case for drawing direct paths between U and U' and S and U' as well as Y and U'. For heuristic and computational reasons only was the latter ($p_{U'Y}$) included rather than any or all of the other possible direct paths. Had these other or additional direct influences been included, however, the magnitude of $r_{AU'}$ surely would have been less. Of course, any such calculated (hypothetical) correlation must be substantiated by sample estimates from real data.

Nevertheless, one can conclude from Figs. 7.6 and 7.7 that by themselves, mother's aspirations for her children's education cannot account for the educational attainment of her son as it is influenced by the education of both parents and the occupational status of the father.

7.2 On the Development of Parents' Aspirations

The results in the previous section leave open the question of how and how much the aspirations of parents for their children's success may influence the children's achievement, although these results suggest that maternal aspirations can hardly be the sole variable mediating the intergenerational correlation of socioeconomic variables. It was noted that maternal aspirations are expressed in the FGMA data as of the time the offspring is still in infancy. We must reckon with the possibility that parental aspirations have a developmental cycle of their own which responds to characteristics of the child becoming manifest only as he matures. Our discussion of this question will be quite tentative, and it seems appropriate to stipulate at the outset the spirit in which the discussion is offered.

In sociological literature one frequently finds discussions based on the juxtaposition of results from several studies. These discussions include conjectures to account for discrepant results of hypotheses suggested by the comparison of findings: "Investigator A found such and such, while Investigator B discovered so and so; putting the two results together, we would conclude this and that."

Our contention is that such discussion is valuable but that much of its value usually is lost for lack of a disciplined approach to the combination of sets of findings. Exploration of the implications of a specific causal model will often serve to rule out some conjectures while lending credence to others. The latter, then, become prime candidates for empirical testing.

This contention is illustrated here by considering a causal model pertaining to the development of parental aspirations for children's higher education. Two sets of apparently disparate data on the subject are at hand. In Section 7.1 we presented an analysis of the FGMA data relating wife's stated aspirations for her children's college education to her own educational attainment, that of her husband, and his occupational status. We also have access to a second set of correlations (WISC data set) computed by William H. Sewell from his study of Wisconsin high school seniors. Only the data for boys are considered here; these boys were asked in 1957 to indicate the degree to which their parents encouraged them to think of going to college.

The results in Section 7.1 indicate a multiple correlation of $.26 = R_{A(YUS)}$ for the relationship of wife's aspirations for children's education to the composite of the three socioeconomic status variables. Sewell's data indicate a correlation of .40 between parents' encouragement and a composite SES score, which includes mother's education, father's education, father's occupation, and some items concerning the boy's perception of the family's financial resources.

For purposes of discussion we shall assume that these two results are comparable in respect to both the definition of a composite SES variable and the reporting of parental aspiration. Flaws in the assumption will be evident, but this is only the first of several assumptions that must be made in order to draw *any* conclusion from a comparison between the two studies.

The most evident discrepancy between the two inquiries—or, at any rate, the one on which the present discussion turns—is that they pertain to different stages in the family cycle. The FGMA respondents were interviewed shortly after the birth of the second child and, in most cases, the older child would have

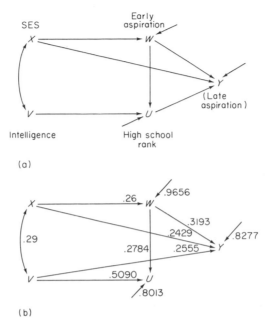

Fig. 7.8. Development of parental aspiration for child's college education, depending on background factors, as represented in two models. (Path coefficients estimated from WISC data set; see Table 7.4) (a) Rejected model; (b) tentatively accepted model.

been still of preschool age. The Wisconsin seniors reported parents' aspirations as of the time the respondents were almost old enough to go to college. The substantive assumption for our discussion is that parental aspirations, while partly a function of socioeconomic background, develop over time and partly in response to the conception that parents form of the child's ability to profit from higher education. (We are neglecting the fact that the family's socio-economic status may also change during this period, though with some additional evidence, it should be possible to incorporate this development into a model as well.)

Figure 7.8 presents two models which embody this interpretation. In both cases it is assumed that family socioeconomic status is correlated with the child's intelligence (though the source of this correlation is not explicated by either model). At the time the "early aspiration" of the parents (actually, in the FGMA data, the mother) is reported, presumably the intelligence of the child is still indeterminate so that the only reason why intelligence and parental aspiration should be correlated is because of their common correlation with socioeconomic status, taking the latter as a cause of aspiration. By contrast, when the "later aspiration" is ascertained, the parents will be reflecting in their encouragement of the son not only their status position but their knowledge of how bright or dull he may be. At the same time it is assumed that there is a carryover or persistence of the aspirations as they were tentatively formed at the earlier date. The degree of persistence is one of the quantities to be estimated by the model.

While they are the same with respect to the foregoing interpretations, the two models exhibited in Fig. 7.8 differ in regard to the role of the child's actual performance in high school, as indicated by his rank in his high school class. The first model, which has to be rejected for reasons which will be noted shortly, assumes that the formation of parental aspirations at the later date depends directly (in part) on high school rank but only indirectly on intelligence. The second model, which cannot be rejected with the data at hand, makes the contrary assumption, that parental aspiration directly depends in part on the son's intelligence and is correlated with high school rank only because school rank and aspiration have common causes.

Still another assumption shared by both models is that parental SES influences school achievement (high school rank) only indirectly, via its initial correlation with child's intelligence, or by way of its influence on aspirations for the child's educational success. In this respect, early aspiration is treated as an intervening variable partially accounting for the correlation of SES with high school rank.

The operational role of the assumptions stated in the last two paragraphs is to set at zero two of the possible path coefficients in a system comprising two initial variables and three dependent variables. In both models, $p_{UX} = 0$; in the rejected model, $p_{YV} = 0$, while in the nonrejected model the alternative assumption that $p_{YU} = 0$ is made. It should be mentioned that some alternative values of the omitted paths might be assumed, but some such assumptions must be made, for there are ten pairs of variables in the system, but only 7 observed correlations (see Table 7.4). One may be skeptical of the assumption that the two omitted paths are identically zero, but our interpretation suggests that one might well have conceptual reasons for thinking them to be of quite secondary significance.

A note on the solution for the numerical values of the path coefficients in the nonrejected model appears at the end of this section. The procedure is much the same for the two models, but the results are quite different. The solution for the rejected model includes a value of $p_{YW} = -1.06$ and one of $r_{YW} = -.76$. This is neither a mathematically impossible result (since a path coefficient may take on an absolute value greater than unity) nor one that can be absolutely ruled out on substantive grounds since we have no independent evidence on the persistence of parental aspirations. The result is, however, quite incredible, for it would imply that parental aspirations tend to reverse themselves over a period of a little more than a decade: Parents with initially high aspirations

TABLE 7.4

Correlation Matrix for Analysis of Parental Aspirations[a]

Variable		X	V	W	U	Y
		Variable (see stub)				
Socioeconomic status	(X)	–	.29	(.26)	.22	.40
Intelligence	(V)	s	–	[.0754]	.53	.35
Early aspiration	(W)	w	d	–	[.3168]	[.4017]
High school rank	(U)	s	s	d	–	.29
Late aspiration	(Y)	s	s	d	s	–

[a] Sources: s, preliminary, unpublished correlations for male high school seniors in WISC data set. Some of these correlations differ from those reported subsequently by Sewell *et al.* (1970), owing to slightly different definitions of variables. w, Computed in Section 7.1 from FGMA data. d, Derived in obtaining the solution shown in Fig. 7.8.

come to have low aspirations, while those with initially low aspirations come to have high aspirations. On the basis of the data at hand, therefore, this model is rejected as implausible. It is not out of the question, however, that a data set free of some of the factors of noncomparability between the FGMA and Wisconsin studies would prove to be compatible with the first model.

The numerical values entered for the second model in Fig. 7.8 are not on the face of the matter implausible, nor do the three derived correlations shown in Table 7.4 arouse suspicion. It appears that the strongest direct influence on later aspirations is the persistence of early aspirations, as represented by a derived correlation, $r_{YW} = .40$. One might have expected this to be higher, but the essence of the interpretation advanced here is that the early aspirations are not crystallized, in view of their remoteness from the actual decision point and in view of the absence of information on the child's ability, one of the significant determinants of the more realistic aspirations. Socioeconomic status affects later aspirations, not only indirectly via its correlation with intelligence and its influence on the initial formation of aspirations but also to an appreciable degree via a direct path.

There is some interest as well in the path p_{UW} representing the effect of early aspiration of parents on school achievement and one of the ways by which parental status affects that outcome. The path coefficient is appreciable, .28, and the corresponding derived correlation is .32. This sector of the causal diagram, of course, merely represents in a drastically summarized fashion the end result of a complex and continuous process. Presumably, parents with high educational aspirations begin to encourage their children's school work from the earliest ages and continue to reinforce behavior producing success on the child's part.

The derived correlation between early aspiration and child's intelligence is a mere .08, reflecting the assumption that parent's knowledge of the intelligence of a child of 2 or 3 years can hardly be accurate and can hardly have much to do with aspirations for his further education as formulated at that time. The reader might wish to insist that how bright the parents *think* the child is may affect their early aspirations. If actual brightness is only slightly correlated with parental assumptions about intelligence, however, we could acknowledge this possibility without having to alter the diagram in any essential way. Perhaps parental assumptions about intelligence may serve as an intervening variable between socioeconomic status and educational aspirations for children.

One significant difference between the two models, as it relates to the use of the empirical data, may be noted. The rejected model, on the one hand, posits a direct causal role for high school rank in producing later parental aspirations, and this factor, therefore, could not be dropped from the model. In the non-rejected model, on the other hand, a complete system would still be present if variable U and the two path coefficients, p_{UW} and p_{UV}, were simply erased. In this instance, variable U merely plays the role of an auxiliary variable which implicitly conveys certain information about the relationships among the other variables in the system, given that knowledge of their intercorrelations is incomplete. Once the solution is reached, U may be dropped, but it (or some other variable playing a similar role) is required to obtained the solution.

Note on the Solution. Making use of the basic theorem of path analysis, we may write down the various equations providing components of the several correlations, known and unknown, in the system. These appear in the order in which they are used in obtaining the solution for the second (nonrejected) model.

1. r_{XV} is given.

2. $r_{VW} = p_{WX} r_{XV}$. But $p_{WX} = r_{WX}$; hence $r_{VW} = (.26)(.29)$.

3. $r_{UX} = p_{UV} r_{XV} + p_{UW} r_{WX}$

   $r_{UV} = p_{UV} + p_{UW} r_{VW}$.

By virtue of step [2], all the correlations in these two equations are known; hence they may be solved for p_{UV} and p_{UW}.

4. $r_{WU} = p_{UW} + p_{UV} r_{VW}$, yielding r_{WU} immediately.

5. $r_{YU} = p_{YW} r_{WU} + p_{YX} r_{XU} + p_{YV} r_{VU}$

   $r_{YV} = p_{YW} r_{WV} + p_{YX} r_{XV} + p_{YV}$

   $r_{YX} = p_{YW} r_{WX} + p_{YX} + p_{YV} r_{VX}$.

Correlations are known or obtained from preceding steps, so that these three equations may be solved simultaneously for p_{YW}, p_{YX}, and p_{YV}.

6. $r_{YW} = p_{YW} + p_{YX}r_{WX} + p_{YV}r_{WV}$, which, on entering previously obtained values, yields r_{YW}.

7. Residual paths are obtained by the usual method. Thus, for example, residual for W is

$$\sqrt{1 - p_{WX}^2}$$

and residual for U is

$$\sqrt{1 - p_{UW}r_{WU} - p_{UV}r_{UV}}.$$

It may be noted that this solution includes no set of equations with the symmetrical form of the normal equations for multiple correlation. The "Doolittle method" of solution is not available, therefore, but one can use any convenient routine involving determinants or matrix inversion available at a computing center. The solution includes derived correlations which fill out the correlation matrix. If one uses all the correlations, including these, in a recursive regression setup—regressing W on X and V; U on W, X, and V; and Y on U, W, X, and V—he will, in fact, obtain the path coefficients as *beta*-coefficients in the regressions, including (within errors of rounding) zero values for the two omitted paths.

Caveat. The reader should be clear about what is here attempted and not attempted, what is achieved and what is not achieved. By our juxtaposition of data from two sources, implemented by a set of assumptions needed to deduce any relationship between them, we have not "proved" anything about how aspirations develop. We have only taken the best evidence we know of in a suitable form and shown that one account of this process cannot be rejected out of hand, given the assumptions made. The work is to be described as conjecture, speculations, or "theorizing," as may be appropriate in the light of the reader's terminological taste. We have carried out this phase of "interpretation" by the exercise of what some critics might well term "methodological virtuosity" rather than by purely verbal means. There is no virtue in virtuosity as such—and there is actually little virtuosity here in any event—but there is virtue in trying to make an interpretation cogent and self-consistent. As such, it is more readily rejected when additional evidence comes to hand than is one that enjoys the cloak of verbal ambiguity.

7.3 Parents and Peers

The most comprehensive model of social influences developed in this project is depicted in Fig. 7.9. The properties of this model and techniques of estimating its parameters are described in detail by Duncan *et al.* (1968) and Duncan

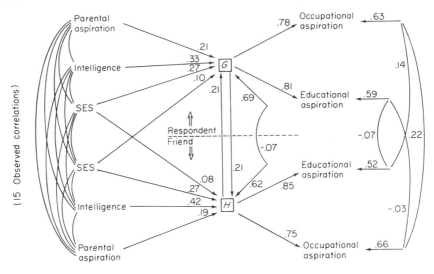

Fig. 7.9. Aspirations of respondents and best friends related to family background, parental aspiration, and friend's aspirations. (Source: Duncan *et al.*, 1968; Duncan, 1970a; based on MICH data set.) $r_{GH} = .56$.

(1970a), and the discussion here summarizes only a few salient points. The data pertain to a population of 17-year-old boys in the MICH data (cf. Section 2.3).

This model, like those suggested in Section 6.5, takes expressed aspirations as indicators of some underlying motivational state, symbolized as G or H; the term Ambition is used as a convenient label in Duncan *et al.* (1968). Here it is assumed that the hypothetical motivation variable depends on family socioeconomic status (SES), intelligence, and parental aspirations for the son's success. In addition, it is influenced in two ways by interaction with peers. First, it is allowed to be influenced directly by the SES of the *friend's* family, an assumption that fits with the notion that role models may be found in a family other than one's own. Second, the motivational variables of respondent and friend are taken to be simultaneously or jointly determined within the model so that each may be thought of as influencing the other. This kind of "reciprocal causation" is a good deal more difficult to handle than is the "one-way causation" represented in recursive models. Hence, the present results are presented quite tentatively, having been secured by procedures that have some heuristic appeal but not a tight statistical justification.

The results are not without interest, if accepted provisionally for the sake of discussion. Both parental aspiration and friend's motivation bear upon the development of motivation in a boy, and the coefficients suggest that they are about equal in importance. This conclusion, however, is somewhat suspect because the data on parental aspiration were obtained from the respondent whereas the data on friend's aspirations were obtained from the friend. The former, therefore, may be subject to an unknown degree of contamination. It is only a coincidence that the two reciprocal paths, p_{GH} and p_{HG}, came out equal to the second decimal place since the format of the data and the technique of estimation did not force such an equality. There are some differences in the paths to H and the corresponding paths to G which may reflect the fact that the friendship used to pair the reports of respondents was identified only by the respondent's choice of "best friend," a choice which was not necessarily reciprocated.

Perhaps the most interesting feature of the model is the perspective that it puts on peer influences. Sociologists have made much of "youth culture," "school climates," and the like; and one sometimes has the impression that socialization to the norms and expectations of peers is all powerful, obliterating the effects of family background and parental influences. This does not appear to be true. There is a modest reciprocal influence or positive feedback that tends to produce homophily with respect to aspirations (or the hypothetical under-lying motives assumed to be reflected therein). But the more basic source of such homophily is that lads tend to become associated with others resembling them in socioeconomic background and mental ability.

7.4 Peers and Schools

A sizable literature of recent years (for example, Sexton, 1961; Rogoff, 1961; Herriott & St. John, 1966) has pointed out ostensible "school effects," "con-textual effects," or "school climates" as influences on achievements and aspirations of youth. In some of this work, investigators have been content to exhibit differences in means of pupil characteristics between schools, classify-ing the latter on some measure of their social characteristics. In the more detailed studies, however, there has been an effort to separate the effects of school characteristics from the effects of the characteristics of individual pupils themselves (Wilson, 1959; Turner, 1964; Sewell & Armer, 1966, Wegner & Sewell, 1970; Hauser, 1969, 1971).

Whether school effects are indexed by the gross association between school characteristics and educational outcomes or by some measure of the net association of the two, holding constant personal and family characteristics of the pupils, the interpretation is seldom governed by an explicit model which represents at once the several presumed sources of variation in achievement or aspiration. The need for such a model is made quite obvious by an encounter with the hypothesis that "structural effects of school status are best conceived of as due to the interpersonal influences of an individual's significant others" (Campbell & Alexander, 1965, p. 288). These investigators (see also Alexander

& Campbell, 1964), in effect, have sought to erect a bridge between studies of "school effects" like those just mentioned and studies in which "peer influences" are scrutinized directly (for example, Haller & Butterworth, 1960; Simpson, 1962). Our intention here is to suggest that this kind of effort is facilitated by systematic extensions of the models treated in this project.

The first such extension is accomplished by means of the algebraic theorems underlying analysis of covariance. Suppose Y_{ij} denotes the score of the ith boy in the jth school on some measure of educational aspiration, where $i = 1, \ldots, n_j$ and $j = 1, \ldots, m$. We define

$$\overline{Y}_j = \sum_i Y_{ij}/n_j, \quad \overline{Y} = \sum_j \sum_i Y_{ij}/\sum_j n_j, \quad \text{and} \quad y_{ij} = Y_{ij} - \overline{Y}_j$$

(the deviation of the given boy's score from the mean score for his school). Let analogous definitions be given for a variable X, where X_{ij} is (say) the family socioeconomic status score for the ith boy in the jth school. The usual correlation between Y and X, computed without regard to the classification by schools, will be referred to as the "total" correlation and written

$$r_{Y_{ij}X_{ij}}.$$

Now, suppose each boy is assigned one Y score which is equal to the mean for his school, that is, $\overline{Y}_j$, and another which is his own score, Y_{ij}. If we compute the correlation, over individual boys, between these two scores, denoting it

$$r_{Y_{ij}\overline{Y}_j},$$

we will have computed, in effect, the correlation ratio of Y scores on school, a better-known formula for which is the square root of the proportion of the total sum of squares of Y that lies between schools,

$$\left[\frac{\sum_j n_j (\overline{Y}_j - \overline{Y})^2}{\sum_j \sum_i (Y_{ij} - \overline{Y})^2} \right]^{\frac{1}{2}}.$$

It is useful to note that

$$r_{y_{ij}\overline{Y}_j} = 0$$

identically and that

$$r_{Y_{ij}y_{ij}} = (1 - r^2_{Y_{ij}\overline{Y}_j})^{\frac{1}{2}}.$$

The latter is, in fact, the square root of the proportion of the total sum of squares of Y that lies within schools, that is,

$$\left[\frac{\sum_j \sum_i (Y_{ij} - \overline{Y}_j)^2}{\sum \sum_{ij} (Y_{ij} - \overline{Y})^2} \right]^{\frac{1}{2}}.$$

Similar definitions can be given, of course, for variable X. Moreover, we can define the "average within-school" correlation of Y and X as

$$r_{y_{ij}x_{ij}},$$

computed from the formula,

$$\frac{\sum_j \sum_i y_{ij} x_{ij}}{(\sum_j \sum_i y_{ij}^2)^{1/2} (\sum_j \sum_i x_{ij}^2)^{1/2}},$$

and the "between-school" correlation as $r_{Y_j X_j}$, which may be computed as follows:

$$\frac{\sum_j n_j (\overline{Y}_j - \overline{Y})(\overline{X}_j - \overline{X})}{(\sum_j n_j (\overline{Y}_j - \overline{Y})^2)^{1/2} (\sum_j n_j (\overline{X}_j - \overline{X})^2)^{1/2}}.$$

From these definitions there follows a useful identity:

$$r_{Y_{ij}X_{ij}} = r_{y_{ij}x_{ij}} r_{Y_{ij}y_{ij}} r_{x_{ij}x_{ij}} + r_{Y_j X_j} r_{Y_{ij} \overline{Y}_j} r_{X_{ij} \overline{X}_j}.$$

Suppose we regard X as a cause influencing Y. The foregoing decomposition of the total correlation may then be represented by a path diagram like the one shown in Fig. 7.10. The situation is such that each of the 6 correlations on the right side of this equation can be regarded as a path coefficient, if that seems

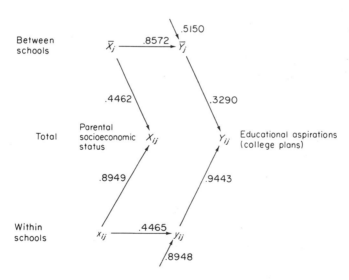

Fig. 7.10. Causal interpretation of the within-school and between-school components of the correlation between educational aspirations and parental socioeconomic status in unpublished data of Campbell and Alexander. Y, Educational aspirations (college plans); X, parental socioeconomic status; $r_{Y_{ij}x_{ij}} = .5032$; $m = 30$ schools; $N = 1137$ senior boys.

appropriate in terms of one's causal scheme. The validity of the decomposition, however, does not depend on the plausibility of assumptions as to causation.

Several interesting calculations can be made from this diagram. It will be noted that there is no path from X_{ij} to Y_{ij}, but the total correlation of .50 between the two variables is nevertheless implicit in the diagram as the sum of a within-schools component

$$(.9443)(.4465)(.8949) = .38$$

and a between-schools component

$$(.3290)(.8572)(.4462) = .12.$$

The contrast in the size of the two components is already a caution against any tendency to exaggerate the socioeconomic influences on aspirations that work through schools as units.

A second calculation reveals that the total variation in Y_{ij}, set at 1.0, has components of $(.9443)^2 = .89$ within schools and $(.3290)^2 = .11$ between schools. One implication of the latter should be obvious at once. Only one-ninth of the variation in Y lies between schools (in the particular population studied here). Hence, no matter how many measurements are made on school composition, school "climate," school "norms and values," school "inputs," and the like, no combination of such characteristics of schools as units can ever "explain" more than one-ninth of the variance in Y. Again, we are well advised to entertain modest expectations for explanations couched in terms of "school effects," rhetoric (for example, Sexton, 1961) to the contrary notwithstanding.

It is useful to note that the decomposition of the total correlation involves only four independent quantities, since

$$r^2_{Y_{ij}y_{ij}} = 1 - r^2_{Y_{ij}Y_j} \quad \text{and} \quad r^2_{X_{ij}x_{ij}} = 1 - r^2_{X_{ij}X_j}.$$

If the total correlation and three of these quantities are given, it is, of course, possible to solve for the fourth. In particular, given the total and between-school correlations and the two correlation ratios,

$$r_{Y_{ij}Y_j} \quad \text{and} \quad r_{X_{ij}X_j},$$

the average within-school correlation may be obtained from a simple calculation. It was possible to take advantage of this fact in working with the WISC data set. The investigators had assigned certain school means as scores for individuals and the correlation matrix involving such variables, therefore, provided the requisite information for computing average within-school correlations.

In the analysis of covariance there is a procedure termed "adjusting Y means for X." The null hypothesis is that all the variation in $\overline{Y}_j$ is due to differences between schools in $\overline{X}_j$, given that Y depends on X within schools to the extent indicated by the "average within-school" regression coefficient, which is defined as

$$b_w = \sum_j \sum_i y_{ij} x_{ij} / \sum_j \sum_i x_{ij}^2.$$

This procedure suggests the possibility of a decomposition of $\overline{Y}_j$ into two components, writing $\overline{Y}_j = \tilde{Y}_j + Y_j^*$, where $\tilde{Y}_j = b_w(\overline{X}_j - \overline{X})$ and Y_j^* (the "adjusted mean") $= \overline{Y}_j - \tilde{Y}_j$. Since variation in $\tilde{Y}_j$ is due solely to variation in $\overline{X}_j$, this term may-be said to represent the component reflecting X composition of schools. Then Y_j^* is a component reflecting factors other than X composition. It is important to note that $\tilde{Y}_j$ and Y_j^* are not, in general, uncorrelated. Indeed, in practice, they are often so highly colinear that interpretation is difficult. Another way of putting the matter, if a causal phraseology is allowed, is that $\overline{X}_j$ affects $\overline{Y}_j$ both in terms of the X composition of schools and via a path involving influences other than composition.

A diagram representing such an interpretation is shown as Fig. 7.11. Except for the additional detail in the between-school segment, this is the same as Figure 7.10. To secure this detail, we must have the average within-schools regression coefficient, b_w, which was defined above. It should be noted that this statistic cannot be computed from a correlation matrix alone, even one that includes within- and between-school correlations. It must be obtained as part of

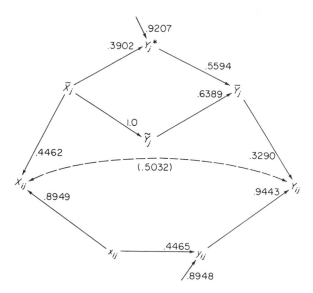

Fig. 7.11. Data of Fig. 7.10 with between-school variation in Y due to X allocated to compositional ($\tilde{Y}_j$) and noncompositional (Y_j^*) components. (Correlation depicted by dotted line is implied by the remainder of the diagram.)

an analysis-of-covariance computing routine. The necessary data for its calculation were kindly made available by Professors Campbell and Alexander.

We have defined components $\tilde{Y}_j$ and Y_j^* such that $\bar{Y}_j$ is completely determined by their sum. These quantities are in raw score form. Path coefficients
are defined by considering their relationship in standard form; we obtain

$$\frac{\bar{Y}_j - \bar{Y}}{s.d.(\bar{Y}_j)} = p_{\bar{Y}_j\tilde{Y}_j}\frac{\tilde{Y}_j - M(\tilde{Y}_j)}{s.d.(\tilde{Y}_j)} + p_{\bar{Y}_jY_j^*}\frac{Y_j^* - M(Y_j^*)}{s.d.(Y_j^*)}$$

where

$$p_{\bar{Y}_j\tilde{Y}_j} = s.d.(\tilde{Y}_j)/s.d.(\bar{Y}_j) \quad \text{and} \quad p_{\bar{Y}_jY_j^*} = s.d.(Y_j^*)/s.d.(\bar{Y}_j),$$

using $M(\;)$ to denote "mean of" and $s.d.(\;)$ to denote "standard deviation
of." The first of the two path coefficients is easily computed, for $s.d.(\tilde{Y}_j) =$
$b_w[s.d.(\bar{X}_j)]$ and $s.d.(\bar{Y}_j)$ is defined in terms of between-school sum of squares
of Y. Hence,

$$p_{\bar{Y}_j\tilde{Y}_j} = b_w\left[\frac{\sum_j n_j(\bar{X}_j - \bar{X})^2}{\sum_j n_j(\bar{Y}_j - \bar{Y})^2}\right]^{1/2}.$$

In the data at hand, this works out at

$$p_{\bar{Y}_j\tilde{Y}_j} = .6389.$$

We also have some further information: the complete determination of $\bar{Y}_j$ by
its two components; the path coefficient and correlation,

$$p_{\bar{Y}_jX_j} \quad \text{and} \quad r_{\bar{Y}_jX_j},$$

both set at unity; and the value of $r_{\bar{Y}_jX_j}$ (the between-schools correlation
already computed). To simplify notation, let $\bar{Y}_j$ be variable 1, $\tilde{Y}_j$ be variable 2,
Y_j^* be variable 3, and $\bar{X}_j$ be variable 4. Let unknown paths be denoted $p_{13} = g$
and $p_{34} = h$. We now know $p_{12} = .6389$, $p_{24} = 1.0$, and $r_{14} = .8572$. Theorems
on path coefficients allow us to write

$$r_{14} = gh + (1.0)p_{12}$$

$$r_{11} = 1 = g^2 + p_{12}^2 + 2p_{12}gh.$$

The solutions are $g^2 = 1 + p_{12}^2 - 2p_{12}r_{14}$ and $h = (r_{14} - p_{12})/g$. From the data
at hand we find $g = .5594$ and $h = .3902$. The residual for variable 3 (or Y_j^*)
is, of course,

$$\sqrt{1 - h^2} = .9207.$$

If the reader prefers, he may regard all this exercise with path coefficients as a
means of partitioning variance in Y_{ij}. We began with the within- and between-
school components, summing to unity, which are, respectively (as already

noted), $(.9443)^2 = .8917$ and $(.3290)^2 = .1082$. The within-school portion has two components of its own, that due to regression on X, which is $(.4465)^2 = .1994$, and the residual $(.8948)^2 = .8007$. To express these as proportions of total variance, each must be multiplied by .8917.

Partitioning of the between-school variance is messier. First (as in Fig. 7.11) we break out the part that is uncorrelated with with $\bar{X}_j : [(.5594)(.9207)]^2 = (.5150)^2 = .2652$. This leaves the part due to correlation of $\bar{Y}_j$ with $\bar{X}_j$ as $(.8572)^2 = .7348$. But the purpose of our somewhat formalistic procedures was precisely to indicate that the latter is not correctly regarded, in causal terms, as all of a piece. Figure 7.11a indicates that

$$r_{Y_j X_j} = .8572 = .6389 + (.5594)(.3902).$$

Squaring both sides we have

$$.7348 = (.6389)^2 + [(.5594)(.3902)]^2 + 2(.6389)(.5594)(.3902).$$

Thus the variance due to $\bar{X}_j$ may be broken down into .4082 due to the "pure effect" of X composition, .0476 due to the between-school operation of X other than in terms of composition, and .2789 due to the correlation of the two arising from the fact that X is the ultimate source of both. All the fractions of variance obtained in this paragraph must be multiplied by .1082 if they are to be converted to proportions of *total* variance in Y_{ij}.

We may summarize our results in the following tabulation:

Total variance of Y_{ij}	1.0	
1. Within schools	.8917	
a. Regression on X		.1778
b. Residual		.7140
2. Between schools	.1082	
a. X composition		.0442
b. Other effects of X		.0052
c. Joint effects of a and b		.0302
d. Residual		.0287

If one chooses to regard the magnitude of residual factors as an indication of the importance of causes as yet unknown, it would seem obvious that much more is to be learned about sources of variation within schools, while there is a comparatively small incremental payoff even for securing a complete accounting for variation between schools.

It is tempting to consider alternative consolidations of the foregoing components in the light of emphasis on the fact that "school districting tends to segregate youths of different social strata" (Wilson, 1959, p. 837). The allusion to a process of "derivation of values from the immediate school milieu" (p. 836) is evidently intended to refer to differences that do not merely reflect the direct operation of socioeconomic factors in such a way that "modally different attitudes" of "school populations" (p. 837) are merely the outcome of differences in socioeconomic composition. It seems relevant, therefore, to sum components 1a and 2a, obtaining $.1778 + .0442 = .2220$ as the proportion of variance in educational aspirations due to socioeconomic status within schools and sheer compositional differences between schools. This leaves components 2b plus 2c, or $.0052 + .0302 = .0354$, as the proportion that one might take as an estimate of effect of "the climate of the school society" (p. 836). This is no negligible figure, of course. However, schools differ in composition on factors other than socioeconomic status, and the Campbell-Alexander data do not permit an evaluation of the degree to which such other compositional factors may be masquerading as "school climates."

In the remainder of this section we shall not retain the foregoing elaboration of the between-school sector of the model. The requisite information for these calculations is not available in the WISC data set. Moreover, the implications of this procedure are far from obvious. Fortunately, the whole matter has been thoroughly studied by Hauser (1971).

Returning to the simpler (though less informative) point of view on between-school effects represented by Fig. 7.10, we now bring into the picture data on the respondent's first choice in answer to the question "What students here in school of your own sex do you go around with most often?" (Campbell & Alexander, 1965, pp. 286–287). For both respondent and best friend, the investigators ascertained information on two variables of interest here: educational aspiration (plans to attend college); and family socioeconomic status (a composite score derived from mother's and father's educational attainment). Thus we can construct a diagram for friends like the diagram for respondents in Fig. 7.10. Moreover, correlations between characteristics of respondents and characteristics of friends can be indicated when the two diagrams are juxtaposed. These two steps are carried out in Fig. 7.12. The prime symbol, as in X'_{ij}, indicates that the variable pertains to the friend. This diagram does not make explicit any such causal assumption as $X \to Y$. While this particular assumption is attractive, there is little or no basis for either of the assumptions $X \to X'$ or $X' \to X$. Without such assumptions, the deductions we can draw from the diagram are somewhat limited but nonetheless instructive.

One property of the diagram is significant in view of the emphasis of Wilson (1959, p. 845) on schools as providing "unequal moral climates" owing to "concentrations of social classes." Let us compute the correlation between the aspirations of friends that arises from their attendance at the same school. Suppose from a whole population of respondents and friends, pairs were formed at random within each school. Given the between-school components of sums of squares of Y_{ij} and Y'_{ij} in the population studied by Campbell and

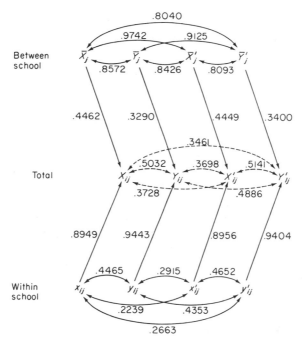

Fig. 7.12. Total, between-school, and within-school correlations for respondents' and friends' educational aspirations (Y) and socioeconomic status (X), computed from data of Alexander and Campbell. (Correlations depicted by dotted lines are implied by remainder of diagram.)

Alexander, we can compute, on this null hypothesis, what the correlation between friends would be. The appropriate calculation is

$$p_{Y_{ij}\bar{Y}_j} r_{\bar{Y}_j\bar{Y}'_j} p_{Y'_{ij}\bar{Y}'_j} = (.3290)(.9125)(.3400) = .1021,$$

according to the data in Fig. 7.12. By contrast, the within-school correlation

$$(r_{y_{ij}y'_{ij}})$$

is .4353 and the actual total correlation is .4886. If the phrase "unequal moral climates" refers to the variation in aspirations of boys going to different schools, we can infer from these results that factors producing homophily with respect to aspirations other than moral climates are much more important in the aggregate than are moral climates per se.

If, on the argument of Section 7.3, we think of homophily in regard to SES as possibly giving rise to homophily with respect to aspirations, then it is of interest to learn to what extent "concentrations of social classes" (Wilson, 1959, p. 845) can be held responsible for the former. [This topic was systematically considered by Rhodes, Reiss, & Duncan (1965).] On the null hypothesis just suggested—friendships formed by random choice within schools—we compute the implied correlation of SES scores:

$$p_{X_{ij}X_j} r_{X_j X'} p_{X'_{ij}X'_j} = (.4462)(.9742)(.4449) = .1934,$$

according to the data in Fig. 7.12. Hence if SES homophily is productive of homophily in regard to aspirations, it is pertinent that the extent of the former within schools, as indicated by

$$r_{x_{ij}x'_{ij}} = .2239,$$

is somewhat larger than that produced solely by between-school variation in SES, .1934.

Interesting as all these observations may be, they do not come to grips with our problem in its full complexity. In Section 7.3 we suggested a model that represents more or less effectively our ideas about "peer influences"; the data pertained to lads in a single school district and, therefore, were tantamount to information for the within-school sector of a model to be applied to a broader population. Since the MICH data set does not supply between-school data, we have resorted to a merger of the WISC and MICH data sets. The former provides between-school data and a portion of the needed within-school data. To fill in the gaps, certain items are borrowed from the MICH data set (see Table 7.5). Moreover, some simplifying assumptions are required. We assume identity of the school means for respondents and friends, that is,

$$\overline{Y}'_j = \overline{Y}_j, \quad \overline{X}'_j = \overline{X}_j, \quad \text{and} \quad \overline{Z}'_j = \overline{Z}_j.$$

Or, if one prefers to state it differently, we assume that

$$r_{\overline{Y}'_j \overline{Y}_j} = r_{\overline{X}'_j \overline{X}_j} = r_{\overline{Z}'_j \overline{Z}_j} = 1.0,$$

$$r_{Y_{ij}Y_j} = r_{Y'_{ij}Y'_j}, \quad r_{X_{ij}X_j} = r_{X'_{ij}X'_j}, \quad \text{and} \quad r_{Z_{ij}\overline{Z}_j} = r_{Z'_{ij}\overline{Z}_j}.$$

That these assumptions are not too far from the truth is suggested by data in Fig. 7.12. In fact, we can compute both

$$r_{Y_{ij}\overline{Y}_j} \quad \text{and} \quad r_{Y'_{ij}\overline{Y}'_j}$$

respectively (cf. the corresponding values of .3290 and .3400 in the data of Campbell and Alexander).

Another simplification is compatible with the foregoing. This is the procedure of estimating data for friends in such a way that the data become symmetrical in respondent and friend. If all friendship choices were reciprocated and each respondent had just one friend, the observations would, of course, take a symmetrical form. Where this constraint is lacking, the MICH data and those of Campbell and Alexander show some appreciable departures from

TABLE 7.5

Average Within-School Correlations in WISC and MICH Data Sets

Variables correlated[a]	Correlation	
	WISC	MICH
yx	.3871	.4047
$y'x'$	(.3871)[b]	.4105
$y'x$	.2807	.3054
yx'	(.2807)[b]	.2407
yz	.4012	.4043
$y'z'$	(.4012)[b]	.5191
$y'z$	.2761	.2903
yz'	(.2761)[b]	.2863
xz	.2316	.2220
$x'z'$	(.2316)[b]	.2950
$x'z$	[.2082][c]	.1861 ⎱[d]
xz'	[.2082][c]	.2302 ⎰
yy'	.4347	.3669
xx'	[.2707][c]	.2707
zz'	[.3355][c]	.3355

[a] Deviations of individual scores from school means. y, Educational aspirations; x, socioeconomic status; z, intelligence. Prime (') denotes variable defined for friend.

[b] Assumed same as correlation on line above.

[c] Borrowed from MICH data set.

[d] Correlations averaged for entry into WISC data set.

symmetry. The assumption of symmetry in the present case is merely a heuristic device to allow us to make some interpretation of the WISC data on a model of peer influences within schools.

In the WISC data, information on friends' educational aspirations derives from a question to respondents phrased: "Most of my friends are: —— going to college; —— getting jobs; —— going into military service; —— other." It might seem likely *a priori* that the format of the question together with reliance on the respondent's perception rather than the friend's independent report would tend to exaggerate the correlation between respondents' and friends' educational aspirations. Indeed,

$$r_{y_{ij}y'_{ij}} = .4347$$

in the WISC data as compared with only .3669 in MICH data. However, this within-school correlation is .4353 in the data of Campbell and Alexander, where respondent's and friend's college plans were independently ascertained. The factor of perceptual distortion, therefore, does not seem serious.

The discrepancy between the WISC and MICH correlations just mentioned is actually a relatively extreme one, as a comparison of the two colums of Table 7.5 will reveal. The risks incurred in a merger of the two sets seem relatively minor.

The model for the within-school sector in Fig. 7.13 is the same in form as one shown in Duncan, Haller, & Portes (1968), where the MICH data were used with quite similar results. It is a simplified version of the model shown in Fig. 7.9 and discussed in the previous section. There is some cause for dissatisfaction with this model, arising primarily from the correlation of $-.42$ between the residuals for y_{ij} and y'_{ij} which must be postulated for the remainder of the solution to be consistent. It would appear that this negative correlation, difficult as it is to rationalize, is in a sense compensating for an exaggeration of the size of the path coefficients running from respondent's to friend's and from friend's to respondent's educational aspiration. The coefficient of .35 here is

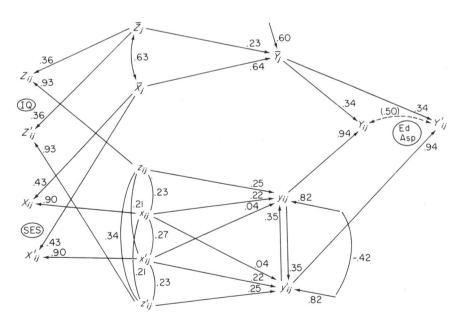

Fig. 7.13. Model of peer influences and effects of intelligence and socioeconomic status on educational aspirations within schools combined with within-school vs. between-school decomposition of correlation between friends' aspirations. (Source: Table 7.5 and 'WISC data set.)

appreciably larger than the corresponding coefficient of .21 in Fig. 7.9, where the correlation between residuals, although negative, is quite negligible in size. Another way to put the matter is this: If the correlation between the residuals for y and y' in Fig. 7.13 were to be zero, given the other coefficients in the diagram, the correlation between y and y' would have to be as high as .72. If the correlation between residuals were to be positive—a relatively easy situation to rationalize conceptually—$r_{yy'}$ would be even larger than .72. In Fig. 7.9, the corresponding correlation (between the constructed variables G and H) was as high as .56. That model not only involved hypothetical variables (of which educational aspirations were regarded as a somewhat fallible indicator); it also contained an additional predetermined variable, parental aspiration, for both respondent and friend. Apparently, the somewhat more elaborate version of the model in Fig. 7.9 has real advantages over the simplified version in Fig. 7.13.

Actually, there is no conceptual reason why the model of Fig. 7.9 could not be used as the within-schools model for Fig. 7.13. The only reason why this was not attempted is that the WISC data set does not provide information on the within- vs. between-school decomposition of all the correlations required for the former model.

One other feature of the model in Fig. 7.13 may be useful for evaluating it. The model implies a total correlation between the aspirations of friends of

$$r_{Y_{ij}Y'_{ij}} = .50,$$

in agreement with the observed total correlation in the WISC data. This agreement is coerced by the estimation procedure used. The model also implies an interfriend total correlation with respect to intelligence of

$$r_{Z_{ij}Z'_{ij}} = .4237.$$

In effect, this correlation is "predicted" by the merger of the WISC and MICH data sets. Neither set provides an observed value for this correlation and no other such observation on a population like WISC is available. Finally, the model implies

$$r_{X_{ij}X'_{ij}} = .4036.$$

This may be compared with the total correlation of .3728 between SES of respondent and SES of friend in the data of Campbell and Alexander. The difference is not large enough to arouse suspicion.

7.5 Conclusions

Wives, parents, friends, and schoolmates are among the significant others whose influence on occupational ambitions and choices has frequently been emphasized. We looked first at the proposition that wives may or may not spur their husbands to occupational achievement and may thereby introduce variance into occupational outcomes that is substantial and independent of other measured factors affecting these outcomes. The answer obtained, in conformity with the findings of previous research, is that the proposition holds to only a very slight degree. We next considered the wife as mother, inquiring whether the data available to us shed light on the extent to which the socio-economic characteristics, intelligence, and personality traits of mothers influence the aspirations they form for their children. It may perhaps be regarded as disappointing that only 5.7 percent of the variance in mothers' aspirations for children's college education can be attributed to such factors. The measurements are, however, on mothers of very young children.

Another body of data can be juxtaposed with the preceding set to construct a model representing the hypothesis that parents' aspirations are crystallized under the influence of the child's own ability, as it becomes manifested in his performance in school. The interpretation illustrates how rigorous inferences can sometimes be made when an explicit model is proposed to reconcile apparent discrepancies between results from different studies. The interpretation remains, of course, conjectural; but the conjectures are rather more carefully disciplined than is usually the case.

Perhaps the most elaborate model constructed in this project concerns the hypothesis that in a pair of friends each influences the development of the other's educational and occupational ambitions. The peer effect had been detected in previous research; here we were concerned to estimate its relative weight in a comprehensive model of the development of aspirations. The significant feature of the model is that it allows reciprocal influences. Such a feature gives rise to rather formidable problems of identification and estimation of parameters. But the process of solving these is instructive in itself. The exercise in question may be considered a demonstration of the potential power and scope of the kinds of models proposed here.

In the discussion of "school effects," emphasis is placed on the initial partitioning of variance of both independent and dependent variables into within-school and between-school components. The latter may seem surprisingly small, in view of the considerable emphasis on "school effects" in earlier writing. A systematic exploitation of the analysis-of-covariance perspective, moreover, indicates the possibility that "school effects" are in considerable measure only the reflection of differential school composition on variables operating at the individual level. The models exhibited in this part of the chapter illustrate how this perspective can be exploited in the context of path analysis and how the "peer effects" noted earlier can be imbedded in a model relating to "school effects."

Chapter 8

Career Contingencies

The notion of career contingencies used in this research is that of events, occurring subsequent to the determination of family background, that may have a bearing upon the level of ultimate occupational achievement. Any one of an indefinitely large class of such events might legitimately come under scrutiny on this point of view. A man who undergoes a period of poor health, for example, may thereby be handicapped in his subsequent career. A period of service in the Armed Forces may, according to the particulars of the case, prove advantageous or disadvantageous for future occupational success. Since there are no well-defined limits to this class of variables, there can be no pretense of exhaustive coverage. The career contingencies selected for study here are those on which data happen to be available from the OCG study. These include the status of the first job, the age upon entering that job, the experience of migration, the possibility that a marriage was disrupted, the size of the family of procreation, and the timing of its initiation. In not all cases can these variables be neatly or readily entered into the format required for a formal extension to our basic model. We have, therefore, followed opportunistic strategies in regard to the analysis, leaving various results in a form that might be regarded as preliminary to a more fully developed model.

8.1   First Job

In the original version of the basic model (Blau & Duncan, 1967), the occupational status of the first job reported by the OCG respondent was treated as an intervening variable, located in a causal chain between educational attainment and occupation as of 1962. The authors noted the problem of ambiguity with respect to the temporal ordering assumed in this arrangement, but the exploration of the implications of such ambiguity was left as a task for this project (see Section 8.2). The outcome of this work suggested the advisability of deleting first job from the basic model, to avoid conveying an oversimplified impression of how this particular career contingency actually operates. This is not to suggest that it is an unimportant variable but rather to indicate that a separate treatment is advisable.

Before raising the question of the timing of first job with respect to schooling, we may briefly indicate the degree to which first job status depends on family background and the degree to which it relates to current occupational status. In Table 8.1 both current occupational status and the status of the first job are related to the three standard family background variables. The point of the presentation is to compare the two measures of occupational achievement in regard to the relative degrees to which they depend on family background. Actually, there is a great deal of similarity in the two sets of results. Both first job and the current occupation as measured for each of four age groups depend positively on father's education, even more so on father's occupation, and

TABLE 8.1

Partial Regression Coefficients in Standard Form for Relationships of First Job and Current Occupational Status to Family Background Factors, by Age, for Non-Negro Men with Nonfarm Background, in Experienced Civilian Labor Force: March 1962[a]

Age and dependent variable[b]	Independent variables[b]			Coefficient of determination
	T	X	V	
25–34				
W (first job)	−.1696	.2632	.1405	.187
Y (1962 occupation)	−.1438	.2263	.1928	.181
35–44				
W	−.1535	.2376	.1696	.185
Y	−.1703	.2842	.1198	.196
45–54				
W	−.1038	.2945	.1404	.179
Y	−.1467	.3126	.0646	.169
55–64				
W	−.1525	.3063	.0971	.189
Y	−.1624	.2486	.1255	.168

[a] Source: OCG data set.

[b] V, Father's (or family head's) educational attainment; X, father's (or family head's) occupational status; T, respondent's number of siblings; W, status of respondent's first job; Y, respondent's occupational status, March 1962.

negatively on number of siblings. The degree of dependence on family background, if reduced to the single figure of the coefficient of determination, is much the same whether we are looking at first jobs or current occupations or whether, in regard to the latter, we are looking at results for younger men or those for older men.

The surprising thing about these results is that it apparently makes no appreciable difference at what age or career stage we measure occupational achievement, at least as far as estimating the degree to which achievement depends on family background is concerned. (It does, of course, make a difference in regard to the average level of achievement since there is a substantial amount of net upward mobility from first job to current occupation as measured for any of the four age groups.) Despite the fact that first job and current occupation depend in much the same way and to much the same degree on family background, they are by no means perfectly correlated with each other. The correlation, r_{YW}, is as follows: .5783 (for men in the population covered in Table 8.1, age 25–34), .4944 (age 35–44), .5123 (age 45–54), and .5054 (age 55–64).

In earlier work there was an effort to reconcile these findings with the assumption that the four age groups may stand for successive observations on a synthetic cohort (Blau & Duncan, 1967, pp. 177–188). The synthetic cohort model was not wholly successful, though apparently it had some heuristic utility.* Figure 8.1 indicates the nature of the difficulty in the synthetic cohort interpretation. In preparing this version of the synthetic cohort interpretation, we carried out the following steps. The value of r_{UW} for each cohort was taken to be equal to the average of the four such correlations for the several cohorts. This arbitrary step is not unreasonable in view of the fact that the 4 correlations are quite similar; they vary between .545 and .586. Next, Y_1 (occupational status of men 25–34 years old) was regressed on W and U. Then it was assumed that occupation at age 25–34 would have a direct effect on occupation at age 35–44, as would educational attainment; but that first job would have only an indirect effect. These assumptions permit us to write the two equations that must be solved to secure estimates of p_{21} and p_{2U}:

$$r_{2W} = p_{21} r_{1W} + p_{2U} r_{UW}$$

$$r_{2U} = p_{21} r_{1U} + p_{2U}.$$

Note that r_{21} does not enter into these equations. Inasmuch as Y_2 is related to Y_1 only by the hypothesis that data for the two cohorts may be merged into a synthetic cohort, we do not have an observed value of r_{21}. However, given the

---

* Featherman (1971a) provides a comparison of the OCG synthetic cohort model with the same structural equations applied to a real cohort in the FGMA data.

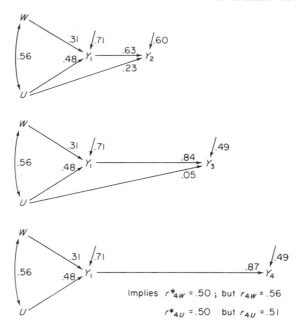

Fig. 8.1. Synthetic cohort models based on combination of data for older cohorts with those for men 25–34 years old. W, first job; U, education; Y_1–Y_4, occupational status at ages 25–34, 35–44, 45–54, 55–64, respectively. (See Table 8.1 for source and population specifications.)

estimated path coefficients obtained from the foregoing equations, we may compute the implied value of this correlation. We obtain

$$r_{21}^* = p_{21} + p_{2U} = .78.$$

While this seems a little high by comparison with the only available estimate of such a correlation (Duncan & Hodge, 1963), it cannot be dismissed as wholly implausible.

Thus far—that is, with the completion of the top diagram in Fig. 8.1—we have found no internal inconsistency in the synthetic cohort interpretation. However, when we proceed to the second diagram, securing estimates by an exactly analogous procedure, such an inconsistency does turn up. We obtain $p_{31} = .84$, and the implied correlation between occupation at age 45–54 and at age 25–34 is $r_{31}^* = .87$. Again, while the latter seems a little high, it is not in itself wholly implausible. However, when we note that the path coefficient representing the degree of persistence of occupational status over the life cycle is $p_{31} = .84$ for a 20-year span while $p_{21} = .63$ for a 10-year span, it appears that there is real difficulty with any simple version of the synthetic cohort interpretation. Of course, it is mathematically possible that current occupational status could depend not only on the last previously measured occupation but also on occupations held at various earlier career stages. Thus one might be tempted to supply an arrow from W to Y_3 in addition to those already appearing in the second diagram. There are not enough known correlations in the data inspected here to produce estimates for such a diagram. In any event, not a great deal would be proved by the carrying out of such estimates.

When we come to the third diagram, a further difficulty arises. If both p_{41} and p_{4U} are included in the diagram and the estimation is carried out with the kind of equations just cited, we secure a small but negative value for p_{4U}. Since this does not seem reasonable, only the one path to Y_4 is shown, and its value is taken to be the average of the values implied by the equations

$$r_{4W} = p_{41} r_{1W} \quad \text{and} \quad r_{4U} = p_{41} r_{1U}.$$

The two values of p_{41} are quite close, .874 and .857, respectively. However, the implied correlations of Y_4 with W and U indicate that some distortion of the data is entailed by this procedure. Apart from this, however, the more disturbing result is that $p_{41} = r_{41}$ is higher than either p_{31} or p_{21}.

Any of several possible conclusions may now be reasonably entertained. First, it may be that an altered form or a more elaborate version of the synthetic cohort model would yield a satisfactory interpretation of these data even though the simplified models studied here do not. Some considerable experimentation with various possibilities does not support this conclusion, but it cannot be rejected nonetheless. Second, it may be that the assumption that occupational status persists over time in a simple causal chain pattern is incorrect. This conclusion receives support from the conclusion of Hodge (1966) that intragenerational occupational mobility is not well represented by a simple first-order Markov chain.* Third, it may be that the simple version of the synthetic cohort model exhibited here would afford a fair representation of the data for a real cohort, if such data should exist, but that the actual cohorts studied here have simply not had comparable experiences in regard to their transitions from first jobs to occupations in 1962. The demonstration that these cohorts could not have had identical intragenerational mobility transition matrixes at comparable ages (Duncan, 1965) is in accord with this conclusion, although it is not precisely relevant because the present type of model considers a more complicated process than one merely involving occupational mobility, for example, in the treatment of education as a predetermined variable of persisting relevance to occupational achievement.

---

* The FGMA data reported by Featherman (1971a) document further that simple first-order Markovian models do not represent the "historical" quality of occupational careers for a cohort of men. At the same time the Markovian model might be fitted to intragenerational mobility data, especially if one were willing to relax assumptions of homogeneity (McFarland, 1970).

8.2 Age at First Job

An apparent inconsistency between the number of grades completed and age at first job in the responses of a sizable number of men was pointed out in an earlier report on the OCG data (B. Duncan, 1965b, Chapter 5). The query on age at first job took the form:

Please think about the first full-time job you had after you left school. (Do not count part-time jobs or jobs during school vacation. Do not count military service.) How old were you when you began this job?

The query did not specify "after you last attended a regular school." If schooling proceeded continuously, with the exception of interruption for military service, however, the age at first job would be the age at which the respondent last attended a regular school plus the elapsed time between school leaving and entry into the employed civilian labor force. A comparison of the "highest grade of school completed" with the "age at first job" for a sizable number of respondents makes it clear that these men either (a) misreported one or the other item or (b) left school, took a full-time job, and later resumed their schooling. Something over a sixth of the men who report having completed at least a year of graduate study, for example, also report that they had taken their first job before they reached the age of 19.

Only responses to a series of questions on school leaving and work-force entry could wholly resolve the apparent inconsistency. When did the respondent first leave school for a term or more? When did he most recently attend school? What were his primary activities between periods of school attendance if schooling did not proceed continuously? The information collected through the OCG survey provides no clues about the sequence of events that occurred, but a check on the internal consistency of the responses can be carried out using information provided by the respondent about the nature of both his first job and the job currently or most recently held.

If "inconsistent" respondents describe as their first job one similar to the first job of a sizable number of "consistent" respondents who took a job at the reported age and their current job as one similar to the current job of a sizable number of "consistent" respondents with the reported level of educational attainment, misreporting in the usual sense does not seem a likely explanation of the inconsistency. A more likely explanation is a period of flux between student and worker statuses within which school leaving and work-force entry cannot be dated unambiguously. An interruption of schooling by full-time participation in the civilian work force or an interruption of job holding by a resumption of schooling occurred or is perceived to have occurred among inconsistent respondents. Consistent respondents, in contrast, did not experience such interruption or, at least, do not define their experience in this way.

Any attempt to interpret substantively an inconsistency which cannot be shown conclusively to be anything more than an error in reporting is open to question. Nonetheless, the social background and occupational achievement of inconsistent respondents may provide clues for investigators who undertake to identify the causes and outcomes of interrupted schooling or "dropouts who came back," to use Eckland's (1964) phrase.

Special tabulations of the OCG data were obtained which permit separate analyses of the process of occupational achievement for inconsistent and consistent respondents of like educational attainment. The study population is made up of native civilian non-Negro males whose family head had not been engaged in a farm occupation when the respondent was 16 years old and who were between the ages of 25 and 64 on the 1962 survey date.

Relatively complete reporting of age at first job for the study population was assured at the time the tabulation specifications were designed. (Earlier tabulations showed that only 1 percent of the native civilian white males age 20–61 on the survey date who reported a nonfarm occupation for their first job failed to report the age at which they took the job.) Nearly all men in the sample can be assigned to an age-at-first-job stratum (Table 8.2). Only among functional illiterates does nonreporting on the item exceed 2.6 percent, and the

TABLE 8.2

Percentage Distribution by Age at First Job for Native Civilian Non-Negro Males Aged 25 to 64 with Nonfarm Background in Eight Strata Defined by Educational Attainment: March 1962[a]

Age at first job	Grades completed as of March 1962							
	0–4	5–7	8	9–11	12	13–15	16	17+
All	100.0	100.0	100.0	100.0	100.0	100.0	100.0	100.0
Under 14	14.9	4.9	2.5	1.0	0.4	0.1	0.1	0.2
14	10.9	16.1	8.8	3.4	1.0	0.7	0.2	0.4
15	6.2	10.9	11.0	5.4	2.0	1.6	0.9	1.1
16	20.4	33.0	33.9	28.7	10.2	6.3	4.0	1.7
17	11.2	12.5	18.6	24.8	18.0	13.4	6.1	5.2
18	14.4	9.0	15.4	19.6	32.8	23.0	14.4	8.8
19	9.2	4.1	2.5	5.4	15.8	13.6	6.1	4.5
20	3.5	3.4	1.7	4.9	7.1	11.8	7.8	4.5
21	2.7	1.8	2.2	3.4	5.4	12.0	11.8	9.6
22	1.2	0.7	1.3	1.5	3.1	7.3	14.6	10.1
23	0.2	0.6	0.3	0.6	1.7	3.7	10.5	12.3
24	0.5	0.4	0.4	0.3	0.8	3.2	8.6	12.0
25 and over	4.5	2.5	1.3	1.0	1.8	3.2	14.8	29.6
Nonresponse rate, per 100	6.9	1.7	2.6	1.3	0.8	1.3	0.2	1.5

[a]Source: OCG data set.

nonresponse rate for age at first job is no more than 1.5 percent in five of the eight strata defined by educational attainment.

Age at First Job in Relation to Grades Completed. Given an imagery of grade-mates with a common age, one might expect to find an unambiguous modal age of entry into the civilian work force among men whose schooling had terminated at a given grade level. A modal entry age is most pronounced for men who terminated after completing the eighth or twelfth grade, but even for these strata no more than a third of the men report the ages of 16 and 18, respectively. At the other extreme, a seventh of the men who terminated after 4 years of college report taking their first job at age 18, another seventh report age 22, and still another seventh report an age of 25 or older. The detailed distributions by age at first job within educational-attainment strata appear in Table 8.2.

One can only speculate about the causes of the diversity in age at entry into the civilian work force among men with similar levels of educational attainment. Periods of civilian employment can intervene between periods of regular school attendance. Military service would have intervened between periods of school attendance, between school leaving and entry into the civilian work force, or between civilian job holding and the resumption of schooling for a substantial number of the college-trained men and a lesser number of men with only high school training. Periods of training in institutions outside the regular school system, such as ungraded business or technical schools, also would intervene between school attendance and civilian job holding for a sizable number of men. The tightness of the labor market may influence markedly the time that elapses between school leaving and employment, especially among the poorly educated whose job skills are few (B. Duncan, 1965a). The survey results make it clear that adult males matched with respect to the amount of formal schooling ultimately completed differ substantially in terms of the age at which they perceive their first regular civilian work-force attachment to have occurred. The potential causes of diversity just identified may alone be sufficient to account for the observed variability, although their frequency of occurrence in the study population is unmeasured.

Current and First Occupation. Respondents in the study population who reported an age at first job are grouped for analytical purposes into forty strata defined by educational attainment and age at first job. Functional illiterates (men with less than 5 years of schooling) are treated as a separate stratum without subclassification by age at first job. Respondents in each of the remaining seven categories of educational attainment are subclassified into at least three groups on the basis of age at first job. Each of the forty strata distinguished includes more than a hundred respondents, that is, sample cases. The mean socioeconomic status score of the occupations currently pursued by respondents in each of the forty groups is reported in the upper panel of Table 8.3; the mean score for the occupations of their first jobs is reported in the lower panel.

Men in each educational-attainment stratum are rather sharply differentiated from men in any other attainment stratum with respect to the positions they hold in the current occupation structure. Only two instances of overlap with respect to mean current-occupation scores between age-at-first-job groups in adjacent strata of educational attainment are observed: the mean score of men who terminated schooling with the eighth grade and took a job before their sixteenth birthday is slightly higher than the mean score of men who dropped out of high school and deferred taking a job until they had reached their majority, and the mean score of functional literates who completed no more than seven grades and took a job before their sixteenth birthday is slightly higher than the mean score of men who completed the eighth grade and took a job at the age of 16 or 17. Had substantial overlap between strata occurred, the assumption of accurate reporting with respect to educational attainment and/or current occupation would have become untenable; it remains tenable in the absence of overlap.

If one is willing to assume that ability has a modest positive influence on the status of the first job net of schooling completed at the time of work-force entry and that the probability of resuming schooling is associated positively with ability, the assumption of accurate reporting with respect to age at first job remains tenable when the first occupations of respondents are examined. (This assumption also comports with the supposition that men leaving school at a given age are more likely to resume schooling if they are not seriously age-grade retarded at that time.) College graduates who report taking a job at 18, for example, report first jobs with a mean score of 30. Their points of entry into the occupation structure are markedly closer to the entry occupations of high-school graduates who took a job at the age of 18—a mean score of 27—than to the entry occupations of college graduates who took a job at the age of 22—a mean score of 55.

It should be made clear before proceeding further that the foregoing interpretation of the inconsistency between number of grades completed and age at first job, that is, that neither is misreported in the usual sense, is speculative. The patterns just described with respect to current and first occupations can be considered to be compatible with such an interpretation, but they do not validate it. In further discussion, however, it is taken to be the case that respondents are describing accurately their current educational attainment and the age at which they first took a full-time job after leaving school, although the salient school leaving may have been followed by another period of school attendance.

The effects of age at first job net of current educational attainment on the occupation of the first job and on current occupational achievement are

TABLE 8.3

Mean Socioeconomic Status Score of Occupations Held by Native Civilian Non-Negro Males Aged 25 to 64 with Nonfarm Background in 40 Strata Defined by Age at First Job and Educational Attainment: March 1962[a]

Age at first job	Grades completed as of March 1962							
	0–4	5–7	8	9–11	12	13–15	16	17+
	Current occupation							
Under 16		25.95	30.99	32.43	37.62			
16		23.24	25.41	32.11	42.37	47.89	65.53	
17	20.02		25.18	32.96	44.74	55.62		72.72
18				31.01	42.09	53.25	64.54	
19		21.35	27.93	35.25	44.08	55.93		
20					42.20	49.92	69.73	
21					42.46	53.97	70.93	75.27
22			28.67				69.19	
23					40.61	56.12	66.80	76.84
24								
25 and over							67.88	76.97
	First occupation							
Under 16		16.00	16.68	20.95	24.27			
16		15.38	17.94	21.22	23.37	27.57	32.75	
17	11.92		16.38	21.67	27.96	31.20		34.25
18				22.25	27.32	32.47	30.32	
19		17.00	21.24	22.48	30.00	35.89		
20					29.34	37.60	44.62	
21					32.93	41.92	58.13	52.17
22			22.54				55.16	
23					34.07	42.56	57.29	71.04
24								
25 and over							62.96	76.44

[a] Each entry stands for the mean of all cases in the block of cells outlined by horizontal lines and appears opposite the approximate mean age at first job for that group of cells.

displayed graphically in Fig. 8.2. The interpretation of the net effect of age at first job will differ depending upon whether it is the first or current occupation that is being examined. The amount of schooling completed prior to work-force entry cannot be assumed to be constant within strata defined by current educational attainment. Indeed, there will tend to be a positive association

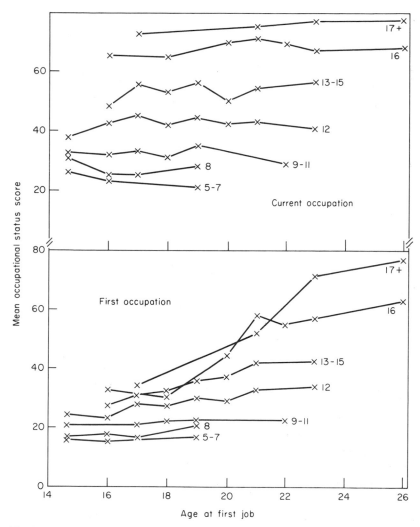

Fig. 8.2. Relationships of mean status of current and first occupations to age at first job, within educational strata (from Table 8.3).

between schooling completed prior to work-force entry and age at work-force entry among men in the same current attainment stratum. Given the floors on age at school entry and age at work-force entry, respectively, the within-stratum association can be presumed stronger among men with high levels of current educational attainment. Thus the effects of educational qualification and age per se are confounded in the effects of age at first job on occupation of the first job net of ultimate educational attainment. When it is the current, rather than first, occupation that is being examined, age at first job can be conceived as a past career contingency which may or may not have a long-run influence on occupational success independently of present educational qualification.

The net effect of entry age on the status of the entry occupation tends to be positive within each stratum defined by ultimate educational attainment, but the magnitude of the effect becomes notably greater as the level of ultimate educational attainment rises. This we presume to represent a more serious confounding of educational qualification and age per se at the time of job taking among men of high current educational attainment. In contrast, a positive net effect of age at first job on current occupation is barely detectable among men who have completed at least secondary school and is absent among men with lesser current educational qualification.

It follows directly from these observations that upward mobility from the point of entry into the occupation structure (the mean score for current occupation less the mean score for first occupation) is more pronounced for men who entered the work force at an early age than for men who deferred entry within each stratum defined by educational attainment as of the survey date. (The mean differences in score between first and current occupation are displayed in the upper panel of Table 8.4.) This should not be taken to mean that deferral of work-force entry depresses advancement within the occupation structure for men entering the work force with the same amount of formal schooling. Instead, the incremental education acquired after work force entry is thought to result in atypically rapid promotion within the occupation structure.

In fact, for several groups whose age at first job relative to current educational attainment unambiguously implies work-force entry prior to the completion of schooling, the socioeconomic status of the current job varies independently of the socioeconomic status of the first job. The lower panel of Table 8.4 shows the regression coefficient measuring the relation of the score of the current occupation to the score of the first occupation for men in the forty strata defined by educational attainment and age at first job. For most strata the positive sign and substantial magnitude of the coefficient suggest an appreciable degree of continuity in career subsequent to work-force entry. No such continuity characterizes the work history of men who were civilian jobholders before they completed college, however.

Social Background. Within educational-attainment strata, early job taking is associated with a social background unfavorable to prolonged schooling. Whether the association comes about through differential work-force participation or differential perception of the participation as a full-time job after school leaving is moot. The possibility of resuming schooling may seem sufficiently remote to the lower status male when he accepts civilian employment for the first time that he defines the event as the first job even when it has

TABLE 8.4

Relation of Respondent's Current to First Occupation for Native Civilian Non-Negro Males Aged 25 to 64 with Nonfarm Background in 40 Strata Defined by Age at First Job and Educational Attainment: March 1962

Age at first job	Grades completed as of March 1962							
	0–4	5–7	8	9–11	12	13–15	16	17+
	Mean increase over first occupation[a]							
Under 16		9.95	14.31	11.48	13.35			
16		7.86	7.47	10.89	19.00	20.32	32.78	
17	8.10		8.80	11.29	16.78	24.42		38.47
18				8.76	14.77	20.78	34.22	
19		4.35	6.69	12.77	14.08	20.04		
20					12.86	12.32	25.11	
21					9.53	12.05	12.80	23.10
22			6.13				14.03	
23					6.54	13.56	9.51	5.80
24								
25+							4.92	0.53
	Regression coefficient on first occupation							
Under 16		.167[b]	.343	.390	.154[b]			
16		.236	.303	.357	.368	.216	.041[b]	
17	.658		.167[b]	.338	.200	.361		−.012[b]
18				.309	.286	.212	.151[b]	
19		.541	.425	.334	.428	.245		
20					.447	.318	.076[b]	
21					.386	.230	.101[b]	.042[b]
22			.410				.108	
23					.502	.298	.284	.307
24								
25+							.290	.696

[a] For men reporting both current and first occupation.
[b] Not statistically significant at the .05 level.

been followed by another period of school attendance. His higher status counterpart who anticipates a continuation of schooling may define the event as only a temporary interruption of his student status.

Differences with respect to both the occupation and education of the family head by the respondent's reported age at first job are to be observed among men with the same current level of educational attainment. The mean socio-economic status score of the occupations pursued by the heads of the families in which young job takers grew up tends to be lower than the mean score of the occupations pursued by the heads of the families in which older job takers grew up. The number of grades completed by the family heads also tends to vary directly with reported age at first job within strata defined by current educational attainment. The frequency with which these patterns recur from one attainment stratum to another can be observed in the tabular presentation of Table 8.5 or the graphic presentation of Fig. 8.3.

Within strata defined by educational attainment, and particularly within strata where the level of attainment is high, it is the early job takers who typically have experienced the greatest upward social mobility over the parental generation. Intergenerational mobility with respect to education can be inferred readily from entries in the lower panel of Table 8.5. Mean changes between the socioeconomic status scores of the occupations currently pursued by respondents and the scores of the occupations pursued by their family heads are displayed in the upper panel of Table 8.6. Inversions in the asserted inverse relation between the amount of upward intergenerational mobility and the age at first job occur with moderate frequency, but they are not patterned with sufficient regularity to invalidate the general tendency.

The differentials with respect to intergenerational mobility which appear when the current occupational achievement of the respondent is contrasted with the occupational status that had been attained by the family head at the time the respondent was an adolescent develop as the respondent's work career lengthens and he increments the schooling completed prior to work-force entry. When the respondent's entry occupation is contrasted with the occupation of his family head, the early job takers within strata defined by current educational attainment are not distinguished by a relatively favorable position in the occupation structure vis-à-vis the positions of their family heads. In fact, the lower panel of Table 8.6 reveals that they are, if anything, distinguished by a relatively unfavorable position.

Another aspect of social background is tapped by two measures on the respondent's siblings: their number; and the educational attainment of the older brother for respondents who have such a sibling. Mean scores on the respective items appear in Table 8.7 for respondents in the forty cells defined by educational attainment and age at first job. A relatively small number of siblings and relatively high educational attainment on the part of older brothers are conducive to prolonged schooling. Within most educational-attainment strata, they also tend to be conducive to late entry into the work force. There are noteworthy exceptions, however. Among men whose schooling has not proceeded beyond the elementary level, few, rather than many siblings distinguish the early job takers. Among men who terminated schooling

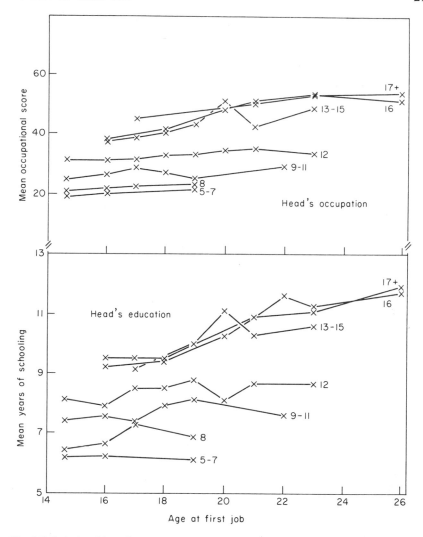

Fig. 8.3. Relationships of mean occupational status and educational attainment of heads of respondents' families of orientation to respondents' age at first job, within educational strata (from Table 8.5).

with the twelfth grade or some college training, the educational attainment of older brothers is not associated with age at work-force entry.

An overall impression can be formed on the basis of these differentials that elements of the family's structure and status which are conducive to high educational attainment also are conducive to continuity in schooling. The groups of men whose schooling is presumed to have been interrupted by a

TABLE 8.5

Mean Socioeconomic Status Score of Occupation and Mean Number of Grades Completed for Family Heads of Native Civilian Non-Negro Males Aged 25 to 64 with Nonfarm Background in 40 Strata Defined by Age at First Job and Educational Attainment: March 1962

Age at first job	Grades completed as of March 1962							
	0–4	5–7	8	9–11	12	13–15	16	17+
				Occupation				
Under 16		19.22	21.65	25.12	31.56			
16		20.14	22.04	26.36	31.58	37.66	37.94	
17	17.34		22.38	28.39	31.75	39.09		44.90
18				26.92	33.00	40.54	41.71	
19		21.54	23.54	25.38	33.23	43.69		
20					34.28	50.73	48.60	
21					34.96	42.27	51.14	50.26
22				29.08			52.16	
23					33.61	48.61	53.17	53.06
24								
25+							51.30	53.66
				Education				
Under 16		6.20	6.47	7.40	8.17			
16		6.22	6.64	7.54	7.91	9.54	9.19	
17	5.97		7.29	7.39	8.50	9.54		9.20
18				7.93	8.56	9.51	9.41	
19		6.14	6.93	8.17	8.79	9.96		
20					8.11	11.09	10.27	
21					8.66	10.33	10.92	10.89
22				7.61			11.60	
23					8.62	10.60	11.27	11.09
24								
25+							11.67	11.93

period of civilian employment, given their current educational attainment and reported age at first job, are drawn disproportionately from families whose characteristics are relatively unfavorable to educational attainment. Inasmuch as these men have achieved occupational success consonant with their ultimate educational attainment, their gains over the occupational status of their family heads have been atypically large.

Several bases of differentiation between "early job takers" and other

TABLE 8.6

Relation of Respondent's Current and First Occupations to Family Head's Occupation for Native Civilian Non-Negro Males Aged 25 to 64 with Nonfarm Background in 40 Strata Defined by Age at First Job and Educational Attainment: March 1962

Age at first job	Grades completed as of March 1962							
	0–4	5–7	8	9–11	12	13–15	16	17+
	Mean change, current over head's occupation[a]							
Under 16		6.51	9.51	7.79	7.49			
16		3.33	4.05	5.96	10.96	9.55	27.74	
17	4.75		2.60	5.06	12.59	17.28		28.44
18				4.33	8.90	14.11	24.19	
19		0.13	4.78	10.22	11.37	12.11		
20					7.85	−0.38	21.75	
21					7.44	11.66	19.52	25.99
22				−1.11			17.75	
23					8.18	7.10	13.43	23.62
24								
25+							16.62	23.22
	Mean change, first over head's occupation[a]							
Under 16		−3.14	−4.54	−4.49	−6.78			
16		−4.38	−4.83	−4.96	−8.25	−10.18	−5.21	
17	−4.08		−6.15	−6.36	−4.82	−7.23		−9.70
18				−4.49	−5.79	−6.79	−10.80	
19		−4.36	−1.88	−2.97	−2.64	−8.14		
20					−4.48	−13.41	−4.14	
21					−1.46	0.55	7.02	2.46
22				−7.32		2.83		
23					1.15	−6.28	4.77	17.89
24								
25+							11.73	22.52

[a] For men reporting both occupations.

respondents with the same level of current educational attainment are summarized in Table 8.8. Among the men whose educational attainment as of the survey date was high, a subgroup of early job takers can be distinguished who must have interrupted their schooling with a period of civilian employment. These early job takers are defined as men who report completing at least seventeen grades and also report an age at first job of 21 or less, and men who report

TABLE 8.7

Means of Respondent's Number of Siblings and His Oldest Brother's Schooling for Native Civilian Non-Negro Males Aged 25 to 64 with Nonfarm Background in 40 Strata Defined by Age at First Job and Educational Attainment: March 1962

Age at first job	Grades completed as of March 1962							
	0–4	5–7	8	9–11	12	13–15	16	17+
	Mean number of siblings							
Under 16		5.30	5.43	4.87	3.81			
16		5.28	5.55	4.48	3.70	3.61	3.48	
17	5.53		5.31	4.18	3.62	3.41		3.20
18				4.42	3.51	3.15	2.69	
19		5.97	5.72	4.35	3.30	2.94		
20					3.44	2.49	2.40	
21					3.28	3.01	2.23	2.73
22				4.38			2.59	
23					3.74	2.71	2.17	2.41
24								
25+							2.47	2.08
	Mean brother's education							
Under 16		7.67	8.23	8.96	12.02[a]			
16		7.90	9.09	10.07	11.13	11.21[a]	11.71[a]	
17	6.74		8.81	10.01	11.13	13.35		13.19[a]
18				10.17	11.44	12.85	12.86	
19		8.26	9.30	10.18	11.85	12.61		
20					11.84	13.11	14.20[a]	
21					11.22	13.36[a]	14.66[a]	13.96[a]
22				10.49			14.39[a]	
23					11.45	13.06	14.54	13.83
24								
25+							13.92	14.45[a]

[a] Fewer than 60 sample cases.

completing sixteen grades and also report an age at first job of 20 or less. The early job takers report first occupations ranking relatively low in the occupation structure; in fact, the difference in mean scores between early job takers and other respondents amounts to a full standard deviation for the first-occupation scores. The point of primary interest here, however, is differentiation with respect to social background and current occupational success.

TABLE 8.8

Mean Scores and Standard Deviations on Selected Variables for College Graduates, by Age at First Job, in the Population of Native Civilian Non-Negro Men Aged 25 to 64 with Nonfarm Background: March 1962

Item	Grade 17 or more		Grade 16	
	Early job takers[a]	All other	Early job takers[b]	All other
	Mean score			
Family head's				
Education (V)	10.11	11.47	9.66	11.38
Occupation (X)	47.68	53.33	43.11	52.08
Siblings (T)	2.96	2.26	2.81	2.36
Older brother's education (E)	13.54	14.06	12.92	14.36
Age at marriage (M)	25.04	26.50	24.97	25.19
First occupation (W)	43.53	73.54	36.03	58.33
Current occupation (Y)	74.04	76.90	66.65	68.46
	Standard deviation			
Family head's				
Education (V)	4.14	4.10	3.69	4.08
Occupation (X)	23.53	23.59	23.10	23.15
Siblings (T)	2.51	2.04	2.36	2.19
Older brother's education (E)	3.28	3.17	3.15	2.88
Age at marriage (M)	4.46	5.52	4.55	3.97
First occupation (W)	23.94	18.39	20.64	21.13
Current occupation (Y)	15.54	14.39	17.60	15.32

[a] Reported an age at first job of 21 or less.
[b] Reported an age at first job of 20 or less.

Within both educational-attainment strata, the early job takers report: a relatively low level of educational attainment on the part of the head of the family in which they were reared; an occupation for their family head which has relatively low socioeconomic status; a relatively large number of siblings; a relatively low level of educational attainment on the part of their older brother, if they have one; and a relatively young age at marriage, if they have married. Although the early job takers also have experienced slightly less occupational success than other respondents in the same educational stratum, they are less sharply differentiated from the other respondents with respect to current occupation than with respect to antecedent social characteristics. Among college graduates, for example, the difference in mean scores with respect to current occupation amounts to only a tenth of a standard deviation for current-occupation scores. In contrast, the differences in mean scores with respect to head's education and occupation amount to two-fifths of the respective standard deviations.

Superficially inconsistent reports on the number of grades completed and age at first job appear to distinguish a group of men whose educational attainment and occupational achievement are relatively high given their social background and whose schooling was interrupted by a period of civilian employment. There is perhaps some justification for looking toward the construction of models of the process of occupational achievement which incorporate not only the amount of schooling but also the timing of schooling with the life cycle.*

8.3 Migration

Migration is treated as a career contingency in view of the way the phenomenon is ascertained in the OCG data. A "migrant" is a respondent who reports that his present community of residence ("city, town or rural area") differs from the one where he lived at age 16. All other respondents are classified as "nonmigrants." Migration at some unspecified time, therefore, intervenes between characteristics of the family of orientation and occupational status as of the survey date. There is no information as to the timing of migration with respect to the completion of formal schooling. Common knowledge suggests that pursuit of a college—or even, under some circumstances, a secondary— education requires or occasions migration. In such a case, it is probably not accurate to think of either migration or educational attainment as a cause of the other. In other cases, of course, migration does not occur until after schooling is completed, although the bulk of the moves ascertained in the type of inquiry described here probably occur during the late adolescent and young adult years.

The main question we try to answer in this brief analysis is whether the occupational achievements of men are favorably or unfavorably influenced by the experience of migration. This question is not lacking in ambiguity since whether an experience is "favorable" or not may depend on the selection of a norm of comparison. One possible comparison is that between migrants and nonmigrants in the same communities of origin. If the migrants enjoy greater success than the nonmigrants, it is inferred that the experience of migration has a favorable influence. In this comparison, however, it is difficult to rule out the hypothesis that migrants enjoy an advantage primarily due to participation in a

---

* One inquiry into such timing effects has been undertaken by Griliches and Mason (1970) for a subset of the United States Army veteran population in 1964. Their analysis decomposed the variance in income due to education both prior to and after military service, as well as to AFQT (intelligence) scores and socioeconomic background characteristics.

more favorable opportunity structure. This hypothesis can be excluded by adopting the alternative strategy of comparing migrants with nonmigrants in the communities of destination. In this case, the opportunity structures are presumably the same.

Whatever type of comparison is effected, however, there is always a further source of ambiguity: whether migration in some sense "causes" achievement or whether migration is merely selective of those men with qualities like energy and ambition which would lead to above-average achievement, irrespective of the decision to migrate. While this ambiguity cannot be finally resolved, it is possible to standardize the comparisons for characteristics already known to influence occupational achievement. These factors, as set forth in our basic model, include the three standard characteristics of the family of orientation and the respondent's schooling.

One other element figures prominently in the present analysis—the classification of migrants according to farm vs. nonfarm background, as ascertained from the question on father's occupation. In earlier work (Blau & Duncan, 1967: Chapter 8) the impact of farm background on occupational achievement was treated in a somewhat unsatisfactory way, and it was not possible to present the proper comparisons with regard to migration status. Most men living in nonfarm areas but having farm background are, of course, migrants. For clarity, they should be compared with both nonmigrants in those areas and migrants with nonfarm background. Moreover, it seems strategic to control the size of the community of residence in such comparisons. Migrants with farm background will have moved in disproportionate numbers to the smaller nonfarm communities, while the other two categories of men will be spread over the city-size distribution. If opportunity structures are more favorable in large places, a comparison between men with farm background and those with nonfarm background which did not control for this factor could lead to an erroneous impression of the influence of background as such.

It is quite clear that the migration classification captures significant variation in occupational status. Table 8.9 shows that migrants with nonfarm background consistently have higher mean occupational status scores than nonmigrants. In urbanized areas the difference is 4-6 points on the status scale; in the smaller urban places and rural nonfarm areas, it is even larger. Almost as consistently, men with farm backgrounds score lower on the average than nonmigrants; in urbanized areas the discrepancy is 6 or 7 points, although it disappears entirely in the smaller urban places and is rather smaller in rural nonfarm areas. Inasmuch as migrants with nonfarm background compare favorably with nonmigrants while migrants with farm background compare unfavorably, there is little question about the comparison between the two categories of migrants: Those with nonfarm background have very substantially higher mean occupational status scores than those with farm background.

TABLE 8.9

Mean Occupational Status Scores for Native Non-Negro Men 25 to 64 Years Old Living in Nonfarm Residences and in the Experienced Civilian Labor Force, by Migration Status: March 1962[a]

Size of place (residence in March 1962)	Nonfarm background		Farm background, migrant
	Nonmigrant	Migrant	
Urbanized areas			
1,000,000 or more	42.7	48.9	36.4
250,000 to 1,000,000	44.6	48.7	38.8
50,000 to 250,000	41.3	47.5	34.7
Other urban places	37.5	47.2	37.9
Rural nonfarm	33.8	42.0	30.3

[a] Source: OCG data set. (*Note*: Men with farm background classed as nonmigrants are excluded because of the small frequencies. "Farm background" refers to men who reported father's occupation as farmer or farm laborer.)

These crude comparisons do not, therefore, provide an unequivocal indication of the effect of migration as such on occupational achievement. The very direction of such an effect appears to depend on farm vs. nonfarm background. Moreover, we have not yet examined any material relevant to the selectivity hypothesis.

To pursue this question, multiple regressions of occupational status on family background and educational attainment were computed for each migration category within each of the five size-of-community classes. The results are shown in Tables 8.10 and 8.11. In planning these computations there was some expectation that the results might show some clear and readily interpretable interactions—relationships, that is, that are much stronger or weaker in one migration category than in another. Apart from fluctuations apparently due to sampling variation and some artifacts of the definitions, there do not appear to be many such interactions to report.

For example, it might be thought that the migrant would be a person who had managed to free himself from the influence of his family of orientation and the social circle within which it moves, and, therefore, that the influence of family background on achievement should be less for migrants than for nonmigrants. The most relevant summary statistics for this hypothesis are found in Table 8.10 in the column of coefficients of determination for migrants and nonmigrants, both with nonfarm background. In brief, the comparisons are not consistent over community-size categories and certainly do not support the hypothesis in question. Similarly, there is not much to be said in regard to the

TABLE 8.10

Regression Coefficients Describing Relationships of Occupational Status (Y) to Family Background, by Migration Status, for Native Non-Negro Men 25 to 64 Years Old Living in Nonfarm Residences and in the Experienced Civilian Labor Force: March 1962. [Parentheses ( ) enclose coefficient smaller than its standard error][a]

Migration status and size of place (residence in March 1962)	Independent variable			
	Number of siblings (T)	Father's occupation (X)	Father's education[b] (V)	Coefficient of determination
Nonmigrants, nonfarm background				
Urbanized areas				
1,000,000 or more	−1.228	.274	1.634	.153
250,000 to 1,000,000	−.965	.367	.594	.176
50,000 to 250,000	−.707	.309	2.753	.209
Other urban places	−.779	.258	1.787	.134
Rural nonfarm	−1.370	.269	1.379	.170
Migrants, nonfarm background				
Urbanized areas				
1,000,000 or more	−1.224	.267	1.294	.154
250,000 to 1,000,000	−1.147	.305	1.646	.188
50,000 to 250,000	−1.292	.259	1.572	.156
Other urban places	−1.382	.297	1.888	.178
Rural nonfarm	−1.606	.273	1.711	.191
Migrants, farm background				
Urbanized areas				
1,000,000 or more	(.060)	(−.162)	2.683	.029
250,000 to 1,000,000	−1.612	1.035	2.818	.118
50,000 to 250,000	−1.284	(.046)	1.564	.050
Other urban places	−1.017	1.077	2.887	.078
Rural nonfarm	(−.089)	.541	3.157	.051

[a] Source: OCG data set.
[b] V is in units of a convenient coding of school years completed.

comparison between the first two panels of regression coefficients in Table 8.10. One might be inclined to conclude that number of siblings has a rather greater impact on occupational achievement of migrants (with nonfarm background) than on that of nonmigrants. There is no suggestion of a consistent comparison with respect to the other two variables, however.

The inclusion of the third panel in each of these two tables involves a calculated risk of creating misleading impressions. The truth is that the regression results for men with farm background cannot be compared directly with those for men with nonfarm background. This is because one of the variables in the basic model—father's occupation—is involved in the very definition of farm

TABLE 8.11

Regression Coefficients Describing Relationship of Occupational Status (Y) to Family Background and Educational Attainment, by Migration Status, for Native Non-Negro Men 25 to 64 Years Old Living in Nonfarm Residences and in the Experienced Civilian Labor Force: March 1962. [Parentheses ( ) enclose coefficient smaller than its standard error][a]

	Independent variable				
Migration status and size of place (residence in March 1962)	Education (U)	Number of siblings (T)	Father's occupation (X)	Father's education[b] (V)	Coefficient of determination
Nonmigrants, nonfarm background					
Urbanized areas					
1,000,000 or more	8.018	−.197	.118	.559	.342
250,000 to 1,000,000	7.482	−.323	.207	(−.451)	.372
50,000 to 250,000	6.684	(.070)	.171	1.719	.350
Other urban places	7.685	(.089)	.132	(.175)	.328
Rural nonfarm	6.058	−.842	.151	(.073)	.295
Migrants, nonfarm background					
Urbanized areas					
1,000,000 or more	8.463	−.240	.105	(.146)	.399
250,00 to 1,000,000	8.000	(−.172)	.171	(−.056)	.426
50,000 to 250,000	8.241	−.356	.128	(.120)	.388
Other urban places	8.346	−.404	.125	(.431)	.430
Rural nonfarm	7.494	−.804	.134	(.026)	.399
Migrants, farm background					
Urbanized areas					
1,000,000 or more	7.460	.871	−.541	(−.149)	.298
250,000 to 1,000,000	8.156	−.636	(.313)	1.388	.432
50,000 to 250,000	6.860	−.677	(−.486)	−1.120	.260
Other urban places	6.417	(−.164)	.830	1.218	.283
Rural nonfarm	6.528	.469	(.076)	(.223)	.255

[a] Source: OCG data set.
[b] V is in units of a convenient coding of school years completed.

background. Men with such background are defined as those reporting their fathers' occupations as farmers, farm managers, farm laborers, or farm foremen. There is comparatively little variation in occupational status within this category, therefore. Although a regression coefficient can be computed for variable X, it is difficult to be sure what interpretation can be placed on it. Moreover, since the variation in X is sharply reduced by comparison with the groups with nonfarm background, coefficients of determination may not be compared between the third panel and the other two. Finally, in view of the small samples of men with farm background in several of the community-size groups, there is a good deal of sampling variation in the results.

Taking account of all these limitations on the comparisons, perhaps the one conclusion that can be tentatively suggested is that the impact of father's education on respondent's occupational achievement is somewhat greater for migrants with farm background than for either nonmigrants or migrants with nonfarm background. Even in this case, not all the comparisons in Table 8.10 are consistent with the summary statement.

If it is difficult to isolate clear interactions of migration status with family background variables, we have some warrant for treating the effect of migration as simply additive to the effects of the family variables. We shall presently take advantage of the convenience of this assumption. One more comparison, however, should be mentioned. In Table 8.11, where educational attainment, along with family background, is regarded as an influence on occupational achievement, it appears that its impact is somewhat greater for migrants with nonfarm background than for either nonmigrants or migrants with farm background (although one of the five comparisons involving the latter does not fit this conclusion). This result is seen not only in the regression coefficients for variable U but also in the fact that the coefficients of determination are uniformly higher in the second than in the first panel of the table.

We should, of course, bear in mind that an apparently consistent comparison over five community-size groups might be expected to occur occasionally as a chance result of sampling fluctuations. Moreover, the magnitudes of the differences in regression coefficients are not uniform and in several cases are virtually negligible. We leave it as a tentative conclusion that nonfarm migrants may be somewhat advantaged in regard to the ease of converting educational attainment into occupational achievement; but a model that assumes no such effect will, nevertheless, not greatly distort the data.

In Table 8.12, therefore, we have standardized the comparisons of mean occupational achievement for family background and education on the assumption of additive effects. Operationally, the "net" effects were computed by substituting the mean values of independent variables for each of the migrant groups into the regression equation for nonmigrants and comparing the implied mean occupational score from this calculation with the actual mean for the migrant group. For example, the regression of occupational status on number of siblings, father's occupation, and father's education for nonmigrants in the largest urbanized areas is as follows:

$$\hat{Y} = 33.0 - 1.2T + .27X + 1.6V,$$

and the mean of Y in this group is 42.7 (as shown earlier). If we substitute into this equation the mean scores of migrants with nonfarm background—to wit, $\overline{T} = 3.48$, $\overline{X} = 36.5$, and $\overline{V} = 3.53$ (V is in units of a convenient coding of school years completed)—we obtain as the expected value of Y, 44.5. But the actual mean of Y for migrants with nonfarm background is 48.9. Hence, the effect of

TABLE 8.12

Gross and Net Effects of Migration Status on Occupational Status, by Size of Place, for Native Non-Negro Men 25 to 64 Years Old Living in Nonfarm Residences and in the Experienced Civilian Labor Force: March 1962[a]

Migration status and size of place (residence in March 1962)	Gross effect[b]	Net effect, net of	
		Socioeconomic background[c]	Background and education
Migrants, nonfarm background[d]			
Urbanized areas			
1,000,000 or more	6.2	4.4	2.4
250,000 to 1,000,000	4.1	2.8	0.5
50,000 to 250,000	6.2	2.7	0.6
Other urban places	9.8	8.2	5.4
Rural nonfarm	8.3	5.4	3.5
Migrants, farm background[d]			
Urbanized areas			
1,000,000 or more	−6.3	2.5	1.5
250,000 to 1,000,000	−5.8	3.6	2.4
50,000 to 250,000	−6.6	2.4	2.1
Other urban places	0.4	6.8	4.9
Rural nonfarm	−3.5	2.9	2.9

[a] Source: OCG data set.

[b] Deviation of mean for given migration class from mean for nonmigrants with nonfarm background.

[c] Includes family head's education (V), his occupation (X), and respondent's number of siblings (T).

[d] See source note, Table 8.9.

this migration category, net of the three family characteristics, is taken to be $48.9 - 44.5 = 4.4$ (the value shown in the first row, second column of Table 8.12). By the same procedure, using the appropriate regression and set of means, we infer that the net effect of this category, when not only the three family variables but also education is taken into account, is 2.4 points on the occupational status scale.

Let us inspect first the top panel of Table 8.12. The difference between gross effects and net effects bears on the hypothesis of selective migration. It appears, in fact, that a substantial part of the differential in occupational achievement is due to the fact that migrants are favorably selected with respect to such background traits as family size and socioeconomic level. The comparison between the two sets of net effects is likewise instructive. The result that net effects are smaller when education is taken into account along with the family variables than when only the latter are standardized for indicates that educational differentials may be a significant aspect of the mechanism by which migration status is converted into differential occupational achievement. Indeed, in two of the community-size groups, the net effects after the education variable has been accounted for are essentially nil. Yet these net effects remain positive—that is, they favor migrants with nonfarm background over non-migrants—in all five community-size groups. The model only partially explains the differential initially observed (see the column of gross effects) and leaves open the question of what other mechanism or principle of selectivity may account for the superior achievement of migrants.

In the second panel of Table 8.12 the results are even more interesting. The column of gross effects shows, as did Table 8.9, that migrants with farm background compare unfavorably with nonmigrants (and, a fortiori, with migrants with nonfarm background) in regard to crude mean occupational scores. This differential, signified by the the negative sign of the gross effect, is, however, reversed when standardization for family background is effected in the middle column of the table. That is, if we could directly compare migrants from farms with a group of nonmigrants who originated in equally large families at equally low levels of socioeconomic status, these results suggest that the farm migrants would actually appear to an advantage. Viewed in this light, migration is a favorable experience—or at least a favorable sign—irrespective of farm vs. nonfarm background. The net effects are much alike for the two groups of migrants. The implication is, moreover, that the substantial difference between the two groups of migrants observed in their crude occupational mean scores is almost wholly due to the advantageous family backgrounds of the nonfarm men.

Finally, we may observe that some part of the superior occupational achievement of farm migrants relative to nonmigrants of comparable family background is effected via education. This appears from the fact that the net effects in the third column of Table 8.12 are slightly smaller than those in the second. This comes about in virtue of the fact that educational attainment of migrants is slightly superior to that of nonmigrants, once a standardization for family background is effected.* The details of the analysis leading to this summary conclusion are displayed in Table 8.13 and do not require further comment since they fall into a pattern of the kind already described.

---

* In a related analysis of the FGMA data, Featherman (1971b) has shown that rearing in a rural or farm area has no direct effect on years of completed schooling for current metro-politan residents (rural to urban migrants). Instead, the disadvantages of rural vs. urban context of rearing can be explained by the larger sibships of those reared in rural areas and a subsequent educational handicap, holding constant paternal occupational status.

TABLE 8.13

Mean Number of Years of School Completed, by Migration Status, for Native Non-Negro Men 25 to 64 Years Old Living in Nonfarm Residences and in the Experienced Civilian Labor Force: March 1962[a]

Size of place (residence in March 1962)	Nonfarm background		Farm background, migrant
	Nonmigrant	Migrant	
		Observed means	
Urbanized areas			
1,000,000 or more	11.6	12.3	10.4
250,000 to 1,000,000	11.5	12.3	10.5
50,000 to 250,000	11.5	12.6	10.2
Other urban places	11.1	12.0	10.5
Rural nonfarm	10.5	11.6	9.5
		Gross effects[b]	
Urbanized areas			
1,000,000 or more	–	0.7	–1.2
250,000 to 1,000,000	–	0.8	–1.0
50,000 to 250,000	–	1.1	–1.3
Other urban places	–	0.9	–0.6
Rural nonfarm	–	1.1	–1.0
		Effects net of family background[c]	
Urbanized areas			
1,000,000 or more	–	0.5	0.2
250,000 to 1,000,000	–	0.6	0.3
50,000 to 250,000	–	0.6	0.1
Other urban places	–	0.7	0.5
Rural nonfarm	–	0.6	0.0

[a] Source: OCG data set.

[b] Deviation from mean for nonmigrants.

[c] Includes family head's education (V), his occupation (X), and respondent's number of siblings (T).

8.4   Disruption of Marriage

Differentials in occupational achievement among men who were living with their spouses on the survey date, men who reported their marital status as divorced, and men who reported that they were separated, that is, married but living apart from their spouses, are investigated in this section. Differential achievement on the part of never-married or widowed men is not explored because the probability of being in the status is so closely linked to age and the only age control in the analysis is restriction of the study population to males aged 25–64 on the survey date. The study population is further restricted by the exclusion of Negro respondents, the foreign born, men reared in families headed by a farm worker, and the men reared in broken families, that is, one or both parents were absent from the home in which the respondent lived as an adolescent.

On the survey date, the men living with their spouses were pursuing occupations with a mean socioeconomic status score some 7 points higher than the mean score of the occupations pursued by divorced or separated men. The difference amounts to about three-tenths of a standard deviation for the score in the study population. There is no difference between divorced and separated men with respect to occupational achievement on the survey date. At the time these men took their first civilian job, however, there had been no differentiation as between the men who were to be found living with their spouses on the survey date and the men who were to report themselves as divorced; both groups had held occupations ranking higher in the occupation structure than the occupations held by men who were to report themselves as separated on the survey date. The difference in mean scores with respect to the occupation of the first job amounted to some 6 points on the socioeconomic status scale, or about a quarter of a standard deviation. Progress in the occupation structure subsequent to entry, as indexed in the mean difference between the scores of the first and current occupations, has been substantially greater among the men currently living with their spouses or separated from them (14 and 13 scale points, respectively) than among the men whose current marital status is divorced (6 scale points). The mean scores and standard deviations on which these observations are based appear in Table 8.14.

Now it must be made clear that marital status is measured at a given point in time. Among the separated men are individuals who will remain in the status for a more or less indefinite period and also individuals who will make the transition into the divorced status and perhaps eventually reenter the spouse-present status, for example. Hence, the differentials cannot be attributed in any direct sense to the fact of separation or divorce. They serve only to differentiate the incumbents of the respective statuses at a given point in time.

With this limitation on the interpretation of the data made explicit, we proceed to examine differentials with respect to other antecedent social characteristics. The current marital-status groups are not notably differentiated with respect to the sizes and socioeconomic levels of the families in which they grew up; the maximum intergroup difference does not take on a value as great as a quarter of a standard deviation for any given family-background indicator. Sharper differentiation is to be observed with respect to the respondent's educational attainment, his age at first job, and his age at first marriage.

TABLE 8.14

Mean Scores and Standard Deviations on Selected Variables for Native Non-Negro Civilian Males Age 25 to 64, with Nonfarm Background and Reared with Both Parents, by Current Marital Status: March 1962[a]

	Spouse present	Spouse absent	
		Divorced	Separated[b]
Variable			
	Mean score		
Father's			
Education	8.61	8.87	8.16
Occupation	34.58	31.21	29.17
Siblings	3.89	3.74	4.24
Education	11.87	10.95	11.51
First job			
Age	18.59	17.88	18.69
Occupation	30.95	30.88	25.21
Age at first marriage	24.20	25.53	24.41
Current occupation	45.12	37.16	37.32
	Standard deviation		
Father's			
Education	3.66	3.94	3.23
Occupation	22.87	20.10	21.38
Siblings	2.92	2.63	3.27
Education	3.22	2.89	3.01
First job			
Age	2.97	2.75	4.29
Occupation	22.43	21.88	19.69
Age at first marriage	4.73	5.96	5.35
Current occupation	24.46	24.24	24.00

[a] Source: OCG data set.
[b] Includes "married, spouse absent."

Educational attainment is relatively low, age at first job relatively young, and age at first marriage relatively advanced for the divorced men by comparison with either the men currently living with their wives or the group of men who report themselves as separated or living apart from their spouses.

Viewed as a set, the mean scores on the several variables for the divorced men are anomalous. Their educational attainment appears atypically low, and their age at first job appears atypically young, given their social background. The socioeconomic status of their first occupations appears high given their educational qualifications and ages at the time of work-force entry. Moreover, the relation of current occupation to respondent's education or first occupation among the divorced males is unusual by comparison with the corresponding relation in most other subpopulations of survey respondents studied. The coefficient of correlation between first and current occupation, for example, takes on a value of .76 for the divorced men, in contrast to .52 for the spouse-present men or .50 for the separated men. The correlation coefficient between education and current occupation takes on a value of .46 for the divorced men, in contrast to .61 for the spouse-present men or .64 for the separated men. Unfortunately, the number of respondents in the divorced status is too small to permit calculation of reliable measures either for populations other than the one under study here or for subgroups within that study population.

On the assumption that the influence of antecedent social characteristics on achievement do not, in fact, differ among the subgroups defined by current marital status (that is, the apparent difference for divorced men represents a sampling fluctuation), we proceed to measure the effect of marital status on occupational success. The gross effect of a broken marital status on occupational success is a handicap of 7–8 points on the occupation scale (first row of Table 8.15). The effect of a separated status appears to be a handicap of about 5 points when allowance is made for slight disadvantages in social background and educational attainment for the separated relative to the spouse-present men. Allowance for the first occupation as well as social background and educational attainment reduces the handicap of the separated to 4 scale points (fourth row of Table 8.15). The difference in social background between divorced and spouse-present men is so slight that the effect of a divorced status on occupational success is reduced by less than a scale point when allowance is made for the background differential. When allowance for the respondent's education or education and first job also is made, however, the handicap of a divorced status falls to about 4 scale points. Overall, then, the observed handicap of about 8 points associated with a broken marital status is reduced to about 4 points when respondents in the intact and broken marital statuses are

TABLE 8.15

Summary of Effects of Current Marital Status on Occupational Achievement, for the Population Covered in Table 8.14.

Item	Spouse present	Spouse absent	
		Divorced	Separated
Gross effect	0.0	−8.0	−7.3
Effect net of social background (father's education and occupation and number of siblings)	0.0	−7.4	−4.9
Effect net of background and respondent's education	0.0	−3.8	−4.9
Effect net of background, education, and first occupation	0.0	−4.6	−4.0

"matched" statistically with respect to social background, educational attainment, and entry occupation. The fact that a measurable handicap remains after such adjustment suggests that disruption of marriage is a significant career contingency, though by no means one that accounts for any substantial part of the total variance in occupational achievement.*

8.5   Marital Fertility

The purpose of this section is to raise for discussion a point of view on the relationship between achievement and marital fertility that makes a different kind of assumption from the standard one in the literature and to report some results obtained on this point of view.

In studies of differential fertility, including those involving measures of social or occupational mobility, fertility (however measured) is usually taken as the dependent variable and measures of status as the independent variables. Thus Census tables on marital fertility show us number of children ever born or number of children under 5 years old per wife or per couple, where the couples are classified by (say) husband's income, husband's occupation, or the education of one or both spouses. Analysts working with these data sometimes note that income or occupation, ascertained as of the Census date (or during the year preceding the Census, as in the case of income) may not accurately represent the income or occupation level of the couple at the time childbearing was taking place. Education, however, can more reasonably be taken as an antecedent to fertility in that most of the childbearing period follows the completion of formal schooling by each spouse. Despite the general recognition of the anomalies generated by taking (past) fertility to depend upon (current) occupation and income, analysts have not often explored the consequences of an alternative assumption.

What is proposed here is that we consider causal models in which the status variables and fertility are ordered with regard to their presumed temporal sequence. On this point of view, we should have to regard the number of children born to a couple as a factor which intervenes between background factors—such as socioeconomic level of origin and educational attainment—and the achievement of current socioeconomic statuses. Since the number of births to a couple is not perfectly predictable from its combination of background factors, fertility would then operate as a "contingency" with respect to

---

* The relationship between marital stability in the parental generation to current marital status of the OCG respondents is reported by Duncan and Duncan (1969). With respect to occupational success, the experience of growing up in an intact family increases the probability that an individual will be pursuing an occupation that ranks relatively high in the socioeconomic structure, although it does not increase the probability that he will be found living with his wife in adulthood. See Section 4.4.

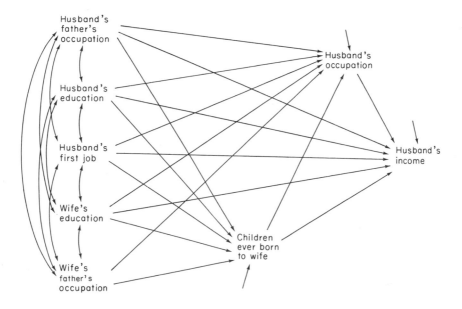

Fig. 8.4. Causal model interpreting fertility as a career contingency.

occupational status or income as observed at the end of the childbearing cycle or (for couples not beyond the age of childbearing) at the end of the period of observation.*

Figure 8.4 presents a causal model embodying these assumptions. The data required for illustrative calculations on this model come from the fertility tabulations prepared from the OCG data set. The following items of "background" information are available: the occupational status of the fathers of the respective spouses, as of the time the spouse was about 16 years old; the status of the husband's first job; the number of years of schooling completed by the husband and by the wife. All occupation items are scored on Duncan's (1961a) scale. The measure of fertility is number of children ever born to the wife. For the minority of couples in which either or both spouses were married more than once, part of this fertility may not be correctly attributed to the couple under observation. This error is assumed to be minor in the present context.

Two measures of achievement pertaining largely if not wholly to dates

---

* Students of population have been investigating the relationship between fertility and mobility for nearly a century (Dumont, 1890), although there have been proponents of both "strong" and "weak" forms of this mobility hypothesis (Blau & Duncan, 1967, p. 367). For an assessment of the role of cumulative marital fertility on the occupational and economic achievements of the FGMA males over the period 1957–1967, see Featherman (1970).

subsequent to the birth of the children are the husband's occupation at the date of the survey (March 1962) and his income in 1961.

The temporal ordering of these variables cannot be completely unambiguous. Childbearing may, of course, have been under way before education was completed, even though for most couples the greater part of it must have occurred subsequently to the termination of schooling. For a few couples, childbearing may have commenced before the husband entered his first job, but again the error in taking first job as antecedent to fertility must be fairly small. With respect to the terminal achievement variables, we have no way of knowing the husband's length of tenure in his 1962 occupation. Conceivably, a substantial minority of husbands may have entered their current jobs a number of years before some of the children were born. We are inclined to guess, however, that such cases are indeed a minority and, at some ages, perhaps a small minority. The postulated direction of relationship between occupation and income (the former preceding the latter) may be in error for husbands changing their line of work within the 15 months preceding the survey.

While Fig. 8.4, therefore, is open to criticism as a literal reading of *temporal* relationships, it is no doubt less open to such criticism than the assumption made in conventional analyses (where the assumption is, by the way, usually tacit). As a *causal* diagram, Fig. 8.4 may seem still more inadequate. One could argue, for example, that couples with a given configuration of background characteristics anticipate the income level they will have at various stages of childbearing and adjust their fertility accordingly. Such an argument, however, should not be taken to justify a reordering of the variables in Fig. 8.4. It should, on the contrary, lead the analyst to insert another variable, "anticipated income," into the diagram in whatever position he believes it should occupy. Presumably, then, the relationship of anticipated income to actual income in a given year would be less than perfect, and part of the analysis would have to be designed to take into account this imperfect relationship.

Let us, however, beg the question of how one might plausibly complicate the causal diagram. The pattern of results obtained with the interpretation offered by the present diagram may prove suggestive as to ways in which such complications should be undertaken.

Our causal model includes the assumptions that fertility depends on five background factors; occupation depends on the same background factors and on fertility along with them; and income depends on occupation, fertility, and the five background factors. We have then to compute a recursive set of three multiple regressions. If the data are expressed in standard from (each variable having zero mean and unit standard deviation), the path coefficients for the diagram in Fig. 8.4 are the standarized partial regression coefficients (or *beta*-coefficients) of these multiple regressions.

In Table 8.16 we show the results of these regression calculations for each of eight cohorts of couples, distinguished according to age of wife. As an aid in assessing the results of the calculations, we have made rough estimates of standard errors of the *beta*-coefficients, taking into account the actual size of the samples and a conjectural allowance for the effect of departure of the sample design from simple random sampling. If anything, the standard errors are perhaps a little too large. Hence we consider any coefficient larger in absolute value than twice its standard error as being clearly significant (that is, too large to attribute solely to sampling variation) and any coefficient at least equal in absolute value to its standard error as being possibly significant.

Before considering the effects of fertility on achievement which are suggested by the results in Table 8.16, we may consider briefly how the background factors appear to affect fertility. The first line of the three shown for each age group provides the path coefficients measuring the direct effects of the variables listed in the boxhead of the table. The factor which is consistently most important, and indeed the only one whose effect is completely consistent over all age groups, is wife's education. Well-educated wives have fewer children than poorly educated wives. Similarly, in all age groups but the last, husband's education is negatively related to fertility, and with the same exception emerges as the second most important direct influence. Husband's first job, where it has a significant effect, likewise relates negatively to fertility, although by comparison with the education effects, first job never has a marked influence. A similar statement can be made for husband's father's occupation. The results for wife's father's occupation, however, are quite erratic. Three of the significant or possibly significant coefficients are positive, as are two of the nonsignificant ones. The remaining three coefficients are negative, although only one is substantially so. In summary, at least four of the background factors relate negatively to cumulative fertility at any age in a reasonably consistent fashion, but only education, particularly that of the wife, has especially strong effects.

According to the model, once fertility has been determined by the background factors in combination with the overwhelmingly important residual factors not explicitly identified in the model, it may in turn influence subsequent status achievement. To facilitate discussion of this influence, a schematic summary of the results is given on p. 242.

Here we show only the sign of the effect; one symbol means that the effect is possibly significant on the criterion previously stated, while the double symbol means it is clearly significant. Nonsignificant coefficients are enclosed in parentheses.

The first conclusion one might reach is that fertility is not a major influence on achievement since only 3 of the 16 coefficients are clearly significant, and the largest of them is no greater than .061. If we accept the signs of the coefficients at face value, however, we can summarize the results in this way: The

TABLE 8.16

Partial Regression Coefficients in Standard Form Relating Fertility, Husband's Occupation, and Income to Socioeconomic Background, for Intact White Couples, by Age of Wife: Civilian Non-institutional Population of the United States, 1962

Age of wife	Dependent variable	Independent variables							Coefficient of determination (R^2)
		Husband's occupation	Fertility	Husband's education	Husband's first job	Husband's father's occupation	Wife's education	Wife's father's occupation	
22–26	Fertility	—	—	−.131[a]	.005	−.058[b]	−.261[a]	−.026	.15
	Husband's occupation	—	.030[b]	.399[a]	.310[a]	.024	.061[a]	.056[a]	.48
	Husband's income	.304[a]	.046[b]	.017	.035	.026	.032	−[c]	.13
27–31	Fertility	—	—	−.064[b]	−.049[b]	−.006	−.178[a]	.043[b]	.06
	Husband's occupation	—	−.001	.419[a]	.242[a]	.081[a]	.069[a]	.101[a]	.53
	Husband's income	.340[a]	.051[b]	.047[b]	−.018	.130[a]	.065[b]	−[c]	.22
32–36	Fertility	—	—	−.096[a]	−.021	.009	−.096[a]	.070[a]	.03
	Husband's occupation	—	−.002	.448[a]	.210[a]	.095[a]	.044[b]	.064[a]	.48
	Husband's income	.272[a]	.061[a]	.054[b]	.106[a]	.123[a]	.152[a]	−[c]	.29

37–41	Fertility	—	—	−.089[a]	−.012	.009	−.115[a]	.019	.03
	Husband's occupation	—	−.029[b]	.387[a]	.195[a]	.091[a]	.064[a]	.070[a]	.41
	Husband's income	.312[a]	.057[a]	.151[a]	.085[a]	.091[a]	.090[a]	—[c]	.32
42–46	Fertility	—	—	−.057[b]	−.044[b]	−.039[b]	−.093[a]	.055[b]	.03
	Husband's occupation	—	.004	.400[a]	.213[a]	.072[a]	.052[b]	.063[a]	.40
	Husband's income	.313[a]	.024	.151[a]	.074[a]	.072[a]	.040[b]	—[c]	.27
47–51	Fertility	—	—	−.120[a]	−.011	.000	−.121[a]	−.012	.05
	Husband's occupation	—	−.051[a]	.383[a]	.199[a]	.118[a]	.070[a]	.027[b]	.43
	Husband's income	.332[a]	.036[b]	.125[a]	.098[a]	.093[b]	.056[b]	—[c]	.31
52–56	Fertility	—	—	−.052[b]	−.070[b]	−.044[b]	−.191[a]	.003	.08
	Husband's occupation	—	−.054[b]	.305[a]	.206[a]	.074[a]	.081[a]	.082[a]	.35
	Husband's income	.354[a]	−.055[b]	.136[a]	.068[b]	.116[a]	−.007	—[c]	.31
57–61	Fertility	—	—	.001	−.090[b]	−.056[b]	−.129[a]	−.100[b]	.08
	Husband's occupation	—	−.031	.319[a]	.251[a]	.149[a]	.038	.071[b]	.42
	Husband's income	.230[a]	−.056[b]	.107[b]	.108[b]	.054[b]	−.006	—[c]	.18

[a] Coefficient greater than twice its standard error (in absolute value).
[b] Coefficient greater than its standard error but less than twice as great (in absolute value).
[c] Not computed; data not available.

Age group	Direct effect of fertility on	
	Occupation	Income
22–26	+	+
27–31	(−)	+
32–36	(−)	+ +
37–41	−	+ +
42–46	(+)	(+)
47–51	− −	+
52–56	−	−
57–61	(−)	−

effect of fertility on occupational achievement (if any) is negative. Except in the youngest age group, the coefficient for the direct influence of fertility on 1962 occupational status is either negative or nonsignificant. By contrast, the effect (if any) of fertility on income is positive, excluding the two oldest age groups.

We are here observing net or direct effects. These need not be comparable in magnitude, nor even the same in sign, as the total or gross associations. Table 8.17 shows, in fact, that the zero-order correlation of fertility with each and every one of the status variables—both those identified as background factors and those taken to be measures of subsequent achievement—is negative, with the single exception of the correlation of fertility with wife's father's occupation for one age group.

Thus the net effect of fertility on occupational achievement is generally consistent as to sign with the zero-order correlation between the two variables.

TABLE 8.17

Simple Correlations between Fertility and Socioeconomic Variables, for Intact White Couples, by Age of Wife: Civilian Noninstitutional Population of the United States, 1962

Socioeconomic variable	Age of wife							
	22–26	27–31	32–36	37–41	42–46	47–51	52–56	57–61
Husband's income in 1961	−.045	−.032	−.008	−.032	−.044	−.084	−.184	−.149
Husband's occupational status, 1962	−.200	−.146	−.093	−.124	−.088	−.184	−.200	−.189
Husband's education	−.326	−.187	−.135	−.148	−.134	−.203	−.223	−.188
Husband's first job status	−.204	−.150	−.089	−.092	−.108	−.130	−.185	−.194
Husband's father's occupational status	−.202	−.101	−.054	−.066	−.090	−.104	−.146	.177
Wife's education	−.370	−.222	−.133	−.158	−.135	−.202	−.259	−.220
Wife's father's occupational status	−.182	−.070	.000	−.054	−.024	−.099	−.106	−.201

In the case of income, however, six of the age groups show a reversal of sign. All simple correlations between income and fertility are negative; the net effects of fertility in this model are positive for the six age groups through age 51.

The meaning of a net effect in this context is, of course, strictly relative to the particular model with which we are working. We are allowing occupation to be influenced by the five background factors as well as by fertility. When their effects on both occupation and fertility are taken into account, fertility is seen to have little direct effect of its own, but such as it is, the effect on occupational achievement is (generally) negative.

Again, occupation and the five background variables are taken to be influences on income. Allowing for these, we seem to detect a slight positive effect of fertility on income. Phrased differently, the negative association of fertility with background factors appears to mask its direct positive effect on income so that the gross association between income and fertility is spuriously negative. When we allow for the operation of other variables in the complex of background and achieved statuses, fertility (with the two exceptions noted) seems to enhance income.

The possibility that income has a net positive association with fertility, once other socioeconomic characteristics are held constant, has been noted in previous research (Freedman, 1963). The interpretation of fertility as a "cause" of certain of these characteristics was, however, not ventured in that research. This interpretation, therefore, is a departure from current thinking and requires justification.

Perhaps the most plausible ground for this interpretation is that a man with many children, if he proposes to support them, is highly motivated to seek and retain such employment as will yield the greatest total income among the alternatives that may be open to him. He is not in a favorable position to trade off some decrement to his earnings for a job with higher prestige or better working conditions, for example. Indeed, he may find it expedient to hold more than one job simultaneously in view of the need for the additional income afforded by the second job. A recent study (Hamel, 1967, p. 18) reports: "Data available for the first time show that . . . the moonlighting rate tends to increase with the number of children under age 18." The rates of multiple job-holding for married men age 25–54, classified as male household heads with wife present and at work during the survey week in May 1966 (Hamel, 1967, Table 0) by number of children in the household under age 18 are shown on p. 224.

The report does not reveal by how much the additional job increased the income available from the primary job.

The OCG data do not include information on multiple jobholding so that it may only be conjectured that this phenomenon contributes to the relationship observed here. Consistent with this conjecture is the fact that the positive net

Number of Children	Percent
None	5.9
1	8.7
2	9.1
3 or 4	9.7
5 or more	9.9

coefficient for income on fertility does not appear for the two oldest cohorts of wives. At these ages at least some of the children ever born are likely to have left home and no longer to represent a claim on the father's income.

While these and other considerations may conceivably rationalize the finding that income is positively related to fertility when occupation, education, and other socioeconomic background factors are held constant, we must not overlook the possibility that the result is a mere artifact of multicollinearity among the independent variables. This problem has been mentioned earlier in this report. Other workers have noted that in such a situation it frequently happens that the coefficient of the independent variable least closely related to the dependent variable will change in sign when the other independent variables are held constant. Systematic illustrative calculations by Fox and Cooney (1954) disclose the arithmetic basis of this result, although their work affords little basis for deciding whether or when it must be regarded as artifactual.

In any event, it must be clear that the data used here force us to take what is undoubtedly an oversimplified point of view on the system of causal relationships involved. We have observations only on current income and cumulative fertility. Presumably, the sequence of events leading up to the observed association between these variables includes a set of complex reciprocal influences between successive increments to family size and decisions to accept or change jobs. It is customary in making such a comment to note that only detailed life history or longitudinal data could resolve the issue of causation. It remains to be shown, however, what form such data must take to permit firm inferences and estimates. The main contribution of the exercise reported here, therefore, is merely the suggestion that the problem of interpreting associations between fertility and socioeconomic variables be conceived in a more flexible way than has usually been done in the past.

8.6 Childspacing

Interest in the pattern of childspacing as a career contingency is stimulated by findings reported by Freedman and Coombs (1966) from their longitudinal study of a sample of white couples in Detroit who were initially contacted in 1962. These investigators summarize their results and some implications as follows (pp. 647–648):

The timing of births after marriage has a strong and consistent relationship to the economic position of a sample of white Detroit couples who recently had a first, second, or fourth birth. Whether measured by current income or by the accumulation of several types of assets, a couple's economic position is substantially better the longer the interval to the first birth or the last birth. Those wives already pregnant with their first child at the time of marriage are particularly disadvantaged economically.

These relationships are not a function of the longer duration of marriage of those with long birth intervals and without premarital pregnancies. . . .

Taking into account such facts as the duration of marriage and the husband's education does significantly diminish (although it does not eliminate) the relationship between rate of family growth and level of income. . . .

These various relationships are especially striking and consistent for the extreme example of short-childspacing couples who were pregnant at marriage. . . .

We suggest speculatively that all of these data are consistent with the following view. Those who have their children very quickly after marriage find themselves under great economic pressure, particularly if they married at an early age. Opportunities for education or decisions involving present sacrifices for future plans, are difficult. They are less able than others to accumulate the goods and assets regarded as desirable by young couples in our society. They are more likely than others to become discouraged at an early point and to lose interest more quickly than others in the competition for economic success.*

It is not possible to perform anything like a strict replication of the Freedman-Coombs study with the data used in this project. The populations are specified by quite different criteria; and, whereas they emphasize current income and accumulated assets as measures of the couple's economic position, the principal dependent variable in the present study is the husband's occupational achievement. Moreover, we are not able to control duration of marriage as Freedman and Coombs did, although we do introduce husband's age at marriage as one of the factors antecedent to current occupational status. In accordance with the general purpose of this report, the present analysis lays heavier emphasis than did that of Freedman and Coombs on characteristics of the husband's family of orientation. Despite these differences, the findings described here may be said to answer in some sense the plea of Freedman and Coombs for additional research on the possible bearing of patterns of family growth on socioeconomic achievement.

We are concerned here with a rather specialized subset of the OCG data. Some of the limitations on the specification of the subpopulation are dictated

* For further explication of the impact of premarital pregnancy on social statuses both before and after marriage, for couples in the Detroit area, see Coombs, Freedman, Friedman and Pratt (1970).

by requirements of the technique for estimating intervals between marriage and first birth. The data are restricted to non-Negro native men 25–34 years of age who were in the experienced civilian labor force in March 1962. There is a further limitation to men who were then married at least 5 years, who had been married only once, and whose spouses were likewise once married. Finally, among couples meeting the foregoing restrictions, the estimates are limited to those in which the wife had borne at least one child and all of whose children were still under the age of 14 and living in the household with the husband and wife.

The sample is clearly not representative of all men in the cohort. It excludes men with unusual marriage histories—those never married by the survey date or whose first marriage was disrupted. It further excludes both those beginning their families only recently as well as those whose families began to grow so long ago that the oldest child has already reached age 14. Altogether, the present analysis is limited to some 48 percent of all native non-Negro men age 25–34 in the experienced civilian labor force or to some 56 percent of the ever-married men in this category. Inasmuch as the population itself is defined by a number of career contingencies, the results bear only upon an ex post facto explanation of patterns of occupational achievement for a selected group and would not be valid as a basis for anticipating future achievement on the basis of currently occurring events in the family cycle of a predesignated cohort of men.

Estimation of the interval from marriage to first birth from the OCG data was made possible by the inclusion of the following questions in the March 1962 Current Population Survey: month and year of first marriage; number of children ever born to ever-married women; and month of birth, age at last birthday, and relationship to household head for each member of the household 0–13 years of age. Given the month and year of the mother's marriage and the month and year (inferred from the age) of the child's birth, the interval from marriage to first birth can be computed with a maximum error of 2 months. Restricting the estimates to households in which all children ever born are still present and under 14 years of age guarantees that the firstborn child is correctly identified.

The gross relationship of occupational status to timing of first birth is depicted in Fig. 8.5. The data are given here with the most detailed classification of the intervals from marriage to first birth available, running by 3-month intervals to 3 years and by 1-year intervals to 7 years, followed by a 3-year interval, 7–9 years, and the open interval, 10 or more years. The very long intervals, as one might imagine, are quite sparsely represented in the sample, which includes approximately 1650 couples.

The figure suggests that there is a quite definite though hardly a simple relationship of occupational achievement to timing of first birth. If we assume that the major irregularities of the regression curve are due to sampling

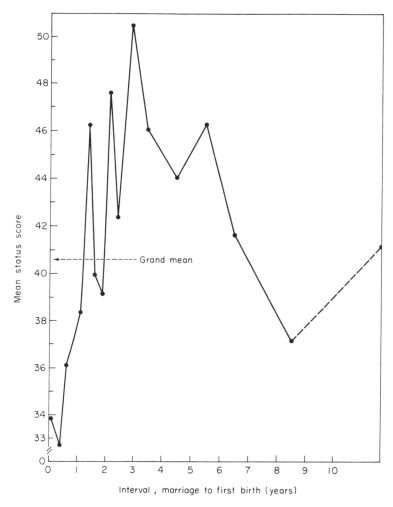

Fig. 8.5. Mean occupational status, by interval from marriage to first birth, for specified (see text) OCG subpopulation.

fluctuations, the relationship can be roughly described as a steeply positive gradient of occupational status with increasing interval, up to an interval of 3 years, followed by a less steeply negative gradient after 3 years. Unfortunately, the data seem to be especially irregular in the region of the apparent optimum so that the latter can hardly be estimated with any great precision. It would appear, however, to be in the neighborhood of 3 years and thus rather higher than the typical interval. The modal interval is actually 9–11 months, and the median is about 17 months.

TABLE 8.18

Means of Selected Variables by Interval from Marriage to First Birth, for Special OCG Subpopulation (Defined in the Text): March 1962

Interval	Number of couples[a] (1000's)	Variable[b]							
		V	X	T	J	M	U	W	Y
Under 6 months	226	8.0	24.4	4.1	17.9	21.5	11.1	24.4	33.3
6–8 months	362	8.1	25.3	4.3	18.2	20.9	11.4	23.3	36.0
9–11 months	791	8.6	29.2	3.9	18.4	21.4	11.8	27.3	37.3
12–14 months	410	8.5	29.7	4.1	18.5	22.1	11.8	26.2	38.5
15–20 months	673	9.0	29.6	3.7	18.8	21.4	11.9	30.8	42.6
21–26 months	477	8.4	30.0	3.9	18.7	21.5	12.1	28.4	41.8
27–35 months	460	8.6	32.6	3.6	19.0	21.6	12.5	33.5	46.1
3 years	264	9.3	32.7	3.7	19.1	21.8	12.4	33.3	46.0
4–5 years	261	8.8	31.9	3.3	18.8	21.5	12.5	31.6	44.7
6 or more years	110	8.2	27.1	3.5	18.4	20.9	11.9	32.9	39.7
All couples	4034	8.6	29.5	3.9	18.6	21.5	11.9	28.9	40.6

[a] Number reporting variables U and M; numbers reporting other variables are somewhat smaller (see Appendix).

[b] V, Family head's educational attainment; X, family head's occupational status; T, number of siblings; J, age at first job; M, respondent's age at marriage; U, respondent's educational attainment; W, occupational status of respondent's first job; Y, respondent's current occupational status.

In the data describing this relationship by itself there is no particular suggestion that premarital pregnancy affords a special handicap to occupational achievement, apart from that pertaining merely to a very short interval. These data, of course, do not identify the couples who had premarital pregnancies with any great precision. Given the intrinsic error of the estimating procedure, we may only assume that the bulk of the couples in the intervals below 6 months were married after the first child was conceived, and perhaps some substantial fraction of those classified into the interval 6–8 months.

To reduce the fluctuations due to sampling error without at the same time obscuring the nature of the relationship, intervals were grouped into a condensed classification, which was used in all further analysis. Table 8.18 shows means of the several variables included in the analysis by this condensed classification of intervals from marriage to first birth.

The patterns by which the nine variables are associated with timing of first birth are somewhat mixed. Father's occupation (X) varies with length of interval to first birth in somewhat the same way as respondent's current occupation (Y). We are thus alerted to the possibility that what may appear in Fig. 8.5 to represent an effect of interval length on occupational achievement may be only a spurious association, in that both are related to family background. Although the pattern is not so regular, men with very short intervals similarly appear to be disadvantaged by low levels of father's education (V) and large numbers of siblings (T). Moreover, short intervals are associated with early entry into the job market (J), with a comparatively low status of the first job (W), and with educational levels below the general average (U). There is, however, no definite relationship between length of interval to first birth and age of the respondent (the husband) at marriage (M). In this connection, it should be remembered that the specifications of the subpopulation place certain limits on the range of variation of M.

The next step in the analysis was designed to estimate the association of the length of the interval from marriage to first birth with selected variables, net of their common dependence on the three family background factors (V, X, and T; father's education and occupation and number of siblings). The method used here was contrived with a view toward economizing on computations at the risk of some bias in the estimates. For the entire subpopulation we computed the regression of each of five dependent variables (Y, M, J, W, and U) on the three background variables (V, X, and T). We then substituted into these regression equations the set of means of V, X, and T for each of the intervals, as shown in the three relevant columns of Table 8.18. Finally, the mean of a given dependent variable in a given interval was expressed as a deviation from that expected on the basis of this calculation from the regression. Such deviations are shown in the lower panel of Table 8.19.

The main result of this work, apparent from a comparison of corresponding

TABLE 8.19

Deviations of Means, by Interval from Marriage to First Birth, from Grand Mean (Gross Effects) and from Values Expected from Regression on Background Factors V, X, T (Net Effects), for Selected Variables Taken from Table 8.18

	Dependent variable				
Interval	1962 occupation (Y)	Age at marriage (M)	Age at first job (J)	First job (W)	Education (U)
Gross effects					
Under 6 months	−7.3	0.0	−0.7	−4.5	−0.9
6–8 months	−4.6	−0.6	−0.4	−5.6	−0.5
9–11 months	−3.3	0.0	−0.2	−1.6	−0.1
12–14 months	−2.1	0.6	−0.1	−2.7	−0.2
15–20 months	2.0	−0.1	0.2	1.9	0.1
21–26 months	1.2	0.0	0.1	−0.5	0.2
27–35 months	5.5	0.2	0.4	4.6	0.6
3 years	5.4	0.3	0.5	4.4	0.5
4 or 5 years	4.1	0.0	0.2	2.7	0.6
6 years or more	−0.9	−0.5	−0.2	3.9	−0.1
Net effects					
Under 6 months	−4.5	0.1	−0.4	−2.4	−0.5
6–8 months	−2.1	−0.6	−0.1	−3.3	−0.1
9–11 months	−3.1	0.0	−0.2	−1.3	−0.1
12–14 months	−1.8	0.6	−0.1	−2.4	−0.1
15–20 months	1.4	−0.2	0.1	1.4	−0.2
21–26 months	1.2	0.0	0.2	−0.3	0.2
27–35 months	4.3	0.1	0.3	3.6	0.4
3 years	3.4	0.2	0.2	2.6	0.1
4 or 5 years	2.5	0.0	0.0	1.2	0.3
6 years or more	−0.1	−0.5	−0.1	4.4	0.0

figures in the two panels of Table 8.19, is that the three family background factors do not fully explain the association of the several variables with interval from marriage to first birth. In terms of both gross effects and net effects, short intervals are associated with relatively low occupational status, early entry into the labor market, and low educational level. Age at marriage, however, shows no association with length of interval, either in terms of gross effects or in terms of net effects. In regard to the other four dependent variables it is true that the net effects are not so pronounced as the gross effects. Thus unfavorable selection on background factors for those with short intervals is part, but only part, of the explanation for their unfavorable subsequent performance.

In Table 8.20 the same type of analysis is carried out with occupational achievement (as of 1962) as the dependent variable. The first column repeats the set of gross effects of length of interval on occupational status. In the second

TABLE 8.20

Gross and Net Effects of Interval from Marriage to First Birth on Occupational Status in
1962 (Y), for Special OCG Subpopulation

Interval	Gross effects	Effects, net of variables[a]				
		U, W	U, W, J, M	V, X, T	V, X, T, U	7 variables
Under 6 months	−7.3	−2.5	−2.7	−4.5	−2.2	−2.2
6–8 months	−4.6	−0.8	−0.5	−2.1	−1.4	−0.2
9–11 months	−3.3	−2.3	−2.3	−3.1	−2.6	−2.4
12–14 months	−2.1	−0.6	−0.9	−1.8	−1.2	−0.9
15–20 months	2.0	1.6	1.8	1.4	2.2	1.7
21–26 months	1.2	0.7	0.8	1.2	0.3	0.7
27–35 months	5.5	1.9	1.9	4.3	2.4	1.8
3 years	5.4	2.3	2.2	3.4	2.7	2.0
4 or 5 years	4.1	1.2	1.2	2.5	1.1	1.0
6 years or more	−0.9	−1.8	−1.7	−0.1	−0.1	−1.3

[a] See list in Table 8.18.

column, the net effects are estimated from the regression of Y on U and W, inserting into that regression the sets of means on these two variables for the several categories of interval from marriage to first birth. Evidently, a substantial part of the association of Y with length of interval is bound up with the fact that short intervals imply unfavorable values of educational attainment and status of first job. It is important to note that the second column, which estimates the influence of interval length on occupational achievement net of education and first job, does not depend for its validity on any assumption as to the temporal order in which first job, educational attainment, and first birth occur—although, to be sure, it would be of interest to clarify the effects of contingencies with respect to the ordering of such variables. Despite the strong overlap of the effects of interval length and those of education and first job, the net effects of the former remain unmistakable, essentially recapitulating the pattern already observed: Short intervals are unfavorable for occupational success, and very long intervals are apparently also unfavorable, with the optimum interval being in the neighborhood of 3 years.

There is no need to comment in detail on the remaining columns of Table 8.20. A comparison of the second with the last column indicates that the net effects of length of interval are much the same, whether only U and W or all the antecedent variables (U, W, J, M, T, X, and V) are taken into account.

While the analysis has emphasized the clear patterning of the apparent influence of interval length on occupational achievement, we should not conclude the discussion without remarking on the need for perspective in interpreting the magnitude of this influence. Looking at the pattern of net effects in

Table 8.20, we see that at most 5 points on the occupation scale can be assigned to the variation between the shortest and the optimum intervals, net of the influence of first job and education.

8.7 Conclusions

The occupational level at which a man begins his career is substantially predictive of the level at which he will be found at any age between 25 and 64. Moreover, first jobs and current jobs depend on background factors in much the same way and to much the same degree in the OCG data for four cohorts of men. Results based on these data cannot be reconciled completely with the hypothesis of a synthetic cohort, to wit, that observations on four age groups represent the pattern of successive measurements on a single cohort.

Detailed cross-classification of data on educational attainment by age at first job suggests that many men interrupt schooling to enter the labor force in what they will later interpret to have been their "first jobs." It is, therefore, an oversimplification to think of schooling as uniformly preceding first job. Men whose schooling was interrupted by the beginning of work are unfavorably selected on background characteristics, as compared with men attaining the same ultimate educational level without such interruption. It is for the latter men, in particular, that level of first job is strongly correlated with subsequent level of occupational achievement.

A third career contingency, migration between attainment of age 16 and the 1962 survey date, involves comparisons of populations in communities of varying sizes, distinguishing among nonmigrants, migrants to these communities with nonfarm background, and migrants with farm background. The pattern of mean occupation scores in each size-of-place category clearly favors the nonfarm migrants by comparison with the "natives" and the "natives" by comparison with the farm migrants. The advantage of the nonfarm migrants is slightly reduced when we take account of their superior family backgrounds, that is, the selective factor in migration. The disadvantage of farm migrants is markedly reduced by the same procedure; indeed, with standardization for family background, the farm migrants are found to be approximately equal to nonfarm migrants in occupational achievement and, therefore, superior to nonmigrants. Thus migration per se is a favorable augury for occupational success, although the methods and data employed here do not permit a decision between alternative hypotheses that may be suggested to explain the observed effects. Migrants may be selected for favorable personality traits, like ambition or persistence, or migration may in itself provide access to favorable opportunities for occupational advancement.

Treatment of the disruption of marriage as a career contingency is handicapped by lack of information on the timing of events in the cycle of family formation and dissolution. Nevertheless, there is a measurable difference in occupational status between men with intact marriages and those whose classification as of the survey date is divorced or separated. No more than half of this difference is accounted for by measured characteristics of family background, educational attainment, and status of first job. Maintenance of the marriage, therefore, is presumed to be a favorable factor.

Size of family of procreation, or marital fertility, has usually been observed to correlate negatively with measures of achieved socioeconomic status. These observations are here confirmed. However, it appears that in a multiple-variable model there is a positive coefficient for the regression of income on fertility once occupational level and educational attainment are taken into account. The interpretation of this result is hazardous since results of this kind may ensue from essentially artificial consequences of high collinearity among status variables. There is, nevertheless, some plausibility in the argument that men with many children are constrained to seek jobs that enhance their incomes, even at the expense of a sacrifice of occupational prestige. It has been observed, moreover, that multiple jobholding (a factor not measured in our data) is more common among men with large numbers of children. This would be reflected in higher incomes, relative to the status of the primary job.

The final career contingency concerns the timing of fertility rather than the cumulative size of family. Specifically, occupational status is found to relate in a curvilinear way to the length of the interval from marriage to birth of the first child. Short intervals are distinctly unfavorable, the optimum interval is around 3 years, and longer intervals are again unfavorable. A significant part of this relationship is explained by the unfavorable selection on family background characteristics for short intervals, and an even more substantial part by the correlation of birth interval with educational attainment and level of first job. However, the persistence of a residual effect of length of interval on occupational status, holding constant all these prior variables, argues that child spacing is indeed a significant (though by no means major) career contingency.

Chapter 9

Epilogue

In the research reported in this monograph, we have sought to build on the results of prior work, taking into account a fairly substantial body of evidence not hitherto integrated into a systematic representation of the processes determining occupational achievement of men in contemporary American society. The notion was to treat such evidence insofar as it was accessible in an appropriate form, as raw material for the construction of interpretive models for which a prototype already existed in consequence of previous research. Each piece of evidence was to be considered for use in attempting an "extension" of this "basic" model. The basic model purported to interpret the association of occupational status, regarded as an "outcome" variable, with characteristics of the family of orientation, regarded as "background" factors. The extensions sought included additional outcome variables, additional background factors, and additional variables believed to mediate between these two categories. The latter, termed "intervening variables" and "career contingencies," were thought of in quite comprehensive terms. Hence the general approach was flexible enough to accommodate all the kinds of variables suggested in the literature as germane to the process under study. The limitations on the scope of our effort were dictated primarily by the availability of data rather than by closure of the conceptual scheme. No new data were expressly collected for this project, although additional tabulations and computations from several already extant bodies of data were made on its behalf.

In one sense, the project clearly met its objectives. In the several chapters of the text numerous examples are offered of "extensions" that develop the original model, clarifying relationships implicit in it or elaborating upon it to give a fuller account of the process under study. These extensions are secured in such a way that the consistency of the several pieces of evidence with the point of view adopted for the purpose of making an interpretation is readily ascertained. The implications of that point of view are made explicit so that both the assumptions and the results of the work are laid open for critical inspection and, perchance, improvement by subsequent research workers.

The project also disclosed weaknesses or limitations of the type of models we were attempting to construct. Some variables of obvious relevance to the process under study are not conveniently treated as quantitative scores on an interval scale; others cannot convincingly be located in a causal sequence with respect to the variables in the basic model; and still others appear to be involved in relationships that are not adequately represented by systems of linear equations assuming additive effects. When confronted with these kinds of difficulties, we have adopted modes of analysis that are less compact and elegant than those suited to the easier parts of the problem. No doubt such improvisation would have to be resorted to more and more frequently with further progress in observation and measurement. In the end we may question whether the causal diagrams and linear equation systems featured in this research can represent the ultimate form of our accumulating knowledge in this area. The use of such models, however, can be an invaluable adjunct to inquiry in our present state of knowledge, where one is as often impressed by an investigator's inability to organize his material as by his difficulties in effecting appropriate measurement.

There is, therefore, no reason to be unduly modest. The models exhibited here do represent an increment of improvement over the schemes, formalisms, and patterns of analysis available in earlier research. That they will, in turn, be superseded by improved models—perhaps by models cast into a radically different form—is not only to be expected, it is also devoutly to be desired. Some readers will undoutedly be disappointed that the new models exhibited here do not result in major increments to the amount of variance "explained" by comparison with the basic model of occupational achievement with which we began. It is implicit in the discussion by Lipset & Bendix (1959, Chapter IX) that a systematic consideration of "Intelligence and Motivation," in juxtaposition with the several sociological variables implicated in the process of stratification, should result in a more nearly complete "explanation" of occupational mobility. Our substantial effort to treat such variables systematically implies agreement with the spirit of their discussion. We were not, however, concerned to move the coefficient of determination much closer toward the asymptote of unity. Instead, we expected to achieve a more thorough understanding of relationships that were already well established, and thus to secure an improved "explanation" in a sense rather different from that conveyed by the magnitude of the multiple correlation. The final judgment of our success is, of course, to be made by the reader; but we would ask that he take as his criterion the cogency of the models and the arguments supporting them rather than the purely statistical norm. There are reasons for believing—indeed, for hoping, in our capacities as members of a relatively open society—that nothing like "complete" explanation of occupational achievement will be secured with variables of the kind we now know how to measure. However, there is still a long way to go in providing a consistent and convincing structure for the knowledge we already have.

We are not alone in this quest for a more integrated understanding of the process of status attainment; indeed, the enterprise spans several continents. In closing this final chapter we shall not undertaken a complete review or critique of these other investigations, nor shall we scan the literature with the aim of constructing some complete annotated bibliography of ongoing research in the area.* Rather, the investigations in the following paragraphs are cited for their current attempts to flesh out a more complete theory of stratification along lines which are congenial to our own. Not all these studies conduct their analyses with the same causal model in the foreground, although most make their interpretations of data from some explicit model. While these current enterprises apply to sometimes rather different age cohorts, population sub-groups, and societal context, each promises to afford greater extensions of our own original model and fuller explanation of the relationships between socio-economic background and achievement. We cite these studies in the hope of stimulating others to consult them and of encouraging more efforts at incre-mental model building.

The continuing work of William Sewell and his colleagues on the WISC data (Sewell *et al.*) is one of the most systematic analyses of the process of status attainment for a cohort as it graduates from high school and either enters the labor force or seeks post-high-school education. Current work on the WISC data follows two lines. First, Sewell's "extension" of some of our own "basic" models which appeared in Sewell *et al.* (1970) is being elaborated. For example, Hauser *et al.* (1971) decompose their index of socioeconomic status for the family of origin to assess the separate impact of each component (for example, father's average income, 1957–1961, paternal occupation and education, mother's average income, mother's education) on son's earnings.

Similarly, the composite variable employed to assess the influence of "sig-nificant others" (parents, peers, and teachers) on the plans to seek post-high-school educational attainment is being disaggregated. This analysis reveals that while parents and peers key their influence and encouragement to the socio-economic background of high school boys, teachers' encouragements for the

---

* The interested reader is directed to Glenn, Alston, and Weiner (1970) for a recent bibliography of stratification research.

lad to seek more schooling are more heavily influenced by performance criteria such as grade-point average (Sewell, 1971). This finding suggests that one fruitful avenue for future studies would be efforts applied to identifying those characteristics of adolescents (or of younger children or of older adults) which act as differential stimuli to the various sets and kinds of significant others who exert social influences at different critical stages of the socioeconomic life cycle. We can envision "extended" models in which structural equations are written for the behavior of significant others (for example, influences of siblings, peers, parents, teachers, or wife) as well as that of ego, and in which the behavior of ego and other are represented by paths of simultaneous, mutual causation (for example, Duncan *et al.*, 1968).

Our own studies have been confined to the status attainments of males. The Wisconsin data set does contain as yet unexplored information on the process of stratification for females. We anticipate that Sewell will explore these data in the near future and thereby will complete the model of status attainment for the entire cohort. In fact, the second line of analysis of the Wisconsin data applies to both males and females and presents timely insights on inequalities of attainments by sex.

Sewell (1971) has addressed the issue of differential attainments by sex in this second line of inquiry by assessing the extent of "talent loss" in his sample (cf. Sewell *et al.*). We have already cited some of the preliminary estimates of loss by sex and by socioeconomic origins. One gains from this variety of analysis a different sense of the impact of socioeconomic background on educational achievement than one obtains from regression analysis. While indeed the partial regression coefficient of socioeconomic background on education in the WISC data is consistent with estimates derived from other studies, and while less of the total variation in schooling can be "explained" by all variables indexing socioeconomic origins than by residual, exogenous influences, the absolute number of able young men and women of lower socioeconomic origins who are "wasted" is striking. Talented females, especially those from lower social origins, are especially vulnerable to the risk of being "lost" in the competition for schooling. One need not necessarily agree with Sewell's (1971) policy recommendations in order to appreciate this mode of data analysis as an enlightening adjunct to causal modeling.

A second research effort which inquires into the extent of wasted talent is being directed by J. W. B. Douglas in Great Britain. This project is rather unique in that it has followed a large sample ($N = 5,362$ in England, Scotland, and Wales) of the cohort born in the first week of March 1946 from birth through primary school, through secondary school, and into university and work careers. Except for the exclusion of illegitimate children and twins, these national data contain an enormous wealth of information on the process of stratification in Great Britain, and they offer in potential an opportunity for comparative analysis along the lines of Sewell's work and that of our own. Douglas and his associates do not specify an explicit model for educational achievement, and their analysis is based largely on cross-classifications and analysis of variance. Their data do address the relationships between the socioeconomic status and other characteristics of the family of origin, on the one hand, and performance in both primary and secondary schools, on the other. Having extensive data on family health, reports from parents about their aspirations and encouragements for their children, and institutional information about and from the schools, Douglas is analyzing among other topics the role of "family climates" and "school environments" as modifiers of educational attainment and performance vis-à-vis ability and socioeconomic differences between families.

We shall not attempt to summarize the findings which are reported in the two monographs written to date (Douglas, 1964; Douglas, Ross, & Simpson, 1968). However, it is noteworthy that the British data confirm relationships established for males and females in the United States between educational attainment and important causal antecedents such as ability, performance in school, parental encouragement, family structure (number of siblings and intact or broken status), and socioeconomic background. In addition, the pattern of talent loss by social origins is similar to the American case. It would be of value for students of stratification to arrange the British data in comparable form to the American, allowing intersocietal generalization about the parameters of a similar causal model of educational attainment and about the relative amounts of wasted talent in the two social systems. In their own right, however, these British data become increasingly unique as Douglas and his colleagues follow the cohort members into and through their occupational careers and adulthood.

A third project which promises to elaborate upon the model of status attainment for an American subpopulation is being undertaken by A. O. Haller in a follow-up of the MICH data set. Although confined to a small sample of 17-year-old males as of 1957, Haller's work parallels that of Sewell in measuring the impact of family background and social influences of significant others in late adolescence on the post-high-school educations and socioeconomic achievements in the early years of the work career (follow-up interview in 1972). The MICH data offer a limited replication of the Sewell et al. model, but at the same time current plans for additional analyses call for an assessment of longer term effects of educational and occupational aspirations on achievements, of the factors bearing on both the timing and spacing of post-high-school education, of influences by significant others (for example, spouse, friends, work associates) on current attainments, and of career contingencies such as military service, marriage and divorce, and pace of family formation.

Two independent panel studies conducted among high school students offer personality and childhood socialization data which augment models of achievement or performance in schools. Bachman (1970) and the "Youth in Transition" project staff sampled tenth-grade boys in 87 schools through the United States in 1966 and conducted follow-up surveys in 1968 and 1970. Data include socio-economic characteristics of parents, family structure, ability measures, school performance and behavior in school, attitudes toward self and schooling, indexes of motivations toward educational and occupational goals, and character of family relationships and parental influence. Supplementary information from the teachers and administrators of the schools is designed to assess effects of "school environments" on the process of achievement both in school and in the immediate post-high-school experiences. Rather similar types of data were collected by Rehberg (Rehberg, Schafer, & Sinclair, 1970; Rehberg, Sinclair, & Shafer, 1970) in a three-wave longitudinal survey of the high school class of 1970 (first wave in 1967) in seven schools in southern New York. Both data sets should illuminate the intrafamilial and intrapersonal factors which account for differential performance in school and in total years of school completed.

As this last chapter was being drafted, we received a final report on a project under the directorship of Alan C. Kerckhoff (Kerckhoff, 1971). Males in the graduated class of 1963 from the high schools of Fort Wayne, Indiana, along with the current (1969) grades six, nine, and twelve, provided the data for an explicit attempt at replicating and extending causal models such as we have offered in earlier chapters for predicting educational and occupational ex-pectations and attainments. Like the two previously cited studies, the Kerckhoff data are especially useful in enlarging the scope of social and psychological factors which can "explain" school achievements. Unlike the former studies, these data include direct measurements of parental variables such as achieve-ment attitudes and parental–filial interaction; since the data are cross-sectional, a synthetic cohort approach is used. Having interviewed parents, Kerckhoff possesses rather unique estimates of the accuracy with which sons of various ages report the educational, occupational, and income statuses of their parents. (These estimates of validity of filial reports are quite naturally limited by the accuracy with which the parent reports his own statuses.) Most studies of educational achievement rely upon the unverified reports by sons of family characteristics; future work should benefit from Kerckhoff's estimates.

We are aware of two data sets in which the complex transition from school to work, involving a number of the career contingencies identified in Chapter 8, can be analyzed in much greater detail than in any of the data sets previously described. One set has been collected as a series of retrospective life histories (Blum, Karweit, & Sørensen, 1969) of men aged 30–39 in 1968. Techniques applied to these data differ in some respects from those used in our work. This enterprise, being conducted at Johns Hopkins University, may show that retrospective life history analysis is a strategic research alternative to panel studies. The second data set was gathered by Herbert Parnes (Parnes, Miljus, Spitz, & Associates, 1970; Zeller, Shea, Kohen, & Meyer, 1970) as a survey of work experiences, conducted annually for a 5-year period (beginning in 1966 for young men aged 14–24 and in 1968 for young women aged 14–24). These data are not exceptionally suited to a replication of models of status attainment such as those developed by Sewell. However, they do provide detailed insight, for example, into the processes of early school leaving and entry into the labor market, and sex differentials in the timing and spacing of education vis-à-vis life cycle events. The latter topics are under investigation in the Parnes data at the University of Wisconsin by Robert M. Hauser, James A. Sweet, and David L. Featherman.

Finally we note that Hauser and Featherman will be replicating the basic Blau-Duncan model and cohort analyses in a survey of the civilian non-institutional male population, aged 20–65 in 1973. One of the chief objectives of the survey "Occupational Changes in a Generation-II" will be the estimation of changes in the process of stratification for specific birth cohorts. Of equal importance will be analyses directed toward policy questions, such as an appraisal of the trends in equality of opportunity for blacks, calculated along the lines of analysis in Chapter 4 and in Duncan (1968b). Currently proposed for OCG-II is an extension of the original analysis to provide more detailed, cohort-specific data, especially for blacks, reflecting a larger sampling fraction than applied to the Current Population Survey design in March 1962. In addition, the extension will attempt to measure more accurately the first job variable* and to augment the OCG supplement with new questions (subject to governmental approval) regarding religious affiliation, maternal education, age at school entry, schooling interruptions, last school attended, vocational education, years of father's and sibling's births, educational attainment of siblings, welfare dependency, on-job training, first marriage, marital fertility, job-seeking behavior, and social class identification. Finally, Featherman and Hauser plan a series of analyses of response errors, using reinterviews, telephone interviews with living parents, state income tax records, and the decennial Census report of father falling closest to son's sixteenth birthday to validate data on crucial status variables. Error estimates will subsequently be employed in reestimating parameters of the models.

In concluding, we submit our own work as reported herein as provisional. We believe that its assumptions and procedures are sufficiently explicit to enable those with continuing interests in the process of status attainment to reconstruct and extend it. Finally, we trust that those current enterprises we have cited in this last chapter not only will serve to rectify deficiencies in our own representations but also will lead to a systematic accumulation of knowledge about the impact of socioeconomic background on achievement and ultimately to a clearer vision of the entire process of social stratification.

---

* See the discussion of the problematic nature of this variable in Chapter 8.

Appendix: Supplementary Tables

Tables A.1–8 present correlation matrixes for selected subpopulations covered by the OCG survey. Some of these correlations have been analyzed intensively in the text; others were not used in any of the formal models presented there. It is thought that some readers may wish to inspect more closely certain of the relationships suggested by the OCG data but not treated in detail in the text.

Each table gives the matrix of correlations among nine variables. The variables are defined as follows:

V, Educational attainment (years of school completed) by the respondent's father or other person who was the head of the family in which the respondent grew up.

X, Socioeconomic score of the occupation of the father (or other family head) as of the respondent's age 16.

T, Number of siblings (brothers plus sisters) of the respondent, including stepbrothers and sisters and children adopted by respondent's parents, and including siblings born alive but no longer living.

E, Educational attainment (years of school completed) by respondent's oldest brother (if respondent had at least one older brother who lived to age 25).

U, Educational attainment (years of school completed) by respondent. Cases in which educational attainment was not reported were allocated by Bureau of the Census imputation procedures.

W, Socioeconomic score of respondent's "first full-time job you had after you left school. (Do not count part-time jobs or jobs during school vacation. Do not count military service.)"

J, Respondent's age upon beginning first job, as defined for W.

M, Respondent's age at first marriage (defined only for ever-married men).

Y, Socioeconomic score of respondent's current occupation as of March 1962, or last previous occupation for the experienced unemployed. Cases with occupation not reported were allocated by Bureau of the Census imputation procedures. Socioeconomic scores are not defined for members of the civilian labor force currently unemployed whose last occupation was member of the armed forces.

Each correlation was computed on the basis of all cases reporting both variables. The entries below the diagonal in each table refer to the percentages reporting the specified combinations. Some approximations are involved here. The base, 100 percent, was taken to be the number reporting both U and Y since the restriction of the universe to members of the experienced civilian labor force meant that all men had a reportable occupation, and the use of imputation for U and Y meant that there were no nonresponses in the tabulations. How-ever, as indicated previously, Y is not defined for former members of the armed forces who have not subsequently taken a civilian job. Hence the number reporting Y may be slightly smaller than the total number included in the tabulation. This is signified by showing the total reporting Y as "100–" percent. Another approximation is involved in estimating the proportion reporting combinations of T with other variables. The correlations here were built up from separate data on number of brothers and number of sisters by the other variables, along with number of brothers by number of sisters. Errors incurred in these approximations are believed to be quite small since there was little nonresponse on number of brothers or sisters.

The means and standard deviations are those computed for the data in the cross-tabulation of the given variable by variable U, or, in the case of the latter, the cross-tabulation of U by variable Y. Because of selective nonresponse, these are not necessarily the same as the means and standard deviations occurring in a given correlation problem. For the most part, differences appear to be minor for the purposes of the analyses conducted here. For the two variables not defined for the whole population (E and M), however, the slippage could assume greater proportions. In connection with variable M, incidentally, the user should remember that the distribution of M is affected by the age limits on the subpopulation; among men 25–34 years old, for example, no man could have reported an age at marriage of 35 or over.

Further explanations of the OCG data will be found in Blau & Duncan (1967). However, some of the variables used here were not employed in that study, and the tabulation scheme devised for the present project involved some variations on the one followed there.

TABLE A.1

Correlation Matrix from OCG Data on Native Non-Negro Men, 25 to 64 Years Old, in the Experienced Civilian Labor Force: March 1962 [Below diagonal: Percent Reporting Combination of Variables]

Variable	Variable								
	V	X	T	E	U	W	J	M	Y
Father's education, V	—	.494	-.292	.465	.418	.328	.250	.017	.321
Father's occupation, X	85	—	-.278	.412	.432	.412	.248	.043	.404
Siblings, T	88	92	—	-.314	-.351	-.265	-.160	-.008	-.261
Brother's education, E	45	47	50	—	.573	.371	.256	.026	.401
Education, U	90	93	98	49	—	.554	.449	.080	.606
First job, W	88	91	96	48	98	—	.442	.092	.534
Age at first job, J	87	89	95	45	96	94	—	.092	.311
Age at first marriage, M	81	85	90	50	91	89	87	—	.072
Occupation, Y	89	93	98	50	100–	97	96	91	—
Percent reporting[a]	90	93	98	50	100	98	96	91	100–
Mean	8.18	28.0	4.30	10.33	11.15	27.1	18.5	24.3	39.6
Standard deviation	3.54	21.3	3.11	3.38	3.40	21.3	3.2	4.9	24.5

[a] One-hundred percent represents 31,133,000 men based on about 14,347 sample cases.

263

TABLE A.2

Correlation Matrix from OCG Data on Native Non-Negro Men, with Nonfarm Background, 25 to 64 Years Old, in the Experienced Civilian Labor Force: March 1962 [Below diagonal: Percent Reporting Combination of Variables]

Variable	Variable								
	V	X	T	E	U	W	J	M	Y
Father's education, V	–	.506	-.275	.449	.393	.322	.285	.022	.306
Father's occupation, X	84	–	-.237	.403	.419	.376	.297	.062	.371
Siblings, T	89	89	–	-.310	-.327	-.250	-.206	-.012	-.254
Brother's education, E	43	42	47	–	.546	.357	.315	.041	.392
Education, U	90	91	98	47	–	.554	.518	.100	.610
First job, W	88	89	96	46	97	–	.485	.117	.526
Age at first job, J	88	89	96	46	98	96	–	.101	.348
Age at first marriage, M	81	82	90	42	91	88	88	–	.095
Occupation, Y	90	90	98	47	100–	97	97	90	–
Percent reporting[a]	90	91	98	47	100	97	98	91	100–
Mean	8.63	34.1	3.85	10.91	11.70	30.4	18.5	24.3	43.5
Standard deviation	3.67	22.7	2.94	3.37	3.30	22.1	3.2	4.9	24.6

[a] One-hundred percent represents 22,638,000 men based on about 10,432 sample cases.

264

TABLE A.3

Correlation Matrix from OCG Data on Native Negro Men, 25 to 64 Years Old, in the Experienced Civilian Labor Force: March 1962. [Below diagonal: Percent Reporting Combination of Variables]

Variable	Variable								
	V	X	T	E	U	W	J	M	Y
Father's education, V	–	.354	–.105	.397	.363	.230	.160	–.044	.226
Father's occupation, X	69	–	–.113	.241	.242	.143	.176	.009	.151
Siblings, T	80	80	–	–.079	–.178	–.075	–.112	–.004	–.102
Brother's education, E	42	42	50	–	.528	.267	.147	–.119	.203
Education, U	81	81	100–	50	–	.271	.314	.029	.410
First job, W	76	76	92	46	94	–	.127	–.026	.329
Age at first job, J	76	75	91	46	92	89	–	–.007	.148
Age at first marriage, M	71	72	90	43	91	83	81	–	.076
Occupation, Y	80	80	99	49	100–	92	90	89	–
Percent reporting[a]	81	81	100–	50	100	94	92	91	100–
Mean	6.31	16.1	5.58	8.18	8.34	14.9	17.7	24.3	17.7
Standard deviation	3.30	12.9	3.74	3.42	3.60	12.7	3.9	5.8	15.3

[a] One-hundred percent represents 3,024,000 men based on about 1394 sample cases.

265

TABLE A.4

Correlation Matrix from OCG Data on Native Negro Men, with Nonfarm Background, 25 to 64 Years Old, in the Experienced Civilian Labor Force: March 1962. [Below diagonal: Percent Reporting Combination of Variables]

Variable		V	X	T	E	U	W	J	M	Y
						Variable				
Father's education, V		–	.396	-.064	.355	.358	.209	.173	-.081	.221
Father's occupation, X		58	–	-.105	.184	.207	.106	.236	.000	.118
Siblings, T		76	68	–	-.042	-.171	-.058	-.158	.008	-.093
Brother's education, E		35	31	43	–	.459	.211	.094	-.186	.166
Education, U		77	68	100–	43	–	.240	.346	.002	.413
First job, W		72	64	90	39	92	–	.150	-.066	.312
Age at first job, J		74	66	92	41	93	89	–	-.008	.162
Age at first marriage, M		67	60	89	37	90	81	82	–	.045
Occupation, Y		76	68	99	43	100–	90	92	89	–
Percent reporting[a]		77	68	100–	43	100	92	93	90	100–
Mean		6.94	19.0	4.86	9.36	9.35	16.7	17.9	24.3	19.7
Standard deviation		3.39	17.2	3.58	3.39	3.51	14.4	3.9	5.8	16.9

[a] One-hundred percent represents 1,870,000 men based on about 862 sample cases.

266

TABLE A.5

Correlation Matrix from OCG Data on Native Non-Negro Men, with Nonfarm Background, 25 to 34 Years Old, in the Experienced Civilian Labor Force: March 1962. [Below diagonal: Percent Reporting Combination of Variables]

Variable	V	X	T	E	U	W	J	M	Y
Father's education, V	—	.489	−.269	.419	.402	.315	.339	.123	.342
Father's occupation, X	88	—	−.229	.379	.413	.371	.330	.116	.353
Siblings, T	93	90	—	−.310	−.326	−.268	−.231	−.081	−.247
Brother's education, E	44	43	47	—	.536	.353	.318	.184	.391
Education, U	94	92	97	47	—	.586	.618	.272	.651
First job, W	92	90	95	46	97	—	.593	.215	.578
Age at first job, J	93	90	96	46	98	96	—	.251	.453
Age at first marriage, M	80	79	84	41	86	83	84	—	.218
Occupation, Y	94	92	97	47	100–	97	97	85	—
Percent reporting[a]	94	92	97	47	100	97	98	86	100–
Mean	9.17	34.6	3.49	11.75	12.38	32.1	18.9	22.2	43.3
Standard deviation	3.53	22.4	2.86	3.23	3.04	23.2	2.9	3.1	25.0

[a] One-hundred percent represents 6,815,000 men based on about 3141 sample cases.

TABLE A.6

Correlation Matrix from OCG Data on Native Non-Negro Men, with Nonfarm Background, 35 to 44 Years Old, in the Experienced Civilian Labor Force: March 1962. [Below diagonal: Percent Reporting Combination of Variables]

Variable	V	X	T	E	U	W	J	M	Y
Father's education, V	–	.530	-.287	.454	.405	.340	.280	.052	.319
Father's occupation, X	84	–	-.248	.440	.434	.366	.293	.060	.390
Siblings, T	89	90	–	-.338	-.331	-.261	-.186	-.033	-.275
Brother's education, E	44	44	48	–	.506	.338	.313	.068	.403
Education, U	90	91	98	48	–	.545	.502	.136	.643
First job, W	88	89	96	48	97	–	.502	.091	.494
Age at first job, J	88	89	96	48	98	96	–	.121	.342
Age at first marriage, M	84	85	92	44	94	91	91	–	.057
Occupation, Y	90	91	98	48	100–	97	97	93	–
Percent reporting[a]	90	91	98	48	100	97	98	94	100–
Mean	8.55	34.4	3.77	11.09	11.95	29.9	18.8	24.0	44.8
Standard deviation	3.72	23.1	2.88	3.17	3.20	21.8	3.0	4.1	24.7

[a] One-hundred percent represents 6,974,000 men based on about 3214 sample cases.

Correlation Matrix from OCG Data on Native Non-Negro Men, with Nonfarm Background, 45 to 54 Years Old, in the Experienced Civilian Labor Force: March 1962. [Below diagonal: Percent Reporting Combination of Variables]

Variable	Variable								
	V	X	T	E	U	W	J	M	Y
Father's education, V	—	.486	−.239	.438	.369	.308	.226	−.006	.252
Father's occupation, X	82	—	−.230	.381	.445	.387	.248	.023	.378
Siblings, T	87	89	—	−.247	−.300	−.205	−.162	−.019	−.234
Brother's education, E	41	41	45	—	.542	.338	.207	.029	.397
Education, U	88	90	98	45	—	.556	.412	.108	.595
First job, W	87	89	97	44	98	—	.346	.077	.512
Age at first job, J	87	89	97	44	98	97	—	.104	.252
Age at first marriage, M	81	83	91	41	92	90	90	—	.058
Occupation, Y	88	90	98	45	100—	98	98	92	—
Percent reporting[a]	88	90	98	45	100	98	98	92	100—
Mean	8.15	33.0	4.09	10.33	11.26	28.8	18.3	25.7	42.4
Standard deviation	3.70	22.3	2.96	3.33	3.29	21.2	3.3	5.4	23.8

[a] One-hundred percent represents 5,633,000 men based on about 2596 sample cases.

TABLE A.8

Correlation Matrix from OCG Data on Native Non-Negro Men, with Nonfarm Background, 55 to 64 Years Old, in the Experienced Civilian Labor Force: March 1962. [Below diagonal: Percent Reporting Combination of Variables]

Variable		V	X	T	E	U	W	J	M	Y
						Variable				
Father's education, V		—	.531	-.275	.504	.353	.302	.275	.077	.302
Father's occupation, X		75	—	-.240	.479	.388	.394	.326	.107	.354
Siblings, T		82	86	—	-.263	-.282	-.253	-.204	-.068	-.257
Brother's education, E		40	40	47	—	.539	.465	.394	.217	.439
Education, U		83	87	98	47	—	.557	.491	.207	.558
First job, W		81	85	96	46	98	—	.498	.220	.505
Age at first job, J		81	86	96	46	98	96	—	.157	.335
Age at first marriage, M		77	81	92	44	93	90	90	—	.141
Occupation, Y		82	87	98	47	100—	97	97	92	—
Percent reporting[a]		83	87	98	47	100	98	98	93	100—
Mean		8.38	34.1	4.46	9.72	10.47	30.4	17.7	26.2	42.7
Standard deviation		3.66	23.2	3.09	3.62	3.61	21.5	3.7	6.5	24.6

[a] One-hundred percent represents 3,216,000 men based on about 1482 sample cases.

References

Alexander, C. N., Jr., & Campbell, E. Q. Peer Influences on Educational Aspirations and Attainments. *American Sociological Review*, 1964, **29**, 568–575.

Anastasi, Anne. Intelligence and Family Size. *Psychological Bulletin*, 1956, **53**, 187–209.

Atkinson, J. W. Motivational Determinants of Risk-taking Behavior. *Psychological Review*, 1957, **64**, 359–372.

Atkinson, J. W. *Introduction to motivation*, Princeton, New Jersey: Van Nostrand–Reinhold, 1964.

Bachman, J. G. 1970. *Youth in transition. Vol. 2*, The impact of family background and intelligence on tenth-grade boys. Ann Arbor, Michigan: Institute for Social Research, 1970.

Benson, Viola E. The Intelligence and Later Scholastic Success of Sixth-grade Pupils, *School and Society*, 1942, **55**, 163–167.

Blalock, H. M., Jr. *Causal inferences in nonexperimental research*, Chapel Hill, North Carolina: University of North Carolina Press, 1964.

Blau, P. M., & Duncan, O.D. *The American occupational structure*, New York: Wiley, 1967.

Bloom, B. S. *Stability and change in human characteristics*. New York: Wiley, 1964.

Blum, Z. D., Karweit, N. L., & Sørensen, A. B. A Method for the Collection and Analysis of Retrospective Life Histories. Center for the Study of Social Organization of Schools Report No. 0048. Baltimore, Maryland: The Johns Hopkins University, 1969.

Bordua, D. J. Educational Aspirations and Parental Stress on College, *Social Forces*, 1960, **38**, 262–269.

Burt, C. Family Size, Intelligence, and Social Class, *Population Studies*, 1947, **1**, 177–186.

Byrns, Ruth, & Henmon, V. A. C. Parental Occupation and Mental Ability, *Journal of Educational Psychology*, 1936, **27**, 284–291.

Campbell, E. Q., & Alexander, C. N., Jr. Structural Effects and Interpersonal Relationships, *American Journal of Sociology*, 1965, **71**, 284–289.

Carlsson, G. *Social mobility and class structure*. Lund: CWK Cleerup, 1958.

Centers, R. Motivational Aspects of Occupational Stratification, *Journal of Social Psychology*, 1948, **28**, 187–217.

271

Coombs, L. C., Freedman, R., Friedman, J., & Pratt, W. F. Premarital Pregnancy and Status Before and After Marriage, *American Journal of Sociology*, 1970, **75**, 800–820.

Crockett, H. J., Jr. The Achievement Motive and Differential Occupational Mobility in the United States, *American Sociological Review*, 1962, **27**, 191–204.

Crockett, H. J., Jr. Psychological Origins of Mobility. In N. Smelser and S. Lipset (Eds.), *Social structure and mobility in economic development*. Chicago, Illinois: Aldine, 1966. Pp. 280–309.

Douglas, J. W. B. *The home and the school: A study of ability and attainment on the primary school*, London: MacGibbon, & Kee, 1964.

Douglas, J. W. B., Ross, J. M., & Simpson, H. R. *All our future: A longitudinal study of secondary education*. London: Davies, 1968.

Duncan, Beverly. Dropouts and the Unemployed, *The Journal of Political Economy*, 1965, **53**, 121–134. (a)

Duncan, Beverly. Family Factors and School Dropout: 1920–1960, Final Report, Cooperative Research Project No. 2258. U.S. Office of Education. Ann Arbor, Michigan: The University of Michigan, 1965.(b)

Duncan, Beverly. Education and Social Background, *American Journal of Sociology*, 1967, **72**, 363–372.

Duncan, Beverly, & Duncan, O. D. Minorities and the Process of Stratification, *American Sociological Review*, 1968, **33**, 356–364.

Duncan, Beverly, & Duncan, O. D. Family Stability and Occupational Success, *Social Problems*, 1969, **16**, 273–285.

Duncan, O. D. A Socioeconomic Index for All Occupations. In A. J. Reiss and others, *Occupations and social status*. New York: Free Press, 1961. Pp. 109–138.(a)

Duncan, O. D. Occupational Components of Educational Differences in Income, *Journal of the American Statistical Association*, 1961, **56**, 783–792. (b)

Duncan, O. D. The Trend of Occupational Mobility in the United States, *American Sociological Review*, 1965, **30**, 491–498.

Duncan, O. D. Path Analysis: Sociological Examples, *American Journal of Sociology*, 1966, **72**, 1–16.

Duncan, O. D. Discrimination against Negroes, *Annals of the American Academy of Political and Social Science*, 1967, **371**, 85–103.

Duncan, O. D. Ability and Achievement, *Eugenics Quarterly*, 1968, **15**, 1–11. (a)

Duncan, O. D. Inheritance of Poverty or Inheritance of Race? In D. P. Moynihan (Ed.), *On understanding poverty*. New York: Basic Books, 1968. Pp. 85–110. (b)

Duncan, O. D. Patterns of Occupational Mobility among Negro Men, *Demography*, 1968, 11–22. (c)

Duncan, O. D. Contingencies in Constructing Causal Models: An Illustration. In E. Borgatta (Ed.), *Sociological methodology: 1969*. San Francisco, California: Jossey-Bass, 1969. (a)

Duncan, O. D. Inequality and Opportunity, *Population Index*, 1969, **35**, 361–366. (b)

Duncan, O. D. Duncan's Corrections of Published Text of 'Peer Influences on Aspirations: A Reinterpretation.' *American Journal of Sociology*, 1970, **75**, 1042–1046. (a)

Duncan, O. D. Partials, Partitions, and Paths. In E. Borgatta (Ed.), *Sociological methodology: 1970*. San Francisco, California: Jossey-Bass, 1970. Pp. 38–47.(b)

Duncan, O. D., & Featherman, D. L. Psychological and Cultural Factors in the Process of Occupational Achievement. Paper presented at the Social Systems Research Institute/Social Science Research Council Conference on Structural Equation Models, Madison, Wisconsin, 1970.

Duncan, O. D., & Hodge, R. W. Education and Occupational Mobility, *American Journal of Sociology*, 1963, **67**, 629–644.

Duncan, O. D., Haller, A. O., & Portes, A. Peer Influences on Aspirations: A Reinterpretation, *American Journal of Sociology*, 1968, **74**, 119–137.

Dumont, A. *Dépopulation et civilisation*. Paris: Lecrosnier et Babé, 1890.

Eckland, B. K. College Dropouts Who Came Back, *Harvard Educational Review*, 1964, **34**, 402–420.

Empey, L. T. Social Class and Occupational Aspiration: A Comparison of Absolute and Relative Measurement, *American Sociological Review*, 1956, *21*, 703–709.

Erlenmeyer-Kimling, L., & Jarvik, Lissy F. Genetics and Intelligence: A Review, *Science*, 1963, **142**, 1477–1479.

Farley, R. & Hermalin, A. I. Family Stability: A Comparison of Trends Between Blacks and Whites, *American Sociological Review*, 1971, **36**, 1–17.

Featherman, D. L. The Socioeconomic Achievement of White Married Males in the United States: 1957–1967, unpublished doctoral dissertation, University of Michigan, 1969.

Featherman, D. L. Marital Fertility and the Process of Socioeconomic Achievement: An Examination of the Mobility Hypothesis. In L. L. Bumpass and C. F. Westoff (Eds.), *The later years of childbearing*, Princeton, New Jersey: Princeton University Press, 1970. Pp. 104–131.

Featherman, D. L. A research Note: A Social Structural Model for the Socioeconomic Career, *American Journal of Sociology*, 1971, **77**, 293–304. (a)

Featherman, D. L. Residential Background and Socioeconomic Achievements in Metropolitan Stratification Systems, *Rural Sociology*, 1971, **36**, 107–124. (b)

Featherman, D. L. The Socioeconomic Achievement of White Religio-Ethnic Subgroups: Social and Psychological Explanations, *American Sociological Review*, 1971, **36**, 207–222. (c)

Fisher, R. A., & Yates, F. *Statistical tables for biological, agricultural, and medical research.* 3rd ed. London: Oliver & Boyd, 1948.

Fox, K. A., & Cooney, J. F., Jr. Effects of Intercorrelation upon Multiple Correlation and Regression Measures, Washington D.C.: Agricultural Marketing Service, U.S. Department of Agriculture, 1954, (processed).

Freedman, Deborah S. The Relation of Economic Status to Fertility, *American Economic Review*, 1963, **53**, 414–426.

Freedman, R., & Coombs, L. Childspacing and Family Economic Position, *American Sociological Review*, 1966, **31**, 631–648.

Glass, D. V. (Ed.) *Social mobility in Britain*. London: Routledge & Kegan Paul, 1954.

Glenn, N. D., Alston, J. P., & Weiner, D. *Social stratification: A research bibliography.* Berkeley, California: Glendessary Press, 1970.

Griliches, Z., & Mason, W. Education, Income, and Ability. Paper presented at the Social Systems Research Institute/Social Science Research Council Conference on Structural Equation Models, Madison, Wisconsin, 1970.

Haller, A. O., & Butterworth, C. E. Peer Influences on Levels of Occupational and Educational Aspiration, *Social Forces*, 1960, **38**, 289–295.

Haller, A. O., & Miller, I. W. The Occupational Aspiration Scale: Theory, Structure and Correlates. Technical Bulletin No. 288, East Lansing: Agricultural Experiment Station, Michigan State University, 1963.

Hamel, H. R. Moonlighting—An Economic Phenomenon, Special Labor Force Report No. 90, 1967 (reprinted from *Monthly Labor Review*, October 1967).

Harell, T. W., & Harrell, Margaret S. Army General Classification Test Scores for Civilian Occupations, *Educational and Psychological Measurement*, 1945, **5**, 229–239.

Hauser, R. M. Schools and the Stratification Process, *American Journal of Sociology*, 1969, **74**, 587–611.

Hauser, R. M. Disaggregating a Social-Psychological Model of Educational Attainment. Paper presented at the Social Systems Research Institute/Social Science Research Council Conference on Structural Equation Models, Madison, Wisconsin, 1970.

Hauser, R. M. *Socioeconomic background and educational performance*. Washington, D.C.: American Sociological Association, Rose Monograph Series, 1971.

Hauser, R. M., Lutterman, K. G., & Sewell, W. H. Socioeconomic Background and the Earnings of High School Graduates. Paper delivered at the annual meetings of the American Sociological Association, Denver, Colorado, 1971.

Heise, D. R. Problems in Path Analysis and Causal Inference. In E. F. Borgatta (Ed.) *Sociological methodology 1969*. San Francisco, California: Jossey–Bass, 1969. Pp. 38–73.

Herriott, R. E., & Hoyt St. John, Nancy. *Social class and the urban school*. New York: Wiley, 1966.

Herrnstein, R. I. Q., *The Atlantic*, 1971, **228**, 43–64.

Hodge, R. W. Occupational Mobility as a Probability Process, *Demography*, 1966, **3**, 19–34.

Hodge, R. W. Social Integration, Psychological Well-being and Their Socioeconomic Correlates. In E. O. Laumann (Ed.). *Social stratification: Research and theory for the 1970s*. New York: Bobbs-Merrill, 1970. Pp. 182–206.

Hodge, R. W., & Siegel, P. M. A Causal Approach to the Study of Measurement Error. In H. M. Blalock, Jr. and A. B. Blalock (Eds.) *Methodology in social research*. New York: McGraw-Hill, 1968. Pp. 28–59.

Hodge, R. W., Siegel, P. M. & Rossi, P. H. Occupational Prestige in the United States 1925–1963, *American Journal of Sociology*, 1964, **70**, 286–302.

Hodge, R. W., Trieman, D. J. & Rossi, P. H. A Comparative Study of Occupational Prestige. In R. Bendix and S. M. Lipset (Eds.). *Class, status, and power*. (Rev. ed.) New York: Free Press, 1966.

Hyman, H. H. The Value System of Different Classes: A Social Psychological Contribution to the Analysis of Stratification. In S. M. Lipset and R. Bendix (Eds.), *Class, status, and power*. Glencoe, Illinois: Free Press, 1953.

Jensen, A. R. How Much Can We Boost IQ and Scholastic Achievement? *Harvard Educational Review*, 1969, **39**, 1–123.

Kahl, J. A. Educational and Occupational Aspirations of "Common Man" Boys, *Harvard Educational Review*, 1953, **23**, 186–203.

Kahl, J. A. Some Measurements of Achievement Motivation, *American Journal of Sociology*, 1965, **70**, 669–681.

Kandel, Denise B. Race, Maternal Authority, and Adolescent Aspiration, *American Journal of Sociology*, 1971, **76**, 999–1020.

Kerckhoff, A. C. Educational, Familial, and Peer Group Influences on Occupational Achievement. Final Report on Project No. 8–0053. Office of Education, U.S. Department of Health, Education, and Welfare, 1971.

Klassen, A. D., Jr. Military Service in American Life Since World War II: An Overview. Report No. 117. National Opinion Research Center, University of Chicago, 1966.

Land, K. C. Principles of Path Analysis. In E. F. Borgatta (Ed.) *Sociological methodology 1969*. San Francisco, California: Jossey–Bass, 1969. Pp. 3–37.

Lipset, S. M., & Bendix, R. *Social mobility in industrial society*. Berkeley, California: University of California Press, 1959.

Mason, W. On the Socioeconomic Effects of Military Service. Unpublished doctoral dissertation, University of Chicago, 1970.

McClelland, D. C. *et al. The achievement motive*. New York: Appleton-Century-Crofts, 1953.

McClelland, D. C. *The achieving society.* Princeton, New Jersey: Van Nostrand–Reinhold, 1961.

McFarland, D. D. Intragenerational Social Mobility as a Markov Process: Including a Time-Stationarity Markovian Model that Explains Observed Declines in Mobility Rates, *American Sociological Review,* 1970, **35**, 463–476.

McTavish, D. G. A Method for More Reliably Coding Detailed Occupations into Duncan's Socio-economic Categories, *American Sociological Review,* 1964, **29**, 402–406.

Nisbet, J. D. Family Environment and Intelligence, *Eugenics Review,* 1953, **45**, 31–40.

Parnes, H. S., Miljus, R. C., Spitz, R. S. & Associates. *Career thresholds: A longitudinal study of the educational and labor market experience of male youth.* Vol. 1. Washington, D.C.: U. S. Department of Labor, Manpower Administration, 1970.

Rehberg, R. A., Schafer, W. E., & Sinclair, J. Toward a Temporal Sequence of Adolescent Achievement Variables, *American Sociological Review,* 1970, **35**, 34–47.

Rehberg, R. A., Sinclair, J., & Schafer, W. E. Adolescent Achievement Behavior, Family Authority Structure, and Parental Socialization Practices, *American Journal of Sociology,* 1970, **75**, 1012–1034.

Reiss, A. J., Jr., & others. *Occupations and social status,* New York: Free Press of Glencoe, 1961.

Reissman, L. Levels of Aspiration and Social Class, *American Sociological Review,* 1953, **18**, 233–242.

Rhodes, A. L., Reiss, A. J., Jr., & Duncan, O. D. Occupational Segregation in a Metropolitan School System, *American Journal of Sociology,* 1965, **70**, 682–694; **71**, 131.

Rogoff, Natalie. Local Social Structure and Educational Selection. In A. H. Halsey, J. Floud, and C. A. Anderson (Eds.), *Education, economy, and society.* Glencoe, Illinois: Free Press, 1961. Pp. 241–251.

Rosen, B. C., & D'Andrade, R. The Psychological Origins of Achievement Motivation, *Sociometry,* 1959, **22**, 185–218.

Sewell, W. H. Inequality of Opportunity for High Education, *American Sociological Review,* 1971, **36**, 793–809.

Sewell, W. H., & Armer, J. M. Neighborhood Context and College Plans, *American Sociological Review,* 1966, **31**, 159–168.

Sewell, W. H., & Orenstein, A. M. Community of Residence and Occupational Choice, *American Journal of Sociology,* 1965, **70**, 551–563.

Sewell, W. H., & Shah, V. P. Socioeconomic Status, Intelligence, and the Attainment of Higher Education. *Sociology of Education,* 1967, **40**, 1–23.

Sewell, W. H., Haller, A. O., & Ohlendorf, G. W. The Educational and Early Occupational Status Attainment Process: Replication and Revision, *American Sociological Review,* 1970, **35**, 1014–1027.

Sewell, W. H., Haller, A. O., & Portes, A. The Educational and Early Occupational Attainment Process, *American Sociological Review,* 1969, **34**, 82–92.

Sewell, W. H., Hauser, R. M., & Shah, V. Social Status and Higher Education. Unpublished University of Wisconsin, Madison, Wisconsin.

Sexton, Patricia C. *Education and income.* New York: Viking, 1961.

Schiller, B. R. Stratified Opportunities: The Essence of the 'Vicious Circle,' *American Journal of Sociology,* 1970, **76**, 426–442.

Siegel, P. M. The American Occupational Prestige Structure. Unpublished doctoral dissertation, University of Chicago, 1970.

Simpson, R. L. Parental Influence, Anticipatory Socialization, and Social Mobility, *American Sociological Review,* 1962, **27**, 517–522.

Stacey, B. G. Some Psychological Aspects of Inter-Generation Occupational Mobility, *British Journal of Social and Clinical Psychology,* 1965, **4**, 275–286.

Stephenson, R. M. Mobility Orientation and Stratification of 1,000 Ninth Graders, *American Sociological Review*, 1957, **22**, 204–212.

Stewart, Naomi. A.G.C.T. Scores of Army Personnel Grouped by Occupation, *Occupations*, 1947, **26**, 5–24.

Svalastoga, K. *Prestige, class, and mobility*, Copenhagen: Gyldendal, 1959.

Svalastoga, K. *Social differentiation*. New York: McKay, 1965.

Terman, L. M. *Genetic studies of genius*. Vol. I, Mental and Physical Traits of a Thousand Gifted Children. Stanford, California: Stanford University Press, 1925.

Thorndike, R. L. Two Screening Tests of Verbal Intelligence, *Journal of Applied Psychology*, 1942, **26**, 128–135.

Thorndike, R. L., & Gallup, G. Verbal Intelligence of the American Adult, *Journal of General Psychology*, 1944, **30**, 75–85.

Turner, R. H. *The social context of ambition*. San Francisco, California: Chandler, 1964.

Tyler, Leona E. Work and Individual Differences. In Henry Borow (Ed.), *Man in a world at work*. Boston, Massachusetts: Houghton Mifflin, 1964.

U.S. Bureau of Employment Security. Guide to the Use of the General Aptitude Test Battery. Section III, Development. Washington, D.C.: U.S. Department of Labor, 1962.

U.S. Department of Labor. *The negro family: The case for national action*. Washington, D.C.: Government Printing Office, 1965.

Warren, B. L. Socioeconomic Achievement and Religion: The American Case. In E. O. Laumann (Ed.), *Social stratification: Research and theory for the 1970s*. New York: Bobbs-Merrill, 1970. Pp. 130–155. (a)

Warren, B. L. The Relationships between Religious Preference and Socio-economic Achievement of American Men. Unpublished doctoral dissertation, University of Michigan, 1970. (b)

Wegner, E. L. & W. H. Sewell, Selection and Context as Factors Affecting the Probability of Graduation from College, *American Journal of Sociology*, 1970, **75**, 665–679.

Westoff, C. F., Potter, R. G., Jr., Sagi, P. C., & Mishler, E. G. *Family growth in metropolitan America*. Princeton, New Jersey: Princeton University Press, 1961.

Wilson, A. B. Residential Segregation of Social Classes and Aspirations of High School Boys, *American Sociological Review*, 1959, **24**, 836–845.

Winterbottom, Marian R. The Relation of Need for Achievement to Learning Experiences in Independence and Mastery. In J. W. Atkinson (Ed.), *Motives in fantasy, action, and society*. Princeton, New Jersey: Van Nostrand–Reinhold, 1958. Pp. 453–478.

Wright, S. Path Coefficients and Path Regressions: Alternative or Complementary Concepts? *Biometrics*, 1960, **16**, 189–202. (a)

Wright, S. The Treatment of Reciprocal Interaction, with or without Lag, in Path Analysis, *Biometrics*, 1960, **16**, 423–445. (b)

Yule, G. U., & Kendall, M. G. *An introduction to the theory of statistics*. 13th ed. London: Griffin, 1947.

Zeller, F. A., Shea, J. R., Kohen, A. I., & Meyer, J. A. *Career thresholds: A longitudinal study of the educational and labor market experiences of male youth*. Vol. 2. Columbus, Ohio: The Ohio State University Center for Human Resource Research. Washington, D.C.: U.S. Department of Labor, Manpower Administration, 1970.

Author Index

Numbers in italics refer to the pages on which the complete references are listed.

A

Alexander, C. N., Jr., 191, 192, 198, *271*
Alston, J. P., 256, *273*
Anastasi, Anne., 95, *271*
Armer, J. M., 191, *275*
Atkinson, J. W., 116, 175, *271*

B

Bachman, J. G., 258, *271*
Bendix, R., 12, 101, 255, *274*
Benson, Viola E., 83, 84, 89, 102, *271*
Blalock, H. M., Jr., 19, *271*
Blau, P. M., 1, 5, 10, 11, 32, 37, 49, 88, 92, 178, 205, 207, 225, 237, 262, *271*
Bloom, B. S., 100, *271*
Blum, Z. D., 259, *271*
Bordua, D. J., 169, *271*
Burt, C., 95, *271*
Butterworth, C. E., 36, 192, *273*
Byrns, Ruth, 79, 81, 82, 89, *271*

C

Campbell, E. Q., 191, 192, 198, *271*
Carlsson, G., 10, *271*
Centers, R., 10, *271*

Coombs (C continued, right column)

Coombs, L. C., 244, 245, *272*, *273*
Cooney, J. F., Jr., 244, *273*
Crockett, H. J., Jr., 10, 35, 106, 116, 117, 166, *172*

D

D'Andrade, R., 179, 180, *275*
Douglas, J. W. B., 258, *272*
Dumont, A., 237, *273*
Duncan, Beverly, 1, 11, 32, 41, 50, 51, 52, 62, 63, 64, 65, 66, 94, 210, 212, 236, *272*
Duncan, O. D., 1, 5, 7, 10, 11, 18, 32, 33, 34, 36, 37, 42, 47, 48, 49, 50, 51, 52, 54, 55, 56, 58, 61, 65, 66, 69, 75, 80, 85, 86, 88, 92, 93, 100, 105, 131, 132, 133, 135, 165, 178, 189, 190, 200, 202, 205, 207, 208, 209, 225, 236, 237, 257, 260, 262, *271*, *272*, *273*, *275*

E

Eckland, B. K., 211, *273*
Empey, T., 108, 109, *273*
Erlenmeyer-Kimling, L., 96, *273*

277

Subject Index